Surfing the High Tech Wave

Books by Roger Bourke White Jr.

Tales of Technofiction Series
www.technofictionland.com

The Honeycomb Comet

Rostov Rising

Tips for Tailoring Spacetime Fabric, Vol. 1

Tips for Tailoring Spacetime Fabric, Vol. 2

Science and Insight for Science Fiction Writers

Business and Insight Series
www.cyreenik-says.com

Surfing the High Tech Wave: A History of Novell 1980–1990

Evolution and Thought: Why We Think the Way We Do

Why We See Beauty

Surfing the High Tech Wave

A story of Novell's early years, 1980-1990

by Roger Bourke White Jr.

authorHOUSE®

AuthorHouse™
1663 Liberty Drive
Bloomington, IN 47403
www.authorhouse.com
Phone: 1-800-839-8640

First published by AuthorHouse 7/1/2010

ISBN: 978-1-4520-2303-8 (sc)
ISBN: 978-1-4520-2304-5 (e)

Library of Congress Control Number: 2010907959

Printed in the United States of America
Bloomington, Indiana

This book is printed on acid-free paper.

Dedication

To the people of Novell in the 1980–1990 period.

Acknowledgements

This story would not have been possible without the inspired work of the people at Novell between 1980 and 1990. They made the magic and I was fortunate enough to be there and watch the magic happen.

My thanks to George Trosper and his fine editing skills. His help and advice have put the professional polish on this work of love for me.

Contents

PRELIMINARIES

Overview

First come some *Preliminaries*. This Overview and an Introduction provide context and define some terms I will be using throughout. If you want to know why this is an interesting story, start with the Introduction.

PART ONE: The Foundation Years, 1980–84, is Chapters 1–4. Here I tell how Novell struggled to find the right vision and the right people to make that vision happen.

PART TWO: Novell Emerges, 1985–88, covers the years when Novell prospered mightily in sales and grew mightily in numbers of people as the vision was implemented. Because this second part of the story is more complex, I break it into two timelines: The technical thread, Chapter 5, followed by the cultural thread, Chapters 6 and 7, including one example of how not all the projects implemented by Novell turned to gold—the story of the NetWare Centers.

The last section is Chapters 8 and 9, *PART THREE: Novell Matures, 1988–94.* At that time, Novell was more complex than ever, still profitable and growing, but no longer a company trying to make an entirely new industry. The story of Craig Burton and Judith Clarke's departure is emblematic of Novell's transition from visionary company to well managed "Statue of Liberty" company.

Introduction

Entertainment, Education, and Employees

Some may wonder what possible use a history of a company might serve. Entertainment, for one: Novell's is a crackling good story. Education, for another: To understand Novell of the '90s and early 21st century, and its flagship product, NetWare—now Open Enterprise Server (OES)[1]—it is useful to understand where the company came from.

Then too, there are the employees, past and present. Novell has a semi-organized alumni association, called LAN—in this case, Life After Novell. When you worked at Novell you felt that you were part of something that mattered, and few people who passed through its doors were worse off for the experience. Working at Novell in the '80s was perhaps the most frustrating, irritating, anxiety-producing career experience that Information Age pioneers ever suffered through, and yet it was an exhilarating and rewarding experience.

Novell has been a place where colossal mistakes were made, where colossal achievements were forged, where some dreams flourished and others died, where lasting friendships were sealed, and where the world was transformed. For the great numbers of Novellians currently in and out of the company, a history may provide a sense of closure and an opportunity to reflect on what has been for all a great adventure.

---

[1] At this writing, the latest version of NetWare is v6.5 Support Pack 8, which is identical to OES 2 SP1, NetWare Kernel.

Roger Bourke White Jr.

The Novell Story

In 1983 a failed business in a small Utah town is turned around. Six years later that business is ranked in the Fortune 1000 and the small Utah town becomes the center of a major computer technology.

A young college drop-out (Craig Burton), a middle-aged former beauty technician (Judith Clarke), and a near-retirement former "company man" (Ray Noorda) become millionaires virtually overnight and lead the creation of a major high tech industry.

A technological innovation so profound that it changes the way the world communicates, yet so esoteric that most people never notice it, is developed in about six months by four young free-lancers trying to put themselves through graduate school.

For sheer amazement, spectacle, drama, and comedy, no work of fiction can surpass the history of Novell, Inc., the Provo, Utah, company that rode the crest of a billion-dollar industry. Novell's is a story of stupendous success—of wealth and power, of victory and conquest, and of the realization of hundreds of individuals' dreams. It is also the story of stupendous failure—of fortunes lost, of the mighty overthrown, of scandal and defeat and treachery. It is a story of human beings who risked all, lost all, gained all, and built a business, day in and day out, that has literally changed the world. It is the legend of red-blooded all-American heroes civilizing a high tech frontier in the 1980s—a legend brought to life by real people.

The story of Novell fascinates on many different levels. It is a study of business enterprise, of people who saw a market opportunity and set out to exploit it. It is a lesson in business management—how managers faced first the challenge of business failure, then the greater challenge of dealing with a concept whose success grew a million-fold in ten years. It is a revealing illustration of how new technology is created, marketed, and sold.

Most interesting of all, Novell's story is a tale of the human spirit— of people who, like people everywhere, cherished visions and hopes of what they might become and of what they might achieve, and who embarked together on a journey of self-fulfillment. It is a story of how these people helped and hurt each other in pursuit of their common and separate goals. Novell's story is an adventure story, as thrilling in its way as any ever told or lived.

What was Novell? From its rebirth in 1983 to the turn of the 21st century, it was a manufacturer of networks that linked together personal computers (PCs).

Its vision as a company has been remarkably consistent through two decades of innovation, although the implementation of the vision has changed dramatically. Novell, like a handful of other companies, successfully rode the technological wave set in motion by the cataclysmic PC revolution—so successfully that it became a recognized industry standard-bearer for a major segment of the personal computing industry: The PC-based local area networks (LANs).

A Brief History of Events
Leading to PC-Based LANs

Computers began their existence as machines of mystery. They were the exclusive domain of computer professionals from the first UNIVAC sold in 1951 through the minicomputers sold in the 1970s. Data Processing (DP) or Management Information Systems (MIS) departments were the keepers of company computers—which were mainframe computers or, after 1963, a mix of mainframes and minicomputers.

Employees who had jobs for the company computer to do would typically submit the work with a request form to the MIS administrator, who would return the processed job upon completion. Knowledge of computer operation was highly specialized and beyond the ken of the ordinary person.

With time and declining costs computers became more widespread and familiar. Minicomputers brought a price breakthrough that pulled computers out of giant institutions, such as the Department of Defense, and made their use practical in medium-sized businesses and in large government and university departments. In the late '70s minicomputers become common in corporations as a solution to department-level data processing needs.

Declining price and increasing familiarity allowed companies to automate more and more functions. The digital computers of World War II were used only for computing artillery trajectory tables. The first post-war commercial computers found use as accounting machines and engineering tools for giant tasks. By the 1970s medium-sized activities such as word-processing telephone books and process-controlling chemical operations were also appearing on a large scale. For example, a marketing department might have its own minicomputer that secretaries could access through terminals. Such minicomputer companies as DEC (pronounced *deck*, for Digital Equipment Corp.), Wang, Control Data, NCR (pronounced N-C-R, for National Cash Register), AT&T, and Vydec prospered in this period.

Although a company's total computer power was a bit more decentralized than it had been in the past, the department-level minicomputers were still centrally administered by the MIS department.

A milestone in computer history was attained in 1969 when Marcian E. Hoff developed the first microprocessor chip, the Intel 4004, containing a miniaturized set of integrated circuits. The microprocessor was the basis of "fourth generation" computers that were developed in the 1970s. (First generation computers used vacuum tubes; second generation, transistors; third generation, integrated circuits; and fourth generation, microprocessors. Current computers are still fourth generation.)

The microprocessor also extended the computer's usefulness by making possible an unexpectedly successful new kind of product: The microcomputer, later called the personal computer or PC.

In 1975, the year moviegoers flocked to see Jaws and *Saturday Night Live* premiered on TV, MITS (pronounced *mitts,* for Micro Instrumentation and Telemetry Systems) started selling the first commercial personal computer, the Altair. By 1977 Apple, Commodore, and Radio Shack were also manufacturing PCs.

The first personal computers were regarded as toys: The playthings of hardware buffs, programming junkies, and the curious. All through the 1970s, conventional wisdom held that playthings were all they would ever be. The real home computer was going to be a time-sharing terminal in the home connected to a centrally located mini-computer, perhaps using the TV as its screen, perhaps with the minicomputer co-located with telephone switching equipment. As a result, prototype personal computers stayed on the shelf at many, many companies in the business of building minicomputers, terminals, and other electronics.

A classic example comes from Sperry Univac in Salt Lake City: One day the engineers needed to test a supplier's ability to provide quality printed circuit boards. They gave the supplier a mask for a personal computer mother board that the engineers had designed in their spare time. The boards came back, were tested—and then became the foundation for their computer club's hobby computer kit.

The toy perception began to disappear only after VisiCalc hit the market in 1979. VisiCalc was the first spreadsheet software for personal computers. It far surpassed in concept and ease of use anything comparable on minis or mainframes, demonstrating decisively how PCs would be different from those and how important *user friendliness* was to become in general-purpose computer applications. As user-friendly accounting, word processing, and other software application programs became available for PCs, people began to look at them as low-cost computers for the office.

In the early days of personal computers, the potential of the technology had been enthusiastically pronounced on, but only a few visionaries acted to realize that potential. Eventually, said the prophets, every home would have its own PC. Families would use the new appliance for everything from balancing checkbooks to shopping to helping with homework. Databases around the world could be accessed from every home. People could even vote by punching in a few commands on the family keyboard.

Twenty years later in 1995, the promise of a PC in every home was close to being realized, but the hottest area of PC proliferation in the late '70s and the '80s—the place where PCs first actually revolutionized modern life—was the office. But back in 1975 almost no one had predicted that personal computers would take over the office, largely because minicomputers and mainframes were already well established there.

Personal computers put computing power on the desks of millions of individual employees with easy, simple access to word processing, spreadsheets, graphics, and sophisticated analytical programs. No MIS department intermediary was required to process work or to control files. "One man, one computer" (as the microcomputer slogan went) was becoming a reality in the offices of the developed world.

It wasn't talked about as much, but those were also the days of "one computer, one programmer". Most users mastered a programming language such as BASIC or Pascal so they could get more out of these machines with such potential. Doing so was feasible because "one man, one computer" eliminated the programming overhead associated with multi-tasking and security.

By 1980 the revolution was beginning but another step was needed. Computers users had been given privacy, simplicity, and user friendliness by the new personal computer technology, but they also needed more access. Users had access to the wide range of application programs, but they needed to share files and have access to databases held on other computers if they were going to take full advantage of this new technology, and this required networking of some sort.

Why Call This a Revolution?

A revolution is a time of rapid, unpredictable change. The development and acceptance of the personal computer has produced changes in our way of life more radical than even those contemplated by the masses cheering "Liberté, Égalité, Fraternité" in the 1790s.

There are fortunes to be made in every revolution—and fortunes to be lost. Change means opportunity to those perceptive, bold, and lucky enough to take the right actions at the right moments.

The first Novell was launched by people with a vision of how they could prosper from the computer revolution underway. This company, Novell Data Systems, Inc., failed: It did not catch the wave of technology but instead was sucked under and squashed by it. The second Novell did rather better and is still riding the crest of the wave.

The Burning Questions

Why did one Novell die while another rose phoenix-like from its ashes? Why do some visions succeed while others fail? What combination of people is necessary to create a winning technology—and from there a winning company? Can lessons be derived from Novell's experience so that the phenomenon of Novell can be repeated in other industries, or be predicted more accurately?

The answers to such questions, if answers exist, are elusive. Before we can speculate about why Novell is a success we have to determine what happened. This is more difficult than one might think, even though the Novell story spans scarcely three decades. Each player saw a different piece of the story from a unique perspective and the rush of events was so dizzying for the central characters that memories have already blurred or faded. Many of those who were in a position to see the big picture are still chasing the technology muse and lack the time and the inclination to discuss the past. A few are discouraged and trying to put the past behind them.

The Enigma

At the core of the Novell story was Ray Noorda, the man who discovered a kernel of greatness in a moribund operation and from it grew a company and an industry. Although he spoke frankly and usually sincerely, although he was a public figure whose contributions to the computer industry were well known, Ray was an enigma even to those who worked closely with him. There was an indefinable, unfathomable quality to the man—a Lincolnesque aspect to his personality. A folksy manner belied a superior, probing intelligence. One did not expect to find in this paragon of homespun virtue a master strategist and a relentless, sometimes reckless entrepreneur. Like Lincoln, Ray was often underestimated by those who dealt with him.

As with Lincoln, opinions of Ray vary widely. To some he was "wily" or "slippery"; some of his key managers described him as "a moody little son of a bitch". Others revered him as a father or benefactor—"a great man with a great heart." A few of his most ungenerous critics considered him merely lucky. But most people in the computer industry agree that Ray was a good man of business. Even his harshest detractors acknowledge that he worked exceptionally hard and that he was an entrepreneur in the purest sense of the word.

PART ONE
The Foundation Years, 1980–84

CHAPTER ONE
Building Ray's Stage

Ray Noorda didn't start Novell, Inc., from scratch in 1983. He bought a company: Novell Data Systems, Inc. (NDSI).

Novell Data Systems was the hopes and dreams of other people. It had been founded in 1980 and grew to 120 people in 1981, but by the end of 1982 had collapsed to 15 people. Things were so bad in late 1982 that NDSI's products were being returned faster than they were being sold.

But those 15 people left at the company had a dream … a dream for a revolutionary product that would save the company. And Ray found that dream so exciting and real that he was willing to invest his time and money in this otherwise losing proposition to make it happen.

The dream was a local area network product that would become NetWare. The founders of the Novell we know today included Harry Armstrong, Craig Burton, Judith Clarke, and the SuperSet group of programmers.

These people made Novell and NetWare. To understand them you need to understand the Novell that they watched grow and collapse. They learned a lot watching that happen. And between what they learned and the experience Ray brought, they developed a winning product and a company that made an industry. To understand Novell, Inc., you need to understand the stage that it was built upon, NDSI.

The Novell Data Systems story is also important as a contrast: The goals of the companies were almost identical, but the results of the implementations were dramatically different.

The Acorn Is Planted

In the summer of 1980 two seasoned computer industry executives got together to start a company, Novell Data Systems. Like all good high tech entrepreneurs they intended for that company to shake the

3

world. Unlike many, their company actually did—but hardly in the straightforward manner that they had envisioned.

Those men were Jack Davis and George Canova. They had been building dreams, experiences, and expectations for several years. Those meshed with the reality of the early '80s to make Novell happen the way it did.

Jack Davis

Jack Joins the Job Market

Jack Davis was born in Utah. He graduated from Brigham Young University (BYU) in 1961 with history and French degrees. Jack first found work in the growing minicomputer industry at NCR, the start of a long career pursuing the Muse of Technology. He moved to Phoenix when he started working for General Electric's disk-drive division. Later in the '60s his career took him to southern California where he joined up with CalComp, a maker of plotters and other minicomputer peripherals, heading up international sales. From CalComp he moved to General Automation and headed international sales there, too.

These were the hotbed days for minicomputers, and southern California contributed no less to the industry's development than Massachusetts ("Route 128") or the northern California Bay Area ("Silicon Valley"—alias Silicon Gulch to wags in Massachusetts).

Jack had wide circles of acquaintances in the southern California industry in the '60s and '70s. These later provided him with the manpower he needed to start Novell.

In the '70s he moved to Utah and became Director of International Sales for Beehive International in Salt Lake City. Beehive at that time was one of the biggest independent manufacturers of CRT terminals. Jack sharpened his skills at selling peripherals and became experienced at dealing with marketplaces that required custom products.

The specialty terminal market had benefits and weaknesses: The benefits were high margins for the products and fewer competitors. The weaknesses were limited market size and higher development costs.

The constraints of these specialty markets caused controversy within Beehive. One engineer I talked with years after Jack left felt that Jack was a good salesman, but he was always bringing back orders

4

for "terminals with purple reset buttons, or some such, when he should have been bringing back orders for the stuff we made already".

Jack's Habit of Electronic Entrepreneurship

Jack liked to start companies and projects. Novell was far from his first. In California he started a company to sell a protocol converter (a box that converts one electronic communications protocol into another). This endeavor was still-born when the company he chose to manufacture the box got wrapped up in legal battles and couldn't produce.

While no product came out of this project, it introduced him to Victor Vurpillat, a southern California hardware designer who had done some work for an East Coast outfit named Safeguard Scientifics. Victor introduced Jack to Adolf "Dolf" Pere and Pete Musser at Safeguard, and Jack did some consulting for them. It was one of many contacts Jack made in the '60s and '70s that would be cashed in on in the '80s.

Terminal Specialties, Inc. (TSI)

Jack's startup just before Novell was Terminal Specialties, Inc., a terminal distributing company. TSI met a need for linking terminal makers with their customers.

In the late '70s many companies from the East Asian "Four Tigers" countries (Hong Kong, Taiwan, Korea, and Singapore) were introducing new lower-cost CRT terminals into the US. This was partly why the price for "dumb" ASCII terminals[2] declined from $1500 apiece in 1978 to $900 apiece in 1982. These East Asian companies knew a lot about manufacturing but very little about marketing in the US. Jack's TSI was providing the service of getting them in touch with their market.

And Jack was effective. He added value for these companies. One of the big companies TSI serviced was TeleVideo Systems. Jack nego-

---

[2] A dumb terminal transmits to a computer what is entered on its keyboard, character by character, with essentially no processing, where an intelligent or smart terminal can display characters that are not on its keyboard (like é) and can store and send a whole page or form at a time. An ASCII terminal uses the now-standard character coding in the American Standard Code for Information Interchange, rather than one of the proprietary codes like IBM's EBCDIC (Extended Binary Code Decimal Interchange Code).

tiated a master distributor agreement with TeleVideo, then proceeded to introduce its people to big name distributors he had worked with previously, such as David Jamison Carlyle out of the LA area.

Jack also worked with TeleVideo on improving the product's features, big things as well as little things to make the product fit US market tastes—such as changing the case color to make it more harmonious with other computer equipment.

Jack was effective but he liked to play fast and loose, and sometimes this caught up with him. TeleVideo was one of those cases. The company prospered but in 1979 they underwent a management shakeup and ceased honoring the master distributor agreement they had with TSI. That had never been formalized with a contract, so TSI was out in the cold—left only with yet another "distributor dumped upon" war story to show for its efforts.

The TeleVideo episode is important because it helped convince Jack that he had to make his fortune somewhere besides distributing. Like many other players in the computer field he planned to migrate up the marketing chain: Customers dream of becoming retailers, retailers of becoming distributors and wholesalers, distributors and wholesalers of becoming manufacturers. Jack was going into manufacturing next.

TeleVideo was one of TSI's big customers. Among its smaller ones was Dobbs and Woodbury—a two-man terminal-designing company based in Salt Lake City that had designed a cutting-edge terminal for the Sperry/Univac marketplace. TSI's terminal was good but they were having trouble marketing it, which meant poor sales. As a result they were out of money.

Jack wanted to market their terminal, but Dobbs and Woodbury needed money right away and they were about to sell the rights to another company that was unlikely to deal with TSI. So Jack offered to buy the rights for the same price as the other company. Woodbury said yes, Dobbs said no. There were other convolutions, but the net effect was that Dobbs and Woodbury split. Dobbs retained control and Jack didn't get his terminal rights. What he got instead was a commitment from Rusty Woodbury to join Jack in his new enterprise when it started up.

Otherwise 1980 was not a good year for TSI. Jack discovered that in addition to losing TeleVideo as a revenue source and failing to acquire rights to Dobbs and Woodbury's specialty terminal, he had gained an unexpected expense: The company accountant had been dipping into the till.

With TSI fighting for its existence and in need of cutting expenses, Jack and his partner, Frank Richins, agreed that Frank would continue TSI while Jack sought his fortune elsewhere. Jack needed a new organization, and that organization would be Novell.

It was time to assemble the team.

George Canova

Jack's Heavy-Hitter

By 1980 Jack had informally lined up many people who were ready to help him start this new company, but he needed what all new companies find hard to come by: Money.

Jack called on George Canova to critique his business plan. He had seen George's handiwork at CalComp, the minicomputer peripherals maker where Jack had worked in the '60s. He knew George had started Century Data, a prosperous disk drive maker, and had made a lot of money when Century merged into CalComp. The merger agreement gave George some stock options based on CalComp's post-merger performance. It did so well that George ended up its largest stockholder.

In 1980 George had just finished an even bigger task. For the last three years as President and then Chairman of CalComp he had been turning the company around.

In the mid '70s CalComp experienced losses. In 1977 George replaced its founder as President and Chairman and worked hard to stem the "red tide". He reduced the debt load partly by selling off divisions. (One of the hardest cuts was selling off the memory products group, which had been the Century Data that George had founded.) He also controlled costs in other ways. For instance, he was the first to implement a four-day work week in a major (1200 employees) California electronics company.

In 1979 George had turned the corner and was thinking about future growth in a way that paralleled Jack's thinking. An article in *Business Week*, Dec. 4, 1978, talks not only about his turnaround efforts but also his vision for CalComp's future.

> Canova's next move will be into an area that he considers full of growth potential: supplying a line of peripherals for minicom-

puter users, who can save substantially by assembling their own minisystem a la carte. … Canova predicts this miniperipherals business venture will produce sales of tens of millions a few years out.

Right Vision, Wrong Place

George's vision was controversial within CalComp. Instead of reselling peripherals, the company devoted resources to building their presence in the CAD/CAM (computer-aided design and manufacturing) marketplace, which was a more logical extension of their already established plotter business.

In early 1979 CalComp got an opportunity to tap a large financial source: Cash-rich Sanders Associates was willing to buy them up at a good price to extend their presence in the non-military marketplace. CalComp stockholders, including George, agreed to the sale. George was given a vice-presidency and a position on the board of Sanders. But in nine months, in the summer of 1980, he resigned from both positions to start up a new company "that wouldn't compete with Sanders or CalComp". That company was Novell.

Great Minds Meet

Although Jack approached George simply to critique his business plan, as George reviewed it he grew more and more enthusiastic. Jack was writing about George's own vision about minicomputer peripherals and the business computer marketplace! He was so enthusiastic he told Jack he'd like to be a part of it.

Jack was delighted. One of the key things he needed for this new enterprise was financing, and here was a man well-connected into the southern California venture capital community who could also bring a heavy-hitting résumé to the Novell effort.

George's price was high: He would come in as President. But Jack decided the promise of access to million-dollar financing made it worthwhile.

George Canova

Bio

George M. Canova, born 1931, was Chairman of the Board and President of CalComp, 1977–80. He was principal founder of Century Data Systems, Inc., in 1968 and served as its President until 1973, when the company was purchased by and incorporated into CalComp a maker of minicomputer peripherals. Before founding CDS, George was a Director of Product Development for Scientific Data Systems (now Xerox Data Systems) and was yet earlier employed in engineering and management positions at RCA and Burroughs Corporation.

Relevance

George Canova is important because he was Jack's partner in starting Novell and brought with him many important innovations to Jack's basic plan, such as adding a personal computer to the product line.

Timeline

George Canova founds Novell Data Systems and stays with the company until March 1982. He is one of the few people who walk away from Novell never to return. In fact, he says he never wants to think about it again.

Jack Davis

Bio

Jack Davis graduated from BYU in 1961. His first job in electronics was working for NCR as a programmer. He gained further experience at Hughes, General Electric, CalComp, Beehive International, and TSI before coming to Novell.

Relevance

Jack Davis pulls Novell Data Systems together to found it and later rescues it by bringing the company to Ray Noorda's attention. His and George Canova's actions in building NDSI provide a rich contrast to what happened at Novell, Inc., under Ray Noorda.

Timeline

Jack Davis stays with the company until November 1981. He then plays behind-the-scenes roles until Ray Noorda takes over in 1983.

The Sapling Grows

Picking the Name

Jack and George were thinking on parallel tracks, but parallel does not mean identical, and both were strong-willed people.

The day Jack and George went to incorporate, Jack got his first surprise. He had been using the name Macro Systems for the business. While they were waiting for the lawyer, George said, "You know, I talked to my wife about this new company and she thought of a nice name for it."

"What's that?"

"Novell."

Jack replied, "Sounds nice. What does it mean?"

"It means 'new' in French," George said.

Jack blanched a bit. In addition to his degree he'd spent two years in France on a Mormon[3] mission and was quite fluent in the language.

"I don't think so, George. There's either *nouveau* the masculine or *nouvelle* the feminine—"

"Well, it sounds good anyway."

Jack, having just read a magazine article saying that the important thing about a business name is that the name isn't as important as what a business does, conceded.

"Yes, it sounds good, George."

For a long time after that the company name meant "new in French" when you asked George and "nothing at all" when you asked Jack.

Moving into the Truck Dealership

Novell started in a vacant truck dealership in an industrial park on the north side of Orem, Utah. From it one had a view of three spectacular sights: Mount Timpanogos, Utah Lake, and the Geneva Steel works, the largest steel mill between the Mississippi and the Pacific coast.

---

[3] The LDS Church requests that in first references it be called by its official name, The Church of Jesus Christ of Latter-day Saints. Consider it done.

Jack, Sherrill Harmon, and Joe Maroney[4] were the first to set foot in the building as employees of the new company. They started the cleanup and transformation of the building into an electronics manufacturing facility.

Picking the Products

Jack started Novell on the vision of manufacturing a multi-CPU minicomputer system and the terminals and printers for that system, and of reselling software for it. (CPU stands for *central processing unit*. It can be a chip, the board that the chip is on, or the box that the board is inside—what most of us call "the computer".)

Part of Jack's vision was to build a minicomputer that would offer more power for less price. That part was conventional. He was going to offer accessories for that minicomputer; that too was conventional wisdom for the time.

There were two unconventional parts of his vision. One was to expand the minicomputer power by adding more CPUs to the box.

The other was to build the accessories he offered as well as the minicomputer. It was conventional at the time to OEM them. (OEM stands for *original equipment manufacturer*. OEMing means either offering your product for other people to put their brand name on, or putting your brand name on other people's product.)

The Minicomputer

The minicomputer was to be the heart of the Novell line. Based on the Motorola 68000 CPU chip, it would be expandable by adding more 68000 processing boards as the customer needed them.

In 1980, this ability—to be useful over a long span of capacity requirements—was a challenge for all makers of mainframes and minis. A user who started on, say, an IBM System 34 could only grow so far before they would have to upgrade to, say, a System 38 or a 4331. When they did they would have to toss out all their old software and much of their old peripheral hardware, terminals, and printers as well. Moreover,

---

[4] Despite diligent inquiry, the author cannot confirm the spelling of Joe's name, pronounced muh-ROW-nee. It could equally well be Moroney or Maroni. (If it had been Moroni, like Joseph Smith's angel, it would have been commented on and mispronounced.)

moving company data from the old system to the new was an elaborate and laborious process.

Even more threatening to the manufacturer, once the customer realized they were going to have to go through all this nonsense whether they bought the same brand or a competing brand, they were likely to shop around: The computer manufacturer "lost control" of the client.

Thus, the difficult transition was fraught with uncertainty for all involved. Offering products with extended capacity spans gave a company a competitive edge.

The Universal Terminal

Jack knew the terminal marketplace, so it would be easy to make money by offering a terminal. In his dealings with Dobbs and Woodbury he had developed a rapport with, and an obligation to, Rusty Woodbury. He called upon Rusty to join the new company to design another Sperry-compatible terminal and then to design a terminal for the Novell minicomputer.

The Printer

Every office computer has a printer. Usually those printers are made by a company specializing in printer manufacture and then OEMed to the computer maker.

But why? Why not make the printer as well as the computer? Jack decided to capture this part of the revenue stream too. He licensed a dot-matrix printer design from Tritel, another contact from his earlier days, and included it in the product mix.

The Personal Computer and the LAN

In Jack's original business plan there was no standalone microcomputer or local area network. These products were added after he and George joined forces.

The "terminal computer" (the company's name for its microcomputer or personal computer, which combined the functions of a standalone microcomputer and an intelligent minicomputer terminal) became part of the plan shortly after incorporation. George proposed it for two reasons: First, the terminal computer—sold as a microcomputer—would be a quick revenue generator financing the larger minicomputer's development. Second, they had a ready customer. A standalone micro-computer would fit more closely than a terminal or minicomputer with what Safeguard wanted as an electronic alternative to its One Write system. (More on this next.)

And in classic terminal-manufacturer logic of the '70s, if they were making a terminal, why not make a standalone computer too? In fact many terminal makers tested the waters of the personal computer market in the late '70s, but none survived the shakeouts of the '80s.

The LAN did not appear in the product mix until the summer of 1981. (That story is covered below, starting on p. 50 with "The LAN Is Born", as part of how the SuperSet group came into being.)

The First Check

As Joe and Sherrill were cleaning up the building, Jack and George were flying to Philadelphia.

No one on the West Coast had been interested in financing this new startup, but on the East Coast Jack had rekindled yet another old contact: Dolf Pere and Pete Musser of Safeguard Business Systems and Safeguard Scientifics. Victor Vurpillat, who was then Vice President of R&D at Safeguard Scientifics, re-introduced them.

Timeline: Dolf Pere and Pete Musser

Pete Musser is Chairman and founder of Safeguard Business Systems. Dolf Pere is its President. Both are Novell board members from the beginning of Novell Data Systems throughout the transition to Novell, Inc., and into the 1990s. Through their holdings in Safeguard Scientifics, they are investors during the same period.

Dolf and Pete had built Safeguard Business Systems and their One Write accounting system into a thriving cash cow. They had used an independent franchise marketing approach to develop a sales force numbering in the thousands.

In years previous Dolf and Pete used the profits to diversify into industrial areas such as metal finishing and transmissions. But in 1980 they could see a much different opportunity appearing: Microcomputers used for accounting might soon supplant some of their One Write manual accounting system demand. They wanted to be prepared by diversifying into high tech, specifically microcomputers.

When Jack and George came to them about investing in a computer company, they were very interested. They wanted a system that they could offer as a high-end migration product for their One Write sales force.

Dolf and Pete knew from earlier experiences that some of their plans and visions weren't in line with what salespeople and customers wanted from Safeguard Business Systems and the One Write product. They solved this friction by forming Safeguard Scientifics as the organization for their diversification. Safeguard Scientifics was to be the venture capital organization for Novell, building Novell into a stable and profitable company, then spinning off its ownership when the shares could be sold for a good return.

But the products Dolf and Pete were interested in seeing come from Novell were for the future development of Safeguard Business Systems.

The meeting ended with Dolf and Pete committing to financing Novell and with George and Jack getting a check for $250,000 so they could go to Comdex (the **Com**puter **D**ealer's **Ex**hibition) that year.

The First Comdex

Going to Comdex in 1980 said a lot about the Novell that was to come.

Novell didn't have a product. It didn't have a plant. It hardly had an organization or money. But Jack felt that establishing a relationship with future resellers of Novell product was important, and that he was going to find those resellers at the Comdex trade show in November.

The choice of Comdex was significant.

This was Comdex's second year. It was still overshadowed by the giant National Computer Conference (NCC) trade show, which centered around mainframes and minis but was felt by many in the industry to be a show for students and tire-kickers. (This complaint was real enough that the NCC show imploded after a famously ill-organized 1983 exhibition in Anaheim, California.)

The Comdex show was directed towards independent reseller organizations—the new wave of retail computer stores that were springing up around the country—and centered around microcomputers rather than minicomputers. Jack felt Comdex might be small compared to NCC, but it was strategic.

14

So George, Jack, and Larry Edwards, the new Vice President of Sales, went to Comdex. They put up an inexpensive but visually impressive booth consisting of nothing but hanging Novell banners and lots of chairs. Dead in the center was an apartment-sized refrigerator (about 3 feet high) wrapped up as a Christmas present, representing products to come.

Jack's hunch paid off: Comdex was strategic. Sitting space was at a premium, so the chairs at the Novell booth attracted hoards of foot-weary resellers. The media stopped in because they were curious and they wanted to see more polished marketing in an industry segment still dominated by inventors wearing T-shirts and jeans while showing off their latest technology. The Novell reputation started to grow even before the product did.

Having made their debut, the Novell team headed back to Utah to plan a blockbuster year for 1981.

The Goals of 1981

In 1981 Jack and George's ideas began their transformation into flesh and blood, and into metal and plastic. For 1981 the goal was to assemble an organization that would start producing revenue.

Safeguard's Goals

Safeguard was looking first at the bottom line. They wanted Novell to lay the foundation for a growing and profitable high tech company. Dolf and Pete were counting on Jack and George's long and successful experiences in the minicomputer industry to make Novell profitable quickly. This goal affected the order in which products would be developed and brought to market: Quick things first.

Safeguard's second focus was integrating a fruit of the computer age into their existing interests. As mentioned above, they wanted their Safeguard Business Systems sales force to have a high tech alternative to their existing paper-based One Write product—they wanted a way to sell computerized accounting. This goal encouraged the addition of a personal computer to Novell's product line.

Jack's Goals

1981 would be a big year for Jack. He needed to finish building his founding team and build a company around that team. That company needed to define, design, manufacture, and sell profitable products within the year.

But this was no simple single-product company. Jack was assembling a comprehensive computer system manufacturer in a locale that had never seen any comprehensive system manufacturer before. His vision was large, and to make it happen would take all the Old West heroism he could muster from his Utah heritage.

George's Goals

George wanted to prove he was right. He had told the people at CalComp that minicomputer peripherals were the market to be in, and they had rejected him. Now Jack had come to him with a business plan that outlined a great way to get into that market. George's goal was another winning company, and whether it was minicomputers or personal computers didn't matter much. What was important was the peripherals business.

George could see that Jack had done his homework in terms of lining up people and making a plan. This would let him concentrate on arranging financing and fine-tuning the manufacturing process—his great loves. 1981 would be a great year.

The People of 1981

Building the Novell Data Systems Team

Between January 1981 and January 1982 Novell grew from 10 founders to 120 people as a steady stream of new faces came in to all aspects of company operations. Many good people came in with Novell Data System's flood tide of fortune and left with its ebb; many of those sailed happily back in on the flood tide of Novell, Inc.

I look at the people who came to be part of Novell in 1981 in this order:

First are the founders of Novell Data Systems, the people who built the stage and then left. The free market system declared that they didn't quite have their act together; they would have to pursue their dreams in other places, a little older and wiser.

After the NDSI founders I consider those who came to NDSI and left it, then came back again to play significant roles in Novell, Inc. These are the people who best know the difference between Novell-before-Ray and Novell-after-Ray.

Finally I look at those who came and stayed—the founders of Novell, Inc.—the people responsible for making the "Ray difference" happen.

The NDSI Founders

Through the years Jack had worked with a lot of computer industry people. He picked from this vast experience base to build the Novell Data Systems team. For years he had been discussing business ideas with people on an informal basis. Those who believed in his dream and were ready for a change joined him. Some of the people joined late in 1980; the rest came on board early in 1981.

Manufacturing from CalComp

Jack drew other manpower besides George Canova from his Cal-Comp experiences. He knew Joe Maroney from his work there. In 1980 Joe was working at Storage Technology in Denver, and Jack invited him to head Manufacturing at Novell.

Timeline: Joe Maroney

Joe Maroney is an NDSI founder. He is with Novell until March 1983, when he leaves as part of Ray Noorda's first reorganization.

Design from BYU

Motorola wasn't the only one excited about the arrival of the 68000 CPU chip. Dennis Fairclough was finishing his Ph.D. thesis, which compared the relative merits of the various 16-bit processors being introduced in 1980. He showed Jack his work—which found that the 68000 was a superior chip to the Intel 8086 or Zilog 8000 offerings—and Jack invited him to help start Novell. Dennis would have been the one who designed the multi-CPU minicomputer if it had been built.

Dennis often moved back and forth between the two worlds of academia and commerce. He had previously been involved in the startup of Praxis, a company that sold minicomputer systems with customized

17

software to dentists and that Jack would head following his term at Novell.

Dennis agreed to be part of starting Novell, but he didn't leave BYU. He still had his Ph.D. to finish and staying at BYU kept Novell's startup expenses down. By the time he was ready to join full-time, Novell was in trouble, so he was involved as a founder but not as a full-time employee.

Timeline: Dennis Fairclough

Dennis Fairclough is an NDSI founder, though never a full-time employee. He is with Eyring Research Institute, a BYU-connected think tank in Provo, Utah. He stops working with Novell in March 1982 during the "March Massacre". At this writing he is Deputy Chair/Professor at the Computing & Networking Sciences Department at Utah Valley University.

Sales from IBM and Praxis

The "people conduit" from Praxis included Larry Edwards. His work experience included stints at IBM.

Larry was born in southern Utah. Every new acquaintance ran into one vestige of that: His name is pronounced "lorry", with the vowel of "barn" or "born" according to taste—in rural Utah, as in various other English-speaking places, those are the same vowel—rather than rhyming with "Harry" and/or "hairy" (which have the same vowel in most of North America).

He was head of Sales for NDSI.

Timeline: Larry Edwards

Larry Edwards is an NDSI founder. He comes on in 1980 as Vice President of Sales and leaves in the late summer of '82, midway through the "Time of Six Presidents".

Engineering from Motorola

Sherrill Harmon was one of those "brightest and best" people that others complain won't stay where they're born, in this case Price, a coal-mining town in the center of Utah. He left to become part of the electronics industry that was springing up in many places in the West, but not in Price. His journeys took him to Phoenix in the '60s, where he joined the General Electric disk drive division where he became acquainted with ... who else? ... Jack Davis.

18

In the late '60s that GE division went through one of those economic convulsions that periodically shake companies in the electronics industry and lead to contraction. As is also common in the electronics industry, one company, GE, was contracting while another, Motorola, was growing. So a "people conduit" was established from GE to Motorola. Sherrill was part of that conduit.

At Motorola he became a project leader on the 68000 chip development. The minicomputer in Jack's business plan was based on the 68000, so he invited Sherrill to join Novell.

Sherrill became head of Engineering for NDSI. And while the multi-CPU minicomputer Jack envisioned was never built, its successor, the LAN file server, was 68000-based.

Timeline: Sherrill Harmon

Sherrill Harmon is an NDSI founder. He lasts until March 1982, when he leaves as part of the "March Massacre".

Design as a Legacy of TSI

TSI provided Novell not just with Jack Davis but a whole legacy of commitments. As noted on p. 6 above, one was between Jack and Rusty. The way that selling the Dobbs and Woodbury terminal was handled had caused acrimony between Dobbs and Woodbury. That and the company's rocky fortunes proved sufficient grounds for a split.

Jack invited Rusty to design Novell terminals, including another for the Sperry marketplace.

Timeline: Rusty Woodbury

Rusty Woodbury is an NDSI founder. He lasts until March 1983, when he leaves as part of Ray Noorda's first reorganization.

A Beehive Connection

Another people conduit ran back and forth between Beehive International and Novell. It included Phil Long. Because of Phil's experience designing terminals for the IBM mainframe marketplace, Jack called upon him to head software design. As head of Software Development, Phil became deeply involved in developing the various low-level programs needed to get the terminal computer going. (Low-level programs are those closest to machine language and therefore needing the highest expertise to produce.)

Timeline: Phil Long

Phil is an NDSI founder. He joins in 1981 and leaves as part of the March Massacre in 1982.

The Forgotten Connection

There was another connection Jack had made in his wide-ranging activities but had forgotten by 1980. Reid Clark, a trainer at GE in Phoenix, remembered working with Jack but not vice versa.

In 1980 he walked into Novell's new office as a representative of another Utah startup company, Billings Computer, to sell floppy disk drives to Novell.

As mentioned on p. 7 above, George Canova's CalComp divestitures to raise cash included the disk drive operation he had himself started. It had been a part of the Memories Division sold to Xerox, but Xerox had declined to take that part, and it got sold to Billings Computer in a separate deal. So Reid felt that there ought to be a good fit between Billings and NDSI.

When he got there and discovered that his old associate Jack Davis was also involved, he asked to join and signed on to head International Sales.

An interesting piece of trivia about Reid: He was a Guinness world record holder for high-altitude survival. While being a pilot in the Air Force, he had been able to function in an altitude chamber with the air at a record-thin level.

Timeline: Reid Clark

Reid Clark is the longest lasting of the NDSI founders, the only one to survive the transition to Novell, Inc. He retires from Novell in 1987.

People who Came and Went ... and Came Again

About a hundred people were cast out of NDSI during its first time of troubles. Many couldn't stay away. As Ray reassembled the Novell dream, they came back for a second try. Here are a few.

Jim Bills headed Novell Data Systems Technical Service. Throughout 1981 he labored to set up maintenance agreements with the big service outfits such as Icot. He left early in 1982 to work with Peripheral Systems, another Jack Davis offshoot, as the magnitude of the crisis was becoming evident.

20

He came back late in 1983 to continue working on service and thrived within the Novell organization until the mid-'90s. Jim wasn't one of the founders who survived the troubles within the Novell organization, but he's an almost founder.

Timeline: Jim Bills

Jim Bills signs on with NDSI in 1981, leaves early in 1982, comes back late in 1983, advances steadily, and by 1991 is a Vice President heading up Sales of NetWare.

Psssst! This is your author, Roger Bourke White Jr. I will from here on refer to myself in the third person.

Roger White came to Novell after spending three years running a ComputerLand retail store. He brought marketing expertise on reaching the retail store channel and technical expertise on dealing with the rapidly developing CP/M applications world. (CP/M meant *control program/monitor*. It referred to the premier operating system before Microsoft's MS-DOS took over the field.)

Roger started as head of Customer Support for the personal computer, then moved to Sales and headed the Dallas regional sales office for six months, when the ebb caught him.

He spent three years at Beehive International working with their personal computer and then returned to Novell's Communications, working on strategic reports and developer relations. He left Novell with the 1989 Organizational Phase Change.

Timeline: Roger White

Roger White is about the 20th person to join Novell in January 1981 and is laid off when the company shrinks back to about 20 people in the summer of 1982. He returns to Novell in the summer of 1986 as Novell tops 500 employees and leaves again in the summer of 1989.

Dave Owens was an NDSI engineer. He left in the summer of 1982 to join Beehive International, but in the summer of 1983 he became head of Engineering at Novell under Ray and continued afterward.

Timeline: Dave Owens

Dave Owens joins NDSI in 1981, leaves in summer 1982, returns a year later, and prospers well into the '90s.

People Who Came and Stayed: Novell, Inc., Founders

The Novell, Inc., founders are the people who survived NDSI's time of troubles. The hard sieve of layoffs and the soft sieve of having the opportunity to pursue other more attractive opportunities had skimmed off about 100 people and left these people behind to carry on the dream. Some of the founders continued on in quite prosaic fashion—they just did their job. A few, the ones this story is about, rose to the challenge of shaping a new company and a new industry. We will follow them throughout this tale.

The Returned Missionary

In 1977, Craig Burton stepped off the plane and took a deep breath of the dry, thick air of home: Utah. He was still over 4,000 feet, but he'd come from a mission in Ecuador where he was riding a bicycle and proselytizing for the Mormon Church at over 10,000 feet. The airport announcements were in English, not the South American Spanish or the native Indian Quechua he'd been hearing for the previous two years.

It was good to be home, but what to do now?

Rather than return to college, Craig started working with his father, LeR Burton, selling real estate. The income was slow in coming. In fact, he only sold one house. But real estate was merely one of many things that interested the Burtons. Computers and electronics was another. LeR, for instance, had worked in the mid '70s with some of the first Hewlett Packard handheld calculators, the HP-35s, and had written some of the examples that HP put in their instruction manuals for doing real estate calculations.

Craig and LeR started doing computer consulting, helping businesses integrate personal computers into their work. Roger White at ComputerLand supplied them a couple Apple IIs. Craig was soon setting up cash flow projections using Apple's Pascal programming language.

By 1981 Craig was out of real estate and into personal computers entirely. He was working with Personal Business Computers (PBC), a thriving retail computer store in Salt Lake, to sell systems to professionals, and he was discovering that while professionals liked the pricing and the office productivity software available on personal computers, they needed more connectivity than personal computers offered.

When Craig saw the first ads for the Corvus computer networking system, he thought he was seeing a godsend. Then he tried to make one work. It didn't. He called many times and even visited their factory once. He wasn't satisfied. By 1982 he knew they were onto something hot, but he could also tell that Corvus hadn't the foggiest idea what it was they were making, and it would be a while before they found out.

By then Craig knew a lot about selling personal computers. He had participated as Apple and the various CP/M-based computers had battled for the hearts and minds of computer retailers and their customers. He had witnessed Commodore shoot themselves in the foot time and time again through ham-handed marketing and introductions of new products incompatible with old ones and with each other, then save themselves time and time again with price reductions that opened markets of new buyers and new store operators who saw those prices and said, "Let's start here."

He had witnessed Apple bobble the Apple III introduction—in part by ignoring how important the Apple II's open bus had been to its attractiveness. And in 1982 he was watching them compound the error with their Lisa product introduction by making it both closed and pricey. (Lisa was the short-lived Macintosh processor that taught Apple how *not* to market Macintosh.)

Craig had also been noticed by several people at Novell. He was interested in local area networks at the same time Novell was interested, and in spring of '82 he got his break. Roger was moving out of Customer Support into Sales and he needed a replacement. Craig came to mind. Roger talked with him. Craig visited, talked with top management, expressed his views on LANs, and was immediately invited to speak at a seminar in St. Louis.

Weeks later he was formally on board doing customer and sales support work.

Craig did a lot of things at Novell but he spent most of 1982 working with Reid on building international sales. The two traveled worldwide. As a result they were partly isolated from the crises that shook Novell in the Time of Six Presidents, discussed in Chapter Two below.

As the crises ended, Craig was working on documentation, customer support and, in what ended up being his most strategic effort, developer relations.

Craig Burton

Timeline

Craig Burton joins Novell early in 1982 at the beginning of the Time of Six Presidents. He stays with Novell until March of 1989 when his departure, along with Judith Clarke's, signals the beginning of the Organizational Phase Change of 1989–90.

Adding from ADDS

Utah has seen its share of electronics failures as well as successes.

There is a straight as an arrow section of I-15 at the south end of the Salt Lake Valley, just before the highway winds and curls by Point of the Mountain—the landmark hill that separates the Salt Lake Valley, which holds Salt Lake City, from Utah Valley, which holds Orem and Provo. Midway along this stretch of highway is a giant brick building that now houses the Utah National Guard—easily identified because out front is a jet fighter mounted on a forty-foot-high pedestal.

This spectacular building is the legacy of a multi-hundred-million-dollar electronics industry failure. The builder of that building had dreams of churning thousands upon thousands of computer terminals out of it. It was ADDS (pronounced *adds*, for Applied Digital Data Systems), a New York company that in the mid-'70s was one of the leading CRT terminal makers, and Harry Armstrong was one of the people who was going to make that happen as its employee. But ADDS suffered the same declining price and declining margin challenges that faced Beehive, Novell, and all the other domestic makers of CRT terminals in the late '70s and early '80s. Even Utah's low labor costs weren't enough to keep them competitive with the East Asian imports. Shortly after it was built, the factory was shut down.

At ADDS Harry was a "metal bender" and "plastic pourer". He was in charge of making the physical manufacturing processes happen, and it was this expertise that attracted Joe. But Harry was another of those people with a rich background in electronics. Before working for ADDS, he had been one of the founders of a personal computer manufacturing company in Ogden, Utah, that didn't make it, and prior to that he'd been in California doing design and troubleshooting work on flying surveillance systems used by the military in Vietnam.

Harry enjoyed working with people, and Novell turned into a perfect stage to exercise his many people and technical talents.

24

Harry Armstrong

Timeline

Harry Armstrong joins Novell in the summer of 1981 to work for Joe Maroney in Manufacturing, survives the Time of Six Presidents, and heads both Manufacturing and Sales under Ray Noorda. He stays with Novell until summer of 1987, when he retires to take up ranching on the Idaho/Wyoming border.

The Wife and Mother

Judy's story began as typical Americana. She grew up in humble backgrounds in the period between "Rosie the Riveter" of WWII and the "Women's Lib" of the '70s and '80s. She was outgoing, ambitious, and constantly driven to make something of herself in a time when this ambition wasn't taken seriously in the average woman.

In her younger days, she had qualified as a beauty technician. By 1981 she had married twice and borne three children, but there was little one could point to on her résumé to predict "Giant success awaits you just around the corner." In 1980 she was in Hawaii working part-time with her husband, Reid Clark, at a company that sold minicomputer-based energy management systems, and before that she had done some presentation work for a small telecommunications company.

Judy met Reid at a church social in Phoenix, Arizona, and they married shortly thereafter. (She added the E to her last name after their divorce.) She followed him as his work took him from Phoenix, to California, to Hawaii, and finally to Provo, Utah.

Judith Clarke

Timeline

Judy Clark (after her divorce, Judith Clarke) starts working for Novell part-time in the summer of 1981, becomes full-time as Ray Noorda comes on in 1983. She heads Communications until March of 1989 when her departure, along with Craig Burton's, signals the beginning of the Organizational Phase Change of 1989–90.

The Programmers

In 1981 Jack Davis was looking for a word processor to offer as "Novell's word processor", and in 1981 BYU was a hotbed of word processing activity. It had a horde of graduate students and professors

25

who had been developing word processors the previous two years for organizations such as Hill Air Force Base, Savin (copiers and other office technology), and Qume (a division of ITT that did daisywheel printers at the time, terminals later).

("Blistering hotbed" is the proper description for BYU that year. Besides those who met their destiny as SuperSet at Novell, another group started what would become WordPerfect.)

Jack consulted with an assistant to the Dean at BYU's College of Engineering about what features the Novell word processor should have. This fellow did some research for Jack and recommended four BYU computer science grads to bring in as programmers. One of them, Dale Neibaur, had done work on a word processor for Jack in 1980—yet another of Jack's entrepreneurial projects.

But before they could work on a word processor, they were directed to a more pressing need: A product introduction for Comdex.

As you will see below, the story of SuperSet reveals a lot about the functioning of Novell management before and after Ray came on board.

SuperSet

Timeline

SuperSet is a group of sometimes three and sometimes four BYU grad students (Drew Majors, Dale Neibaur, Kyle Powell, and often Mark Hurst) who come to Novell as contract programmers in the summer of 1981, form into a distinct entity in the summer of 1982, and continue working for Novell as SuperSet into the 1990s.

People Who Didn't Join in Founding Novell

Jack's list of connections didn't end with people who joined Novell. Many helped Novell without actually joining it.

Motorola Men

These include Sherrill Harmon's superiors at Motorola in Phoenix, who had also been associates of Jack's. Even though he was taking one of their people back to Utah they saw his work as a potentially big market for their chips, so they remained enthusiastic about Jack's work. They helped Jack and Sherrill stay up to date on the 68000's progress. Novell was usually the first or second company in the state to get update information and newly revised 68000 chips.

Ray Noorda

Another person who was aware of Jack's work but not involved was Ray. Jack and Ray had earlier worked together at GE in Phoenix. In the '70s Ray moved on to become President of General Automation and Jack worked for him there, heading up International Sales.

When Jack presented his plan to Ray, Ray was involved in turning around Boschert, Inc., a maker of power supplies for electronics. He declined to get involved.

Ray had another reason for staying out.

Since he'd become head of a company producing a component for computers, he had gained a new perspective on industry trends. When Jack talked about manufacturing hardware in Utah—minicomputers, terminals, and printers—Ray felt Jack was in for some tough sledding. Yes, Utah was a low-wage state in the US, but in 1980 terminals and printers were just the components East Asians were getting good at making. This meant increased competition and declining margins for all involved. In fact, one of Ray's major goals for restoring profitability to Boschert was to move power supply manufacture offshore.

Ray decided to pass on the opportunity Jack offered.

The Products of 1981

The goal of all the people joining Novell was to build computer products that the marketplace would buy. Jack had an impressive list in his business plan and 1981 was the year in which those ideas would be transformed into metal and plastic.

The Printer

The first product out the door was the printer. Incorporating the Tritel design had gone quickly and Image 800 printers were moving off the shipping dock in March. The Image 800 was a medium-duty wide-carriage dot-matrix printer. It printed at 160 characters per second and had a character selection comparable to the early Epson printers: Four basic widths plus double-high and double-wide, with international and extended sets.

Through most of 1981 the printers sold well, and this brought assurance that Novell was on the right track. But printers carry low profit margins, so Novell was going to have to sell more than printers if it was to be the kind of company Jack and George had in mind.

The Terminal

Early in 1981 Rusty had started designing the terminal. Jack's vision was that it would sell to the Sperry-Univac marketplace, but shortly after Rusty arrived he was diverted from designing a Sperry-compatible terminal to one that would be the front end for the personal computer.

In theory this would be no problem. In practice, Rusty took all the Sperry-compatible ideas floating around in his head and put them into the personal computer product. The result was an "engineer's delight": A product with a lot of features that were easy for an engineer to implement but not particularly relevant to the market for which the product was designed.

The terminal Rusty produced had graphics capabilities and two kinds of programmable function keys. It was housed in a large case and the keyboard was broad and detached from the screen. All this was being presented to a personal computer marketplace that was used to working with simple, small, character-only terminals.

The terminal was premium, but how much of the market was willing to pay for a premium terminal? No one knew and top management didn't have the time to find out. They were relying on Jack's experience in the marketplace to lead them through to profitability. Once they were profitable, then they would have time to experiment and do market research. Meanwhile, Jack was busy building a company.

As Rusty finished the terminal for the computer, he turned back once again to working on the Sperry terminal. But before he could finish, the first wave of crisis in the fall of 1981 put it on the shelf.

The Terminal Computer

The terminal computer was a child of the Cynic's Golden Rule: He who has the gold, rules. The Safeguard connection drove this product to the front of the development list. It was a combination of Rusty's terminal plus a 64KB-RAM computer board incorporating Zilog's Z-80 CPU. The computer would run CP/M and have two serial ports for talking with printers, modems, and other peripheral devices.

The terminal computer suffered from being brought into the planning in a hasty way. Novell was structured so that it was counting on Jack's experience in marketing to substitute for batteries of consultants and hours of market research—the company didn't have the time for those if it was going to be quickly profitable.

The flaw was that Jack hadn't paid that much attention to the personal computer marketplace. His attention was focused on terminals, printers, and minicomputers. In these areas his instinct as to what constituted a winning product was sharp. In personal computers it was fuzzy, but the terminal computer was to be the company's second product. As a result, he let Rusty's engineer's delight slip out the door without bringing it sharply into focus with what the market was looking for.

The Novell terminal computer ended up being a high-end feature-loaded personal computer system when all the company needed to produce was a computerized accounting system that One Write salespeople could sell. But by the summer of 1981 that was what they had, and that was what they had to sell.

Ironically, this engineer's delight was a vital step in developing the local area network product.

The Minicomputer

The minicomputer was to be developed with profits from the sales of other Novell products. It went on the shelf (on indefinite delay) almost as soon as Safeguard financing was arranged.

AutoGen: A TSI Software Legacy

Jack's work at TSI also garnered him rights to a program called AutoGen. It never became a Novell product but its evolution gives more insight into Jack's style.

The AutoGen idea started when Jack encountered an earlier program-generator program put together by a group in Hawaii for the Nova line of minicomputers.

The intent of program generators is to allow relatively inexperienced programmers to produce code quickly by automating parts of the code-generating process. A beginner programmer may build a screen with a screen editor, then the program generator scans what the programmer has done and generates code that will tell a high-level language—typically COBOL, BASIC, FORTRAN, or Pascal—to build a similar screen. This leaves the programmer free to concentrate on other parts of the programming task.

The program generator concept has been around a long time, but it is one of those parts of computerdom that rarely lives up to expectation. The concept is highly cyclical. It rises suddenly as a panacea for each new generation of computer programmer wannabes, then dies quickly as those people see the reality of the product and find that programming is still tedious.

(A modern incarnation of this concept that has actually been successful is converting WYSIWYG screens into HTML code for web sites. Dreamweaver is an example.)

Jack saw this Nova program generator and felt the concept was a breakthrough. He wanted to buy the rights to this package and sell them through TSI. He was foiled; the programmers had already sold interests to other companies and one of those objected that selling to TSI would conflict with their interest.

So Jack did an end run. He brought in a programming friend of his to look at the package and asked him if he could reverse-engineer it. "Of course," said the programmer. He developed AutoGen for TSI and Jack put another piece in his minicomputer "hope chest". (In the tight circles of the Utah computer industry, few people disappear. This programmer was Charles Burgoyne, a jack-of-all-[computer-related]-trades who later started one of Salt Lake's most long-lived retail computer stores).

AutoGen shows that Jack was resourceful and his connections were widespread through the Utah and southern California computer industry. It also shows that he was sloppy about his follow-through; he would build fast while leaving lots of holes behind.

The Events of 1981

Now that the stage set has been revealed and the actors introduced, here are vignettes of what Roger White saw in 1981. They show the excitement, the innovation, the compromise, and the coping that went on as Novell tried to make dreams fit reality on a limited budget.

Organizing the Sales Force

Bringing on the Sales Power

Larry came on early, as Vice President of Sales in November 1980. As mentioned on p. 15 above, he was one of the attendees at Novell's first Comdex.

Larry's job was to organize those who would sell Novell products. This is significant because it shows that from day one Jack was bent on selling things. There was no low-overhead development phase at Novell, during which product was developed without the pressure of a sales staff waiting expectantly to rip the finished work out of the developers' and manufacturers' hands and begin hawking it.

Larry knew how to sell minicomputers. He immediately set out to build a national sales force with offices located regionally across the nation.

Larry was a man with experience, so he brought in salespeople he was experienced with. The first on board was Andy Olson, who would handle the southern California area. His experiences with introducing Novell products were typical.

Andy was born and raised in Northern Minnesota. His dad was a mining engineer who worked at exploring and developing the open pit iron mines in that area. But digging giant holes in the ground wasn't a legacy to be passed from father to son.

Ten to fifteen years before, Andy had reached the California coast and flourished. When he signed on with Novell he had two houses and two ex-wives in Manhattan Beach and he was something of a local celebrity. He was into supporting local politicians and he was trying to reach a final settlement with his second wife. He was also a remodeling contractor.

Andy was the kind of guy who was always busy and always on the phone except at lunch, when he went to Orville's, a classy restaurant in the center of Manhattan Beach where Andy knew the owners and the banker that financed the owners and so on. He treated the computer industry the same way he treated Manhattan Beach. He was one of the speakers at and advisors to the first Comdex, Comdex 79, and he had connections all through the southern California minicomputer sales scene.

Andy Olson

Timeline

Andy Olson, one of Novell's first salespeople, comes on in March 1981 and is one of the first to see how deep its problems will be. He leaves in May 1981, shortly after the first personal computer is shipped.

The First Expedition into ComputerLand

When Roger was brought on in March 1981 to head Customer and Sales Support there weren't any customers yet, so he helped in the task of getting some. Roger coordinated with Andy to set up a series of meetings with the five ComputerLand stores in southern California.

The meetings went smoothly enough but the response was reserved: None of the store owners wanted to be a pioneer. They wanted to see product and see customers before they committed.

As they left, Roger hummed "The times they are a-changing". The days had ended when a ComputerLand store owner asked only two questions: "Does it run CP/M?" and "Will it work when I turn it on?"

Andy moved on to Plan B.

Andy's Plan B: Jade Computer

Andy's next stop was Jade Computer, a mail order house pioneering in offering personal computers, where Andy had connections. The Jade people were more responsive. Mail order, it seemed, was still in the two-question era, and Jade was signed up as Novell's first customer.

This left Roger uneasy. Mail order was the low-end whorish competitor to the retail store channel. It wasn't clear that taking on Jade as a reseller would make the task of penetrating the retail channel any easier. It might if it helped generate awareness and demand, but it might not if it started a trend of margin shaving.

What Andy knew that Roger didn't was that Jade had a retail side as well and this made it look attractive to Andy.

So Andy had his first blood and Roger returned to Utah.

Organizing Product

The Quickstep from Visions to Reality

The quickest way to turn Rusty's terminal design into a computer was to add a CPU board to the terminal enclosure and put the disk

32

drives in a separate box. This was the path chosen and it was a good one for at least two reasons: The terminal enclosure was big and heavy already, so having the disks in a separate box made the shipping and handling easier. In the early '80s disk drives were noisy; with a separate box the drives could be moved away from the operator.

The pitfalls in this simple approach involved how these various parts were going to communicate with each other.

The terminal part of the microcomputer was already designed to talk with the outside world, being equipped with the twin RS-232 ports that made that possible. Once again, the simplest solution was to use those ports and let the CPU board do all its communicating through the terminal board. But this was a deviation from standard microcomputer practice in the early '80s. The terminal computer looked like this:

[CPU] - - - - - [terminal] - - - - - RS-232 to outside world

when everyone expected:

[terminal] - - - - - [CPU] - - - - - RS-232 to outside world

Putting a CPU behind the terminal produced several other differences that, like the above, presented subtle challenges. Solving these challenges added overhead to the system. In spite of its size and the impressive claim of four CPUs in the system its performing speed was mediocre.

The Graphic Screen

Rusty had been brought on board to design a high-quality terminal that supported graphics. When the terminal turned into a microcomputer there seemed no reason not to make it a graphics-supporting microcomputer, so he did.

The decision to go with graphics produced another hit against performance. The screen generator didn't use a fast character-generator chip; it relied on slower ROM-based software.

A Z-80 with a Hard Disk

One place that the terminal computer did excel was in offering a hard disk. In the early '80s attaching a hard disk to a microcomputer was not unheard of but it wasn't common, either. Novell took the bold step of making the hard disk an integral part of the system: You always got a hard disk with your Novell computer.

Gaining Intelligence about Retail Computing

Marketing and Promotion

One of the first things Jack and Larry needed to decide was how to approach their marketplace: The newly emerging retail computer store channel. Jack knew such a channel existed because these new stores were buying some of the terminals that he sold at TSI. Since Praxis software was sold to dentists on minicomputers, Larry had had few dealings with dealers.

One of their early sources was Roger, the ex-ComputerLand store owner. With his input about how ComputerLand was organized and what was expected of margins and pricing, the product marketing and promotion features were hashed out.

Margin and Volume Levels

Roger recounted his pricing experiences to Jack and Larry, saying something like this.

In the early years of retail computer stores, the late '70s, hardware products carried margins of 25 to 33%. These were very low. One of the first lessons in the ComputerLand training seminars was a cash flow lesson that demonstrated how important a good margin was to profitable sales. The moral: Don't discount just to increase sales volume. If you do discount, make sure you pick your margin back up on the accessory sales.

One of ComputerLand corporate's major goals was to raise that margin, and by the beginning of the '80s the 25% items were rarely seen and a few 40% items were appearing.

Given this background the terminal computer was priced with a 45% margin and no discount for volume dealing. Novell wanted something dealers could become strong by selling.

Training the Sales Force

As Larry assembled the sales force Roger trained them. He assembled classes in CP/M basics: Booting the system, word processing with WordStar, and showing how these tools could be used in office automation.

Building CP/M Familiarity at Novell

Novell was going to build a CP/M computer but no one in the front office or top management had any experience with one. The only CP/M machines at Novell were two Intertech Superbrains in Phil's lab and they were in the usual state of Superbrains—dead. (Intertech was a company that survived for several years on the new blood entering the personal computer field. Their quality was terrible but they were always the lowest price, so they always got tried first.)

Roger saw this as a big oversight. To give the company some insight into what it was dealing with he brought in his pride from Computer-Land days: A dual-eight-inch-drive Digital Microsystems computer with an IBM 3101 ASCII terminal and a Diablo daisywheel printer. He also brought in his software collection and set the system up near the break room where lots of people could have access to it.

From this system the company management and staff learned their first lessons about CP/M word processing and database management.

Organizing the PC Application Software

Following minicomputer tradition, Novell was going to sell software for their personal computer. Roger, being the most experienced with personal computer software, got involved in picking packages.

WordStar

Novell needed a word processor. The most popular in the CP/M world of 1981 was WordStar. Novell signed a deal with MicroPro and began offering WordStar.

It was a good choice. WordStar was a well-known full-featured package that worked well on the terminal computer. With a little extra work it was customized so that it could take advantage of the function keys on the terminal computer as well and it became a hot package.

Tradition!

Like the course of true love, the course of true business rarely runs smoothly. Jack felt that WordStar wasn't a Novell product. It was okay as an interim solution but Novell needed something that Novell could call its own and get better margins on. He continued the search.

This resulted in a parade of word processing developers coming in to offer their product as something Novell could OEM. It also led to

35

Jack's making the BYU contact that eventually brought the SuperSet programmers to Novell.

Excerpt from Roger White's Diary

And while that was happening, other big changes were occurring. Jack and Mike King's search for "Novell's own" word processor was bearing fruit. A group from Phoenix called Metasoft had reached Jack's ear via Sherrill Harmon. They would build Jack a word processer. As credentials they presented their existing WP [word processor]—Benchmark. They had sold this package to Zenith and Harris.

I had seen Benchmark in its Zenith incarnation and it was no great shakes. It was page oriented and did nothing special in my mind to compensate for that. WordStar was better.

But Jack wanted Novell's own, so he struck a deal: We would give them a machine, they would give us a WP. Like many other deals Novell made during this period, it sounded simple enough, but the implementation was another matter.

In this case we had a chicken and egg problem. Metasoft needed the latest terminal firmware to develop their software on so it could incorporate all the bells and whistles they had agreed with Jack to add. We didn't have the latest firmware released yet. But Jack had a show coming up and he wanted to show the WP off.

So Jack put pressure on Rusty, who would then release preliminary (and buggy) firmware to Metasoft. But as soon as Metasoft found bugs, they would stop work.

At one point I was appointed project manager to see if this could get completed. But there was no way I could get into that loop meaningfully, and after a week or so no one tried anymore. I didn't because I became a sales manager and all I needed was WordStar. NovellWriter was a waste of time as far as I was concerned.

SuperCalc

In 1981 the VisiCalc spreadsheet program had been out for two years. It was immensely popular on the Apple II and had made a business machine of that computer. But its developer, VisiCorp, was very slow about porting the package to other kinds of computers. They had a Commodore PET version out (PET was pronounced, and apparently meant to suggest, *pet*) but nothing for CP/M. Roger called them several times and always got back a "we're considering it" sort of answer.

Roger knew having a spreadsheet was as critical as having a word processor. For weeks he phoned, researched, and networked through his connections in the personal computer world looking for a suitable substitute. Just as the impossible looked like it was happening—that there was no substitute—the Osborne 1 computer, a CP/M machine, was announced. Bundled with it was a spreadsheet package called SuperCalc from an outfit called Sorcim Software. (The Osborne was marketed as the first portable computer. Sorcim later merged with Computer Associates.)

Roger called Sorcim and Novell was probably the first place in Utah to have SuperCalc. The spreadsheet problem was solved.

Moving Applications to Novell

Roger didn't see any way Novell could hope to be a single-source supplier of applications software, and personal computer users and sellers weren't expecting Novell to be one, either. What they were expecting was an easy way to get CP/M applications from many sources onto the Novell disk format.

Some Novell personal computers used 8″ floppy disk drives—which were fairly standardized, so getting applications on 8″ disks that Novell computers could read wasn't a problem. But the 5″ floppy disk situation couldn't be solved so easily. There wasn't a single standard for 5″-drive disk formats, there were dozens.

There were two alternatives: Either Novell was going to become a center for disk conversions or it was going to offer a product that could be sold into the field, where conversion would become a reseller activity—a much faster, more flexible solution.

The solution Novell ultimately offered was an error-checking file-transfer program developed by Gary Byrom, another Utah pioneer in the personal computer industry. This product, BSTAM (the Byrom Software Telecommunications Access Method), could communicate between the serial ports of different kinds of CP/M machines. A reseller could buy 8″ versions of software and use BSTAM to transfer the programs to Novell 5″ disks.

The Accounting Crisis

Bringing in Accounting

Word processing, spreadsheeting, file transfer, and terminal emulation. These were all areas where Novell acquired products that were popular, workable, and easy to install. Then came the quagmire of personal computing in general and Novell in particular: The accounting packages.

One of the hallmarks of personal computing in the '80s was its simplicity. The standalone personal (micro)computer system was simple compared to a minicomputer. It consisted of a CPU, a terminal, and a disk system. The operating system was simple; it had to deal with just one computer and one user. Even buying one was simple: Just walk in a retail computer store and buy one.

Most application software was also simple.

You want to word process? You buy a word processing package.

You want to spreadsheet? You buy a spreadsheet package.

You want to program? You buy a programming language package.

Then comes accounting ...

The difference between accounting and the other commodity applications is you can't tell someone how to keep accounts without telling them how to run their business. Worse, computerized accounting tends to be very deterministic—it's hard on the fuzzy, seat-of-the-pants styles characteristic of small business people who were attracted to personal computers rather than minicomputers. Worse still, people ask for, or at least they're impressed by, accounting packages designed by CPAs— who are the most deterministic of the people who deal with accounting. (It would be better if they asked for accounting designed by a housewife who tends three kids after school!)

The confluence of these trends created a marketing challenge in selling accounting packages that was similar to that faced by the life insurance and funeral plot industries: Selling something that's considered important but rarely used.

Most of the buyers of personal computer accounting packages bought them as justifiers for getting the computer but used them only briefly. They used the computer's word processing and spreadsheeting pretty much as they had anticipated, but because the accounting packages were too procedurally rigid to suit their needs they instead used a hybrid spreadsheet-manual system to accomplish their accounting goals. The accounting package ended up sitting on the shelf beside the BASIC programming language package; the optimistic user might mutter, "Someday, I'll get back to that and make it work."

This use dynamic made the marketing and presentation of accounting packages more important than the content. One of the first to discover this was Ben Dyer, the driving force behind Peachtree Software in Atlanta, Georgia. While other personal computer accounting houses were selling their product in plastic baggies he started offering handsome vinyl binders and spent big money on offices, customer support, and advertising.

One group he attracted was top management at Novell.

They wanted to offer an accounting package. Like WordStar, Peachtree had a reputation as something that would fill the need. The decision was made to carry it.

Roger got the shudders when he heard that Novell would be supporting *any* accounting package.

Peachtree, Plumbing, and Jack Saying "Yes"

The first purchaser of a Novell Terminal Computer was Novell's landlord. They wanted to computerize their accounting and Jack offered them a Novell system. The following excerpt from Roger's diary continues the story.

With the shipping of the first units, my job [customer support] came on line. The first unit we shipped was to our landlord, K&P Plumbing. He bought it direct from Jack Davis at a discount. Jack sold him not just the hardware, but a complete accounting system—and we were going to install it. Trouble City!

Gary Dan Hill [in Technical Support] and I got saddled with the installation. We were to install the full Peachtree system—GL [General Ledger], AR [Accounts Receivable], AP [Accounts Payable], Payroll and Cost Accounting.

Dreams, Dreams, Dreams! Peachtree was just converting from Series 4 to Series 5. All the packages were buggy. Payroll wasn't ready yet and, it turned out, it wouldn't be for months. There was no cost accounting [which K&P specifically needed] planned for Peachtree and no easy way to do it—Jack had not checked before he said, "Yes". Jack was also reluctant to sell K&P anything but

Peachtree since this was to be *our* accounting package. The hardware was also brand new so it was somewhat troublesome.

Finally, the K&P people had hired a new woman to run the system and this was her only job. She was an experienced operator on mini equipment, but new to micros and CP/M. Worst of all, she was new to K&P, so her job depended on the performance of the computer.

The net result was six weeks of constant attention from Gary and me. We were constantly back and forth between Sandra at K&P, and Janice and Janet at Peachtree in Atlanta, and Jim Bills at HQ, trying to get things diagnosed and fixed.

We learned Peachtree. Oh boy, did we learn it! I was also totally discouraged at the stupidity of our getting involved in supporting an accounting installation at an end user site.

It was K&P that drove me out of customer support. I told Larry I needed to make more money and asked him what was the best way. "Go sales, young man, go sales", he told me (I paraphrase). So I began negotiations on getting a position as sales manager.

In the meantime, the heat at K&P finally ended when Sandra gave up. She quit and K&P was slow to refill her position—the system gathered dust.

The problem Novell faced in selling Peachtree accounting was, ironically, that it was selling a big, expensive personal computer. The personal computer had a hard disk; it had function keys; it had a classy case. Purchasers expected more from it. It wasn't the easily forgiven toy that an Apple II was. So while Peachtree could adequately serve the TRS-80 and Apple II marketplace where few users would actually use the product, it wasn't going to meet customer expectation in the Novell marketplace.

Gary Dan Hill

Timeline

Gary Dan Hill is another Novell two-timer. He comes in 1981, leaves in 1982, comes again in 1984, and leaves in 1987.

Applying Old Habits to a New Crisis

In a crisis a person's heart rate quickens, the breathing deepens, and habit short-circuits judgment as a way of making decisions. Peachtree was a crisis at Novell. With the shipping of the first of the terminal computers, top management was finally getting some real—and harsh—feedback about their creation.

The habit that top management followed turned out to be calling on trusted outside consultants for a reality check. Since George was the top manager, the consultants he brought in were people he, not Jack, trusted. Unfortunately the people that George trusted were even more deeply steeped in conventional minicomputer practice than Jack's associates were.

So Novell applied a principle from the good old minicomputer days: "BASIC is a bad platform for accounting and COBOL is a good one". Peachtree was unceremoniously dumped on the excuse that it was running on an interpreted BASIC platform, and because it took too long to switch from one module to the next (about 30 seconds).

George's consultant found a COBOL-based accounting package that had been ported to CP/M, recommended it to George, and it was declared the new Novell accounting package.

The first problem with this decision was that bad programs could be written in COBOL just as easily as in BASIC. This was amply demonstrated in the preliminary assessments of the package made by those who bothered to run it.

Top management didn't listen easily. In fact, Novell was just about to sign on the dotted line when Robert Lundahl, newly hired into the Marketing section, suggested to Larry Edwards that he watch this new package do a close, the process that ends each business month. The close took an hour. Larry got the message; he showed the other top managers and it was finally back to the drawing boards once again.

The second problem was that this fiasco opened up serious questions about management competence. Novell management had goofed twice trying to pick an accounting package. The old saying "Fool me once, shame on you; fool me twice, shame on me" was in the minds of Novell resellers.

It wasn't just resellers who were upset, either. Because of the Peachtree experience, Roger had already decided to depart Customer Service. He moved into Sales. And Robert, with the ink barely dry on his hiring papers, decided to depart the company entirely.

Robert's outrage was deeper than Roger's. When he had heard that Peachtree was going to be dumped in favor of a COBOL-based package, Robert offered Novell an accounting package he had himself written in COBOL. On the advice of George's consultant, they refused it, faulting it as not comprehensive. When Robert saw the trash that the company had almost accepted, he sniffed the air and it smelled.

The Way Out: The Personal Computer Way

Habit hadn't worked, but top management's next step did: They ignored the problem and it went away.

It turned out that in the personal computer marketplace, it wasn't necessary for the hardware maker to provide application software. That was the reseller's role. The reseller could contact applications developers and distributors as easily as the hardware makers could, and so long as the operating system was standard the reseller could also install it just as easily. The simplicity, low capital requirements, and standardization of standalone personal computers had driven a change in marketing channel expectations. It made efficient system integration possible at the reseller level.

Novell stumbled onto this truth, but it was a hard one to recognize because other events were commanding most of the company's attention.

The Safeguard Computer Project

As stated above (pp. 13, 15), Dolf and Pete's reasons for investing in Novell were strategic—high profit and migrating Safeguard Scientifics into high tech—and tactical—offering an automated successor to the manual One Write package that Safeguard Business Systems was selling.

Phil, head of Novell Software Development, was the man charged with making a terminal computer variant suitable for the Safeguard Business Systems marketplace.

Phil was a smart, blunt man who liked talking about the intricacies of the technology. "He was the kind of guy who if you asked for the time of day would preface the discussion by telling you the art of clock building," said Reid.

He was also very conservative in his preference for technological styles, which often put him at odds with Rusty, who was designing the terminal hardware. One such conflict was over the protocol used to have the terminal board talk to the CP/M board in the terminal computer.

Some background: The terminal computer was literally a terminal board plus a computer board housed in the same casing. To make communications between the two boards happen, they had to be connected with appropriate circuitry and a cable. The choice of hardware connection was curious to start with: Given the short distance between the two boards and the fact that Novell controlled the circuitry on both ends of the link, a parallel connection would have been fast, reliable, and inexpensive. However, these boards were a product of their own histories and the link was made serial instead—a slower, more expensive linkage, but one for which the circuitry on both boards was already in place.

This expedient choice would dog the terminal computer throughout its life because it aggravated the slow-screen-display problem. Further aggravating this problem was Phil's choice of how to handle the communications protocol—and this is where he and Rusty locked horns.

Phil said something like, "This is a serial connection, and an important one. We'll handle communication over this link with a formal handshaking and error correction protocol."

To which Rusty replied something like, "Using a formal protocol is going to double our overhead over an already-slow link. That formal protocol was developed for modem use, where lines are presumed to be noisy. Let's presume this line is clean and use an abbreviated protocol that'll double our throughput. We'll add just enough error checking to tell if we've had an error. If we get an error, we'll recover and retransmit."

This was the Phil and Rusty Relation in a nutshell, and dealing properly with this kind of relationship is one of the high arts of keeping a company both alive and creative. In a healthy company, such differences are called "creativity at work", because they insure that all sides of issues, and all relevant issues, are examined. In a company that's on the rocks, these differences are called "interdivisional communications problems" and are said to be the root of the company's inability to face its crisis.

Both views are correct. What leads to success is making sure that such people are communicating and making decisions before, not after, the finger-pointing stage. One of the keys is establishing a good company vision.

NCC 81

The high point of Novell Data Systems was NCC 81, the summer 1981 National Computer Conference show at the McCormick Center in Chicago. Novell wasn't planning to attend until the last moment—a couple months before the show. Once the decision was made, the company went into high gear planning how to make a memorable impact on short notice and short funds. Novell's showing at this NCC was an example of Jack's promoting at its finest.

The first problem was even getting a booth. The waiting list by spring was 150 companies long. If a booth couldn't be found, Novell would have to base from a hospitality suite at one of the hotels rather than be at the convention center—which wouldn't be nearly as effective. Thanks to Andy's connections at Jade Computer, Novell got a 10-by-20 booth on the main floor when Jade decided to back out of the show. A display was designed in short order.

Then Jack came up with his *coup de grace*. He swung a deal with some of the shuttle buses moving convention attendees between the McCormick Center and the hotels. In return for covering their chartering costs, he ran low-key tape-recorded Novell ads through the bus intercoms.

"It's a captive audience," Jack chuckled.

In addition, when the attendees arrived they were greeted with a newspaper insert piece describing Novell.

NCC 81 went quite well for Novell. The printer and the terminal computer were displayed and the LAN was announced. Interest was high.

For Judy the show was also the start of her connection to Novell. For months she and Reid, her husband, had been conspiring to get her involved in Novell. Earlier Reid had proposed taking Judy on one of his business trips to Europe as his secretary. Jack had vetoed it.

As NCC approached Reid proposed bringing Judy along as part of the exhibit team. Once again, Jack was dead-set against it. "It would set a bad precedent—having a husband and wife work at the company."

Jack's wasn't an uncommon feeling among businesspeople, but it had made more sense a decade earlier and in communities larger and less tightly-knit than Utah Valley, where there just aren't that many choices of places to work. And in spite of Jack's protests married couples were already working at Novell.

Then as the show deadline neared the booth shipping deadline was missed. Reid later related:

> The only way to get it to Chicago was to load it in a rented truck and have someone drive straight through. "I'll do it," I volunteered, "but Chicago is 20 hours away. I should have someone go with me. How about Judy?"

Jack relented. And so it was that Judy started working for Novell. She drove, worked at setting up and tearing down the booth, and took her share of booth duty as well.

But the road wasn't smooth for her. She was in again and out again at Novell several times after that NCC assignment. She and Reid would conspire to find a place for her during the relatively good times during 1982, then she would get cut out again at each crisis. She was part of Novell's story in 1982, but it wasn't until after Ray's assumption of the presidency in 1983 that her position became permanent.

The First Cracks Appear

The printer was Novell's first released product. In the first half of 1981 it sold well and the printer division was the most productive part of Novell's sales force.

But in the second half of the year the printer business started having a problem that was later to plague the rest of the product line: There were a lot of returns. Most of the returns were DOA (dead on arrival)—the customer had opened the box, plugged in the printer, and it didn't work.

As printer returns continued at a high level, accusing fingers were pointed at Joe's Production people. Joe in turn pointed at Engineering, complaining that there were too many revisions to the product and too little pre-production testing. Engineering replied that all the revisions were to fix problems that Production said urgently needed to be fixed or to add product features that Sales said urgently needed to be included.

Top management never broke the circle of finger-pointing. Poor product quality plagued Novell throughout its life as Novell Data Systems.

Summer '81: The Cracks Widen

Product Delays

In the summer of 1981 reality began to intrude on the Novell vision. It first showed in a classic way: Lack of coordination. By early summer, Larry Edwards had built a sales force to sell the full Novell product line but there was only the printer to sell. The terminal computer was barely released and the terminal was still in development.

Salesmen Start Moving On

When trouble hits a company, it settles first in one of two places. If the trouble is internal, the Chief Financial Officer leaves—usually about six months before the bad news hits the streets. If the trouble is external, it shows up as turmoil in the sales force.

Salespeople are quick on their feet. When they're on commission, they're paid to be so. Novell salespeople were paid as is traditional for computer companies: A base plus commission.

Commissions are a compensation tool that sends a specific message to the recipient: "The company is interested in what you produce today, not what you *may* produce some time in the future."

So if there are no immediate results, the person should be somewhere else.

Novell's sales were less than planned. Along with all the other problems low sales causes, that sent a message to the sales force that it was time for them to move on. Andy, first aboard, was first to leave. He did so in May.

The First Waves of Crisis

The Move to Post Office Place

In summer of 1981 Novell outgrew the Industrial Park Drive building they had been using in Orem and moved half the company to Post Office Place—twin buildings just being finished near the center of the city, behind the post office. Engineering, Design, and Manufacturing stayed behind. The administration, Sales, Customer Support, and Marketing moved.

That complex, given up during the Time of Troubles in early 1982, was later taken over by WordPerfect Corp and became the home of *WordPerfect Magazine*.

46

George Moves to California, Then Doesn't

With the expansion into Post Office Place came another signal of impending crisis. George announced that he would run the company from southern California. His wife didn't like Utah so he was going back and putting up an office there. Jack Davis was made General Manager to handle the Utah operations. It sounded to those of us in the trenches like George was feeling so comfortable about the company that he was no longer needed on the spot.

This plan lasted for about two weeks, then George was back in town on his old schedule. The handoff had been announced but it didn't happen. There was no new announcement to replace the old one so it added to the confusion. The one clear message: Things weren't going like they were supposed to go and there would be more changes in the future.

Scrapping the Minicomputer and the Terminal

Because products had been slow coming out, as noted above, by fall of 1981 sales were slower than expected. That led to the first shake-out. It was a slight tremor, hardly more than a premonition. Roger felt it because he was in the Bay area, just about to sign on the dotted line of a lease for a Novell sales office he was going to head in the Bay area, when he got a phone call from Larry saying, "Don't. And fly back ASAP."

When he got back they had a meeting. Larry said that due to the slow sales there were some tactical changes: Novell wasn't going to open the Bay Area sales office and the planned terminal and the mini-computer were officially on the shelf.

That had no great impact on Roger. He was a dyed-in-the-wool personal computer man. However, the Bay Area sales office was to have been Roger's transition from Novell Customer Support to Sales. He didn't have to wait long for another opportunity. Two weeks later the head of the Dallas sales office announced he was leaving.

The Consultant Parade

In spring of 1982, another sign of impending crisis was the stream of management consultants parading through George Canova's office door. When a manager doesn't have an answer, he or she seeks one out, and a common source for answers is a consultant. The sign of trouble is when there are a lot of consultants.

The consultant activity goes up when the manager isn't hearing answers he or she likes: Answers that will solve the problem at hand without creating a lot of organizational pain. If the first consultant doesn't have a good painless answer then it's time to find another consultant. If the consultant stream is growing and the turnover is high, then trouble is afoot.

The second sign of trouble is when the consultants aren't experts in the problem area. George's most frequent consultants, for instance, were old business associates of his with extensive business experience but no more experience in this new technology or market area that was the personal computer industry than George had. They could offer general truisms but not the word on the street—the specifics that made this market different from any other. This showed up in the questions the consultants asked of others in the organization as they did their research and it was soon clear that they didn't know much.

It was also clear that some carried great influence. One was Jim Walker, the person who recommended the infamous COBOL accounting package.

Jack Gives "The Speech"

Just before leaving for Dallas, Roger listened to Jack give a speech that sent shivers up and down his spine, for the reason explained in his diary:

> Jack communicated a lot, but it wasn't his habit to give group pep talks. But this particular meeting sounded like that was what it was to be. All the employees at the Post Office Place building gathered in the central meeting room, and Jack stood there in front of us.
>
> A quick summary of the speech was as follows:
> We aren't in trouble
> We need to cut expenses.
> We can't sacrifice service while we cut expenses.
> The suggestions he gave were: Don't use Federal Express when mail will do, and use customers' 800 numbers whenever you call.
> I had the impulse to jump up and say, 'And don't use shipping boxes when envelopes will do,' then turn to him and say, 'That's what I told my people.'

48

The déjà vu came from the fact that I had given the same speech to my staff just nine months previous when I was running ComputerLand, and these were the circumstances that led me to make my speech: I had just completed a series of financial projections—using VisiCalc for my first serious spreadsheet project. The results were discouraging: Using a scaled down projection of sales—based on the real sales I'd generated for the six months previously—and a continuation of expenses as they had been for those same six months, I couldn't see a profit.

For those six months I'd done everything I could think of to boost sales, so I didn't see any way to make any dramatic improvements in sales volume. I still had to buy product to sell, so I couldn't reduce inventory expense much. I didn't feel like there was any "excess baggage" in my staff, so I couldn't see how to make many cuts there. That left administrative expenses, so I called my staff together one day and gave them "the speech": "We need to cut expenses but not service, so don't make long distance calls you don't need to—but if you need to make a long distance call to generate business why be sure you do!"—and lots of other similarly contradictory directives.

The speech was, in effect, an admission on my part that no action I could think of taking would save my ComputerLand store situation. Only a change in the business climate ComputerLand operated in, something that spontaneously picked up sales, fattened margins, or lowered costs could save the day.

The day I made the speech I started looking for a buyer.

Now, a year later, Jack and George were facing a similar situation at Novell. They were nearing the end of their startup money. Sales were below plan, but without a sales force they would never reach plan, so the sales force couldn't be cut. (Much more, that is; in fact, the sales force was cutting itself very effectively as salespeople who weren't making any money left of their own will.)

Development couldn't be cut much because half the products weren't out yet and the other half were still buggy or not quite what the market needed.

Manufacturing couldn't be cut much because products had to be produced to sell and there were a lot of returned goods that needed to be processed and repaired.

In short, Jack finally came to the same course of action I did: First, make a speech about cutting administrative overhead because all the other quick fixes were being done to the limit that they could be done, then plan for some radical change.

As I heard the speech, I knew it signaled a change of heart in Jack, and probably George. Their view of Novell's potential had changed, and some radical change in the company was forthcoming. What form it would take was still a mystery, but it wasn't likely to be pleasant for the founders.

The LAN Is Born

Choosing a New Product

While storm clouds were growing over Novell all through 1981 there was lots of sunshine too. One of the bright spots was the evolution and development of the local area network.

Novell's product line, intended and real, was never static. It evolved from Day One, in logical, internally self-consistent ways. Jack started the company on his vision of a multi-CPU minicomputer—something that would break out of the limited-applicable-size constraint that minicomputers of the '70s offered. This minicomputer would need terminals and printers—something Jack was particularly experienced at selling, so why not build these too? Build them first, in fact, to finance the development costs entailed in designing the minicomputer.

So in the summer of '80, that's what the potential product line consisted of.

By fall of '80 it was clear that Safeguard would be doing the bulk of the financing. They wanted something their Business Systems dealers could sell. George said, "These people certainly can't sell a multi-user mini. This means a standalone microcomputer … no problem, we'll convert our terminal into one. Doing so is an industry trend right now." Thus the terminal computer was born and added to the product line as another way of bringing in revenue to support the minicomputer development.

In the spring of '81 Jack was still pursuing his NovellWriter dream. Since none of his commercial contacts had born fruit, he decided to end-run, the same way he had with AutoGen, and he contracted with some BYU grad students to develop a word processor.

Just days before the BYU programmers who would become Super-Set drove into the sparsely populated parking lots at Industrial Park Drive, Novell's top management conducted a brainstorming session.

The subject: Sales of the terminal computer were growing too slowly and something needed to be done. (It was clear that the mini would be a long time coming, so that couldn't be part of the solution.)

The managers assessed the terminal computer they had created:

- It was a graphics terminal with a big screen and programmable function keys. The terminal it had been based on was a feature-rich design intended for the Burroughs/Univac marketplace, where big screens and weighty terminals were traditional.
- It was competing in a microcomputer market accustomed to simple, small-screened, light-weight character-only terminals. This made the terminal computer look big, feature-rich, slow—because of its graphics capabilities—and expensive. (It was in fact a pricey unit.)
- The way chosen to speed its performance so it didn't look slow was to add a hard disk; it was one of the first CP/M computers to come with a hard disk as standard equipment. But this increased the expense even more.
- One way to cut the expense of adding the hard disk was to split it among several terminal computer units—develop a local area network.

Among those top managers, the LAN idea had a lot of supporters:

Jack was aware that two startup companies, Corvus and Nestar, were selling PC-connecting LANs, so he could see a market developing.

For Jack and Sherrill the LAN was a way to keep the 68000 chip as part of the product line, even if the multi-CPU minicomputer product was delayed.

For Dennis (the Ph.D. candidate and part-time Novell advisor), the LAN was a different way to transcend the limited-range-of-users problem that afflicted all traditional minicomputer designs. Instead of adding CPU power by putting additional cards into the central box, the CPU power would be added with each terminal computer added to the system.

For Larry it meant something to sell sooner rather than later.

With so many top managers going for the idea, it turned out that when the programmers from BYU arrived Jack's word processor was never mentioned.

Comdex was coming!

Horseshoe Nails, Motorcycles, and Turf Wars

The temporary BYU programmers—Drew, Dale, Kyle, and Mark— reported to Phil, the head of Software. He and his regular staff were working long and hard on making the terminal computer a suitable Safeguard product.

Phil introduced the expression "creeping feature creature" into Roger's lexicon. When new ideas came up he was often the one to say, "Sure it's nice, but do we really need it to sell product?"

When the LAN project came to his doorstep it was just another feature-adding project that Phil didn't have the resources to devote to. So Jack borrowed his new temporary talent, the BYU boys, to get a LAN demonstration built for Comdex 81.

Dale and Kyle started working on the terminal computer side. Their task was to pry the CP/M operating system apart far enough so they could get disk requests to flow out over a wire to a remote file server rather than go to an internal disk controller. The programmers needed something to test their work on, so Drew took another of the terminal computers and started developing a test-bed file server.

Dale related, "We'd been in this position once before. A year earlier we were working as part of a team project and the other part of the team failed to deliver. We had no way of proving our part worked, so we didn't get paid. This time we weren't taking any chances."

Fate proved the wisdom of this strategy. The fellow that was developing the 68000 file server side had a motorcycle accident. In a flurry of long hours and last-minute hustle it was the Z-80–based test-bed file server, stuck over the top of the 68000 board and using RS-232 connections, that was shown at Comdex.

Blue Smoke and Mirrors

This demonstration system was an example of the "blue smoke and mirrors"—an expression Andy liked to use—that Novell used to make a point at Comdex 81. That first system was never built to be sold, but solely to show what Novell was going to be up to in the coming months.

This practice is controversial: To some it is fooling the public because the thing being demonstrated may or may not come to fruition.

The value of showing off such a may-become-a-product is that it reduces risk to both vendors and consumers. It's a test-marketing step that helps vendors find out how valuable potential customers perceive a product to be and what adjustments need to be made to make it even more valuable.

Not bringing such prototypes to a trade show raises the cost of product introductions by forcing companies to spend more money before demand is proven. We end up with more Edsel cars and Premier cigarettes (a forerunner of the electronic cigarettes of the 2010s), where a lot of money is spent making a product that won't sell. Or we end up with more situations like America losing out on fax machines, where a market isn't tapped because the demand looks too risky for the amount of up-front money that must be committed.

Blue smoke and mirrors—prototyping—is a powerful cost-reduction and feature-tweaking tool for marketers. But like any other powerful tool, it can be abused. Novell used it well at Comdex 81.

After Comdex 81

The LAN demonstration at Comdex was a hit; lots of people were interested. George and Jack had pulled off another coup. They'd come to Comdex 80 with nothing but promises to be a big company. At 81 they were showing off cutting-edge products: The printer, the personal computer with a hard disk, and the LAN.

It didn't take Jack long to sense that the LAN concept was generating more interest than he had expected. Then, at a lull in the bustle of the show, Drew pulled Jack aside.

"You know, Jack, this LAN business is something we programmers have been thinking about between us before now. And what you've been describing here at the show is close to some of the ideas we've developed."

Drew and Jack headed home from Comdex early. Within a week the temporary programmers who came to build a word processor were formally mustered in as the core of the LAN development team.

Disk Server versus File Server

One of the first issues the proto-SuperSet team faced was the question of how to split the disk-controlling duties between the personal computers and the file server. The simplest and quickest approach was to let each personal computer do the bulk of the work, the most important piece of that work being deciding where on the disk to store the data. This is the *disk server* approach. The disadvantage is that the file server can't coordinate between the various computers easily.

There's a quick and easy way to solve that problem: Don't have any coordination. Allocate each computer a fixed portion of the hard disk with no overlap. This is called **disk partitioning** and it's the simplest of the disk server approaches.

Disk server: Quick to develop; simple in concept. Larry Edwards and the sales force loved it. They could say, "Yes, we have a LAN," and be selling it within months. The benefits were so compelling that most of Novell's early LAN operating system competitors were disk server-based.

The alternative is the **file server** concept: Let the file server operating system decide where to store data on the disk and handle coordination between the various personal computers' requests. This requires it to do more and requires more modification of the personal computer operating system. The benefits are more coordination between the personal computers and more efficient use of the disk storage. Partitions aren't required.

There was one other serendipitous difference between the two: File service requires more horsepower from the processor on the file server than disk service does. Novell's plan to use the more powerful 16-bit 68000 for the file server, while most of the competitive units were based on the 8-bit Z-80, made file service easier for the Novell team to develop than it would be for competitive teams.

Thoughts of disk service versus file service were churning through the minds of the future SuperSet in those weeks after Comdex 81. The more they thought, they more they wanted to develop file service, and not just file service but file service with system fault tolerance (an error recovery system that we'll be looking at in detail later).

Doing this would be difficult in the face of Sales demands for "something I can sell today", but as it turned out other events in the company were going to force themselves into the limelight and give the team the time to follow their dream.

One of those events was the firing of Jack Davis, of which more is said in the next chapter.

The Year in Review

1981 was the year in which Novell defined itself. It transformed from an idea into a company: A company based in Utah, a company that would sell printers, personal computers, and local area networks. It was also a year in which many ideas were cast off: It would not be a company that sold minicomputers or Sperry-compatible terminals. It would not be a company of which Jack was a part.

The challenge that Novell faced coming into 1982 was that what had been defined as Novell, thus far, was not profitable: It was still consuming more resources than it was creating. With Jack's firing, the writing was on the wall. The company would have to become profitable soon.

What Had Worked

Larry had been able to assemble an experienced sales and support staff very quickly. Novell never lacked for salespeople in 1981.

Jack's promotion and marketing efforts border on legendary. A company that didn't even exist in 1980 was getting media attention at Comdex 80, and by Comdex 81 was promoting like a well-established minicomputer company.

Rusty and Phil had created a high-end, innovative personal computer that any ex-IBM mainframe or ex-Burroughs terminal user would feel comfortable with.

Finally, the company as a whole had recognized that local area networks were going to be important to the company's future. The LAN was never a "skunk works" project that had to be developed in secret because part of the company was dead set against it. Everyone knew the LAN would be important. It just wasn't getting there soon enough.

What Hadn't Worked

Jack and George had assembled a highly professional team but couldn't supply the vision to keep them all pulling in the same direction. These people, including George and Jack, brought with them old habits and old experiences that were appropriate for the minicomputer world. Some were also appropriate for the personal computer world, but some were not. Mistakes were made, many of them costly.

The evolution of product had produced results that were different than what the mainstream of personal computer users were expecting. The Novell system was high-end at a time when the market was still more interested in low-end solutions. These features added cost, but didn't add customers. For instance, the system offered graphics but no way for average users to access them. They could get more graphics use out of an Apple II because there were software packages available that utilized the Apple II's graphics.

Jack was fast at assembling a plan but he was poor at checking for holes in his logic. George didn't have the background to fill in those holes.

For instance, Ray Noorda pointed out that manufacturing electronic hardware in Utah was a fundamentally risky proposition in the early '80s. Jack wasn't oblivious to this. He had helped TeleVideo import their terminals and every day he drove past the abandoned ADDS terminal factory that Harry Armstrong had once worked in. But on the other hand, even in the early '80s there was lots happening in electronics in Utah, and George's background was in manufacturing. If anyone could make domestic manufacturing happen, it was George, and he was willing to try.

One of the most costly mistakes was the inability to resolve the quality issue. Finding fault is only important inasmuch as it's a step towards resolving the problem. But top management never finished resolving the quality problem, so the organization wallowed in the fault-finding stage and its customers stayed away in droves.

Sunshine and Rain

So by the end of 1981 Novell already had a checkered past. Some of its efforts were hits and others were misses. It would take another year, 1982, to sort out its future.

CHAPTER TWO
1982: The Time of Six Presidents

Summary

"The Time of Six Presidents" was a time of chaos for Novell and all those involved. The chaos lasted from the dismissal of Jack Davis in December 1981 until Ray Noorda's arrival as President in January 1983.

The crisis started because the company was not meeting its original goals and it was not profitable. The board responded to the crisis by shuffling top management, again and again, to find a winning combination. During this period approximately six men were declared President of Novell ... no one knows the actual number.

The chaos of 1982 was exciting and dramatic. New developments were happening weekly. But it weakened lines of communication, lines of authority, and lines of coordination. This period was exciting and it allowed great change to take place within Novell, but it sure was hard to do business as usual!

Many companies miss a market on the first try. The company must recover and either try again or abandon the effort and try something else. When a startup company misses it is often fatal, because there are no reserves to recover and try again. Because it had deep pockets backing it, Novell did not fail in 1982. But it was on the brink because at times those deep pockets needed a lot to convince them they weren't throwing good money after bad. By late 1982 there was a lot of doubt and the company was on the block. Time and time again in 1982, only the promise of the LAN saved Novell from oblivion.

A time of chaos is a time for heroes. It is a time for great change, a time for people to do surprising things. In the end the heroes finally came through for Novell, but not without some cliffhangers.

The First Crisis: Jack Davis Departs

December 1981: The Time of Troubles Begins

Jack and Drew flew back from Comdex 81 flush with success.

The printer was out and selling well; the terminal computer was out and was one of the fanciest being shown at Comdex; the LAN was introduced and there was great interest in it. It looked like they were finally on the track of something the market really needed from Novell, and it looked like Drew and the other programmers had put enough thought into this concept that they could produce superior results.

But the news waiting in Utah wasn't good. The first shoe had finally fallen and Jack was no longer a part of Novell. The hard times "the speech" had foreshadowed were happening, and the first casualty was Jack Davis, the founder.

All through the summer, the Safeguard people had been watching a lot of money go out to Utah and little come back. The reports weren't encouraging: The terminal introduction had been delayed yet again and product sales were slow.

Late in the fall, Dolf and Pete sent a Safeguard Scientifics executive, Jack Messman, to find out what was happening and to do something about it. Jack was an ex-IBMer and a businessman, but he didn't understand this new personal computer industry and he had no love for the mountains or Mormons of Utah. He came; he listened to George and a couple other senior managers finger Jack for the company's problems; he made his recommendation and George, the Novell President, acted on it.

Upon his return from Comdex, Jack found himself on the street.

In Messman's eyes, the incident was now finished: He'd done the nasty job of cutting out the source of the acrimony and now Novell should settle down and become profitable. He flew back East.

Timeline

Jack Messman is actively involved with Novell from the beginning of 1982. He eventually becomes a member of the board and his involvement with Novell continues through the '90s and beyond. He becomes President and CEO from 2001–2006.

The Wound Doesn't Heal

Jack Davis's firing was meant to be a surgical strike, getting rid of the one man causing the problems. Now it was up to George to make things happen right. As Dolf later told Jack in justification of their decision, "Jack, we didn't have time to be referees."

But Jack, not George, had built the Novell team, and Jack had not been discredited in the eyes of those people he had brought on board. For the next five months George worked at straightening out the company but there was a lot of grumbling while he did so.

Jim Walker

Through the winter of '81/'82 George labored diligently to solve Novell's problems. His first act was to bring on a replacement for Jack Davis. This man, Jim Walker, was the consultant George had been working with closely for the six months previously, one of those who recommended the unfortunate switch to the COBOL accounting package. Jim began his tenure by bringing the Post Office Place employees together for one of those rare pep talks.

The talk was a good one. He spoke encouragingly about developing "a sense of closure" in what Novell did. "Follow up, make sure the customer is satisfied," Jim encouraged. It was a welcome change from the pace that Jack had set—"Don't worry about the details, they'll take care of themselves. We've got other high priority items that need to be taken care of." People were looking forward to a lessening of the tensions that the George-Jack feuding had caused.

How Jim's actions would have compared to his words we'll never know. That weekend he flew with George to Philadelphia to present his plan to Safeguard. The morning of the big presentation he was found dead in his motel room of a heart attack.

As far as the people of Novell were concerned this was a perverse twist but no more. For George it was a big setback. He never found another replacement for Jack Davis.

The Winter of Endless Sales Meetings

The winter of 1981–82 was marked by endless sales meetings.

There were meetings to discuss new products and meetings to discuss the meanings of management shakeups. Roger, first as Manager of

Customer Support and later as manager of the Dallas sales office, recalls emergency meetings held monthly. Sometimes the news was good, such as when the LAN was declared ready to demonstrate, other times it was to explain yet another management crisis.

Jack's departure gave George a free hand to solve the company's problems but he was constrained by what he and Jack had already created.

The months-long run of the George-Jack feud had allowed many people in the company to take sides. George was President, but Jack was considered company founder by most of those who joined first. He had invited them in and it was his vision they had hitched their dreams to.

That winter those who sided with Jack grumbled that George was an absentee manager, spending much of his time and the company money jetting back and forth to southern California.

George was further handicapped because two of his important allies in the feud were Joe and Phil—the fellows in charge of Manufacturing and Software Development. Those areas were generating the most heat in terms of customer complaints and dashed expectations.

George had about ninety days to overcome Novell's problems. The challenge proved too daunting.

The White Paper

By February it was clear that George's problems had run deeper than just "Jack Davis is not getting with the program."

Safeguard was once again turning its Baleful Eye from the East upon the Utah enterprise and it wasn't pleased with what it saw: Money was still flowing out. Pete and Dolf still couldn't understand this industry. Neither could Jack Messman. So they fell back on *their* old habits and turned to one person they knew who might understand what was going on: Jack Davis.

Jack remembers:

In early '82 I was in Philadelphia on a business trip for Praxis. [Jack became President of Praxis upon leaving Novell.] I visited Safeguard and asked Dolf, "Do you want to know what's *really* happening out in Utah?"

"Sure," he said.

I wrote him a 20-page "white paper" explaining my side of the story, and I don't know if that opened his eyes or not, but three months later George was out.

The March Massacre of '82

The New Line-Up

In 1982 the problems came right on time, but the solutions were a day late or a dollar short.

On Tuesday, March 2nd, Jack Messman came to Utah again. This time George's head was on the block. He was cast out. There were layoffs, and by the end of the month, half of Novell's founding management was gone, as well as half the company.

Gone: Jack Davis, George Canova, Dennis Fairclough, Phil Long.

Still left: Larry Edwards, Joe Maroney, Rusty Woodbury, Craig Burton, Dave Guerrero. (We'll meet that last man on p. 63.)

New: Jack Messman.

Novell Fibrillates

In retrospect, the March Massacre was a necessary step in keeping Novell alive long enough for the LAN product to evolve into a technologically superior product. It allowed the programmers time to develop the software to support file service, instead of freezing development at the disk service level.

But in the short term it did little to improve Novell's prospects. In retrospect, the short-term shock was too great for the organization to bear. Instead of responding by everyone getting organized and making a great leap towards profitability, the organization fibrillated instead.

The people who had generated many of Novell's problems were gone, but these were the same people who had created many of Novell's solutions, too. People from both sides of the George Canova–Jack Davis feud had been swept out and people from both sides remained. After the massacre Novell was a lot smaller as a company, but no more unified.

The problems remained, and the people who remained had to face them. But each had a vested interest in solutions he or she had already recommended prior to the massacre. The new situation just seemed to pile new problems onto the old ones.

The People of 1982

Jack Messman: The President in Search of a President

In November of '81, Jack Messman had had a simple task: Go to Orem and find out what the problem was. The simple task received a simple answer. George Canova, the President, said in effect that the root of all evils was his relation with Jack Davis and if Jack was gone things would get better. Jack Messman had liked this simple answer, seen it implemented, and flown back to Philadelphia with his mission accomplished.

When he returned in March '82, the answers didn't come so simply. George was out, Jack Davis was out, and Jack Messman became acting President. So who was there for Jack Messman to listen to and explain this business to him? The company needed a permanent President; that was about all Jack knew for sure.

Larry Edwards and the Sales Force: Jumping Ship

What the sales force knew for sure in early 1982 was that status quo wasn't going to work. Months before the Massacre the brightest and most experienced salespeople started leaving. By the time the axe fell, only the inexperienced and ambitious were left.

Larry was still in position as VP of Sales but the sales force under him had changed entirely. Gone were the likes of Andy Olson and those who had worked beside him, Don Whatcott and Winston Lee. In their place were people like Roger White, transferred in from Support, and Dave Guerrero (see below).

Larry had been a close friend of Jack's. He was clearly unhappy with Jack's departure and George's choice of an outsider to replace him. When George bypassed him, and Jack Messman then bypassed him, it was time for Larry to find a new company.

Joe Maroney and Manufacturing: State of Siege

Manufacturing was still being hammered about poor quality. The returns and the horror stories of DOAs continued, but now Joe pointed past Engineering at Sales. Most of the returns in the summer and fall of 1982 weren't DOAs, he explained, they were evaluation units that salespeople had placed. Accounting would call up to collect money but get a pile of boxes sent back to Manufacturing instead.

Fault in the returns problem cannot be clearly assigned now and could not be then, but that is the most important point: *The mystery never was solved.*

Dave Guerrero: The Man from Pick

Novell's image in the computer community was changing. It was getting older; it was getting more widely talked about; but it was also known to be a company in turmoil. As a result, the kinds of people that were attracted to a Novell opportunity changed. The pioneering types were less interested; so were the careful types. But the ambitious and risk-seeking types were taking their place.

Dave Guerrero was ambitious and risk-seeking, a short, energetic man originally from Guam. He was also a talker and he'd found that talking and acting had advanced him further than good looks or knowledge, which he also had.

Before joining Novell as the regional sales manager for southern California, Dave had been selling minicomputers that used the Pick operating system. He was one of the last salespeople brought on by Larry Edwards.

Timeline

Dave Guerrero joins Novell in the spring of 1982 and leaves in the fall of 1982, after having briefly headed the company.

Harry Armstrong: Beyond Metal Bending

Harry was a surprise to the company. Having come on board as a "metal bender" to help Joe in manufacturing, he suffered much of the same heat that Joe did as the quality crisis evolved. But rather than get defensive, Harry remained open and approachable. Harry hadn't always been in Production and in the days of crisis his people skills allowed him to handle the finger-pointing differently than Joe did.

That by itself would have gotten Harry little, but in late '82 he started doing the exceptional: Whenever production duties were not requiring all his time (as more and more they didn't), he phoned customers personally and asked for orders. Word of this bizarre behavior quickly spread through the remaining ranks. In 1983, it reached the ear of Ray Noorda, the new President, who liked what he heard.

Craig Burton: Selling the LAN

From his first day with Novell, Craig had been a network spokesman. His experiences trying to make real-world things happen with some of the pre-Novell LAN products had sensitized him to what was really relevant to making LANs for personal computers effective. Reid was the first manager to get ahold of Craig, and for the first six months of 1982 Craig was overseas touring with Reid, boosting international sales.

This proved good for Novell. It kept Craig out of the fire while the worst of the cutting back and finger-pointing was happening, and it provided a valuable boost to Novell's international sales effort. By the end of '82 international sales was providing 40% of all the feeble sales that Novell was able to maintain.

In the second half of '82 Craig transitioned from selling abroad to improving the marketing of the LAN. He started grappling with questions of what was going to be said about the LAN and who had to hear the message.

Judy Clark: On the Edges

All through 1982, Judy grappled with the problem of how to become part of Novell at all. As the company's fortunes declined, she found more and more opportunity to help out, but always on a temporary basis. By the end of 1982, she was well known within the company and she knew the company well, but she was still not a full part of it.

SuperSet Incorporates

During 1982 Drew, Dale, Kyle, and Mark were watching the Novell crisis intently. They knew they were onto something exciting in this LAN concept they were developing, but their vehicle for implementing this exciting concept—Novell—was as shaky as they come. All through 1982 they watched it get shakier and more confused. But important people at Novell and Safeguard had the LAN vision, too, so as crisis after crisis roiled the company these programmers were spared.

In the summer of '82 they incorporated as SuperSet.

"This was on the advice of Dave Guerrero," said Dale. "Dave may have had his problems dealing with the rest of the company, but he treated us well. He told us that Safeguard and Novell would have an easier time dealing with us if they were dealing with an organization rather than a collection of individuals. So we incorporated, and he was right. Our negotiations with Novell and Safeguard went easier as a result."

While the walls of PCs, printers, and terminal products were falling down around them they continued to develop the LAN product. It was during this period that what would become NetWare transitioned from being a disk server product to a file server product. It was also during this period that SuperSet recognized it would have to handle more than CP/M files, so they developed their own universal file format to allow the server to support CP/M, MS-DOS, and UNIX file structures. Finally, it was during this period that Drew first recognized the need for fault tolerance in the product: "I was talking with you [Roger] about some necessary networking features. The question of disk errors came up, and that got me to thinking."

So the only basic architecture concept in NetWare 2.x or 3.x that waited until 1983 to be introduced was hardware independence, the ability to function with many different kinds of networking hardware. (Much more on this in Chapter Four, under "Hardware Independence", p. 112.)

Getting the First IBM PC

In early 1982 Drew hustled out of ComputerLand in Orem carrying one of the first IBM PCs. He was one of the earliest in a long line of personal computer software developers who wanted to see what IBM had wrought. His burning question: Would this be a good platform to act as a LAN server? He and the rest of SuperSet spent the year toying with it to find out.

IBM's original floppy disk–based PC wasn't suitable but its successor model, the PCXT, with a hard disk, had potential. That finding brought Novell to one of its 1983 crossroads: Should Novell continue developing only dedicated file servers based on the 68000, or should it also develop an 8088-based version of NetWare that could use an IBM PCXT as the file server?

After the Massacre

When Jack Messman became Novell's acting President, he had no desire to run a computer company, a field he had little interest in, in Utah, a place he had little interest in. He set about the task of finding a permanent President to lead Novell out of its time of troubles.

He started by looking for local talent. He talked with Jack Davis. Davis was certainly interested and knew the situation, but he had just accepted the presidency at Praxis and felt he needed to follow through on that commitment.

He talked with Reid, the VP of International Sales. International was one of the company's bright spots of the time, providing 30 or 40% of Novell's sales. Reid declined.

He talked with Dave Guerrero. Dave was a good talker and Dave had a plan. It sounded good enough that Jack made him acting CEO while he continued the search for a permanent President.

The Spring of Endless Layoffs

It was on Dave's shoulders that the unpleasant task of bringing Novell's costs in line with its revenue fell most heavily. He conducted the series of layoffs in 1982 that followed the March Massacre. He shrank Novell to about twenty people by June of '82.

It was a thankless task, and no one thanked him.

At each layoff cycle (there were three) he would say, "We've cut deep so we won't have to cut again."

Even among those who survived there were bitter complaints that he was doing hare-brained things. Dave was a man of action. In his mind action, good or bad, was better than no action. He was desperate, and with good reason. Novell sales were dropping as fast as the employee count.

The Summer of Endless Plans

After the layoffs Dave pursued long-shot ideas because there were no sure-shot ideas available. The printer and the computer had both proved wanting in the general market so trying to boost sales of those products there was fruitless. The LAN was coming but it wasn't ready so no sales gains could come from it.

The choices he saw were pursuing specialty markets, niche market-places, and the foreign marketplace.

Dave was not exceptional in this thinking. Niche markets and foreign markets are time-honored places for electronics companies to survive when the mainstream US domestic market rejects their products. For instance, Wang word-processing machines were sold for years after personal computers had overtaken their capabilities, to customers who already had installed bases of Wang equipment. Commodore, Digital Research, and Atari survived and prospered for years after their products were no longer in demand in the mainstream US personal computer market. Commodore, in particular, used profits from their European sales to try again and again to penetrate the US market. So Dave's strategy of abandoning the mainstream domestic market might have been disappointing, but it might have been viable.

After May, while Reid and Craig pursued the general-purpose markets overseas, Dave spent most of his time looking for specialty deals to cut domestically. One such niche deal involved turning the terminal computer into a point-of-sale system.

Dave's actions staved off Novell's collapse by perhaps six months. But that wasn't all that Novell needed. It needed vision and a plan that the remaining organization could buy into. It was never clear to those left at Novell what Dave was planning and he produced no vision that others could coordinate with. He could act but he couldn't end the chaos; by fall 1982 he was out of grace.

Meanwhile Jack Messman continued the hunt for a President.

The First LAN Demonstrations

While the calamities of spring and summer were crashing in, the roots were being deepened for the one product that would in the end save Novell. By summer the LAN was being demonstrated to the sales force and selected customers.

What a Great View of the Vultures You Have from This Office!

By fall 1982 Novell's Presidential office looked out onto bare branches from which vultures looked in.

One of the strengths of the free market business system is its handling of failure. In some social systems the failure of an organization is

67

hard to officially recognize so it lurches on, consuming resources but producing little value from them. In other social systems the phrase "head on a platter" isn't a metaphor. In the fall of 1982 Safeguard was ready to put free market theory to the test. Through the spring and summer they had been unable to find a President who would treat Novell as a going concern, so by fall they were looking for someone who would take the company for salvage value.

The first to come along was a businessman who'd done some pioneering work in bar code readers and was now head of a company in Hauppauge, New Jersey. His original introduction to Novell had been through the point-of-sale project Dave had worked on. He proposed buying the company and taking the LAN technology he was interested in back East, to meld it into his New Jersey operations. He had no intention of marketing it as a PC network. He would have had a deal but Safeguard decided his offering price was too low. They continued looking.

Next Jack Messman saw a light part the clouds and cast off the gloom. He was contacted by Sandy Shipley, a man with considerable interest in a floppy disk–drive maker, looking for a captive outlet for his drives. Sandy liked Novell and he agreed to become President in October '82.

"I still remember the day," says Reid. "I looked out my window and there was a limousine, one of the stretch kind, with a uniformed chauffeur, and out steps Sandy Shipley."

Sandy was the President who took Novell to Comdex 82. He was also the President who gave Dave the axe. But his tenure was short. A week after Comdex, the dark clouds hovering over Novell came back together with a snap. It turned out Sandy had "exaggerated some of his claims" and he was moved out quickly.

This left Safeguard with a rudderless company once again. Depending on your point of view, the man from New Jersey was still waiting politely in the wings offstage or gliding pitilessly overhead while the relentless sun beat down on orphaned Novell. Each time Safeguard handed off their orphan to a new father it came back whining for more attention.

Comdex 82: The Slough of Despair

According to Judy, Comdex 82 that fall was Novell's low point.

For weeks prior to the show we weren't sure if we were going or not. We'd paid for the booth space and the booth, but even so it'd be on one moment and off the next.

Those weeks were the period in which the Novell founding team was forged, the survivors and the believers who got to know each other's measure. They had faith that the network was a sound product and useful to the market. What they needed now was a way to get it out from under the heap of other Novell products the market had rejected, and the heap of other obligations Novell's existence had created over the last two years.

Judy remembered how they affirmed their dedication.

There was a meeting, I remember, in particular. I don't know exactly when it was or much other detail about its circumstance. I do remember that Drew, Kyle, Dale, and Craig were there. I was there and we were going over the spec sheets that I'd just put together for Comdex. It was for Comdex Fall and we had had eight Presidents that year. And we were just fed up.

We knew we had a good product. We knew that it was the LAN. And by that time I was so involved in it that I was really excited and determined. And I wasn't—at that time I wasn't—interested in making any money out of it, or anything. I just thought it was "a cause".

But all these Presidents would come flipping through there and they didn't [know what they had here]. Sometimes we didn't even know who they were! They'd just walk in and say, "I'm your new President."

We thought, "They don't care about us. The owners of the company don't care about us. They don't care about the product. They just want to get rid of us." They were trying to sell us. And we were holding the threads together.

So we were sitting in the conference room going over the spec sheets and reading them and we were talking about the show and how we were going to do it with no money. They [Safeguard] kept ... every other day they would call up and say, "Cancel. You're not going to go." And we had just about everything all put together and all we had to get was the printing done.

So we all just said, "We're going to do this even if we don't get paid." They thought ... they were telling us they were going to cut all our salaries. They were going to close the doors. They weren't going to make the next payroll.

And so we said, "We're going to do it! We're going to do it! Not even if we don't get paid, we're still going to do it because we know it's a good product." And so we all just looked at each other and we just said, "Now, we're going to do it. No matter what, they're not going to stop us from doing it."

And I don't know if the others at the meeting even remember it, but it was so significant to me because I thought, "These guys are really believing in this technology. They know how good it is." And they were not fools, they knew what they were doing.

And it just got me so excited to this cause. "Save this, this software! We're going to take it to Comdex!"

And we did it. And I think that right there was the big turning point because there was just a group of a few people and we were absolutely determined to let the world know about this product—almost like a rebellion. I felt their dedication. It won me. I really wanted to be a part of this and make it happen.

The Story the Booth Told

Novell's booth at Comdex chronicled the company's fortunes. In 1980 Jack and George were in a booth without product. In 1981 the booth had the wrong product for the time. In 1982 the booth was filled with the right product for the time but Jack and George were gone.

The differences between Comdex 81 and Comdex 82 were ironic. In '81 Novell had money but no LAN product. In '82 they had a LAN product but no money. In '81 they had a big booth filled with lots of high-powered high-priced talent. In '82 the booth was a simple wall of screens showing a Novell network in action and the high talent left after the year of crisis was strictly high tech.

And, most of all, Novell needed a President.

The Comdex show went smoothly. The LAN worked and booth visitors were impressed. The big news of the day was that Sandy took this as the moment to can Dave. Remembered, but unnoticed at the time, was an older visitor to the booth who introduced himself as Ray Noorda.

After the show, Sandy left and Jack Messman was back again. Behind him was the New Jersey man who was still interested in Novell and still offering his low price. A letter was sent to the remaining employees stating that it was likely the company would move to New Jersey and asking who was interested in relocating. Novell was about to become part of this other company.

Harry Armstrong remembers those days.

"I got the letter and told Messman that my cowboy boots were stuck on too tight. I wasn't going back. I'd worked in Hauppauge ten years earlier when I was in aerospace. I knew what I'd left behind, and I'd left for good reason."

The First LAN Ships

In December of 1982, just before Ray took over, the first two production LANs were shipped, one domestically and one overseas. Novell's LAN era began just as it was to find its permanent President.

Novell Data Systems in Retrospect

For two years Novell Data Systems cut a spectacular swath through the lives of a hundred Utahns. Novell's experience helped define what a domestic electronics manufacturer could do in the personal computer industry by showing many things that didn't work.

It showed that quality was important and that if top management wasn't sensitive to quality problems, and wasn't proactive in solving them, it could kill a company.

It confirmed to Ray Noorda that his vision was correct: That the constraints of the domestic manufacturing environment in the '80s would make producing commodity electronics hard to do, and that terminals, printers, and personal computers were now commodity products.

It didn't confirm George Canova and Jack Davis's vision that Utah's advantages—wages lower than the US average, high productivity, and easy access to electronics designing and developing talent from BYU—could allow a Utah manufacturer to offset the East Asian advantage of even lower wages.

It showed that collecting together experienced high-talent managers with long experience in the *minicomputer* industry, and adding lots of money, was not enough to insure success in the *personal computer* industry. Some other mix of talent, experience, and vision was going to be needed to make a success in this emerging industry.

71

It showed that tracking a moving-target goal is expensive: The products that Novell produced in 1982 changed continuously, but the changes were too often reactive rather than proactive and they generated more costs than sales. There wasn't enough coordination between departments to accommodate the pace of change.

It showed that when partners come together to pursue a common vision they need to make sure they understand where their vision is common and where it is different. The blinding brightness of what is common can hide some deep shadows of difference. If those differences fester the product and the company can suffer.

Novell's experience also confirmed one other thing: Just how hard it is to kill an electronics company. This was a company that had never produced a profit, had spent millions of dollars, in its final months had more returns than sales ... *and yet it didn't die!* There was still a dream and still people willing to invest in it.

In coming upon rocky times after existing for two years, NDSI was in plentiful company. There had been a lot of startups in Utah that had sounded just as good and ended up just as broke. For Utah, Novell was not yet a surprising company; it was doing about average.

Novell Data Systems was a proving ground for Novell, Inc. It taught the Novell, Inc., founders how many things could go wrong. It showed them how to squeeze lemonade out of lemons and how important a good vision about the company and the product is.

Perhaps the greatest chain of irony is that a) the LAN would have never developed at Novell if Novell hadn't first had problems with its personal computer product and b) it wouldn't have had problems with the personal computer product if it hadn't been forced by its financing to have a personal computer in the first place.

In retrospect, Novell's evolution into making the LAN product is logical. But if you had talked to Jack Davis in the summer of 1980 about Novell making its fortune with a PC-based LAN product, you'd have gotten a strange look indeed. And most important of all, the LAN wouldn't have happened if there hadn't been a lot of heroes to help it along the way.

It is sometimes forgotten in the Novell story that the LAN vision at Novell emerged early; it rose from the ashes of the minicomputer product in the spring of 1982. All during its gestation it was supported by the whole company, and the company's owners, as important. But throughout 1982 it was recognized as a product for Novell's future. What NDSI could never find in 1982 was a product for its present.

For Novell, 1982 is the story of a framework being built and heroes being forged. Novell in 1983 tells the story of those heroes in action.

CHAPTER THREE
1983: Vision Unchained

The New Man

A Working President Arrives

On a cold January morning in 1983, Ray drove his car under the I-15 overpass and into the glistening parking lot of the old truck dealership that was now world headquarters of Novell Data Systems, Inc. To the east the rising sun peeped over the snowy top of Mount Timpanogos; to the west, Utah Lake, a vast sheet of ice and chill water, was capped by a light mist. Next to the lake the Geneva Steel plant was unnaturally still. It had been shut down for several months now and the Utah Valley community was hurting. A government report in 1982 had declared Utah Valley to be one of the ten most depressed areas in the country.

As Ray walked towards the warehouse, his steps crunching above the sound of freeway traffic, he remembered how he hated Utah winters.

The company Ray was interested in was depressingly spare in terms of staff and product. The $900 paintings from the Canova days still hung on the walls outside the executive offices—a grim joke. Only 14 employees remained of the 120 who had worked for NDSI a year earlier. A few of the 14 had stayed because they believed in the potential of ShareNet (NetWare's original name) but most were there simply because they had nowhere else to go.

Three of the old management team remained: Joe Maroney, Vice President of Production; Rusty Woodbury, Vice President of Development; and Reid Clark, Director of International Sales.

SuperSet—Drew, Dale, Kyle, and Mark—continued development of ShareNet.

74

Dave Baumgartner handled Domestic Sales. Harry Armstrong worked for Joe in the Manufacturing area as production manager.

Craig Burton's job was basically to explain the virtues of LANing; he also wrote documentation, helped demonstrate the system to prospects, and evangelized ShareNet to software developers.

Judy fit in wherever she could as a secretary, receptionist, warehouse helper, trade show assistant, whatever.

Diane Solberg was a secretary and Lorraine Fitch helped with the bookkeeping. There was also a draftsman.

Ray sat everyone down and introduced himself as a would-be President. For the next couple of months he would be like a consultant to the company, observing and talking with the staff. He reassured them that he was not going to fire everyone and bring in his own people. He was going to see what he had to work with and what they could do. In the next few days he would interview each person to find out what they were doing and what they needed to do their jobs better.

The staff were somewhat skeptical. In the last nine months they had seen at least five Presidents come and go. Ray was merely the latest, and he was another guy with a minicomputer background. On the other hand they were encouraged by his personal investment in the company and by his reputation as a turn-around artist, a savior of failing businesses. Jack Davis called him "a company doctor".

In the beginning, Ray commuted to Novell from the Bay area, until he bought a house in Orem and moved his family in March. Jack Messman was still officially President until Ray was elected President and Chief Executive Officer that month. On February 21, 1983, one of Messman's last acts as President was to reincorporate Novell Data Systems, Inc., as Novell, Inc.

The staff weren't sure how to read that—maybe it was positive that NDSI was dead and a new company had been born, or maybe it was a ploy to deprive them of their shares of NDSI.

There was something reassuring in the style of their new leader, though. He projected a kind of calm confidence, and as a Mormon—like most of the employees and most of Utah Valley—he was more believable than his predecessors. Of the six or more Novell Presidents up to then, only Ray was a member of the LDS church.

For the first two months, January and February 1983, Ray studied his new company carefully; he questioned and listened to his staff and watched them work. He spent a lot of time with SuperSet and a lot of time with Craig.

Ray's most pressing problem was to reverse the plummeting sales of Novell products and he immediately hit the road making calls on prospective customers. Drew, Kyle, and Dale accompanied him on many of these calls, as did Craig. Soon the staff realized that Ray was quite unlike the Presidents who had preceded him: Ray was not just a manager, he was willing to work in the trenches with them. He rolled up his sleeves and jumped into every aspect of the business, from sales to shipping.

Where other Presidents had commuted to Orem, Ray put down roots there. Where Sandy, for example, arrived to work in a limo, Ray drove an old pick-up truck. And no previous President had the depth of experience, the contacts, or the reputation in the computer industry that Ray Noorda had.

Dale recalled his early experiences working with his new boss:

The thing that I saw with Ray that was different right from the start was that he was competent. I don't know any other way to describe it.

Back in those days, Drew, Kyle, and I quite often would travel on sales calls and meet for discussion with nearly every person who considered being a customer of Novell. We almost always got involved in talking about what do we have, what direction we're going, what do you want, how fast do you need it. You know, "We'll have it by tomorrow night."

And when we started going out with Ray, people responded to him a lot differently. He took us into businesses that already knew him, people that had had dealings with him before. And he had an incredible credibility rating. People bought Novell because Ray Noorda was running it. They would buy off on this crazy, unheard-of notion because Ray Noorda was backing it.

I saw that when we went places, he ended up doing a lot of the sales early on. … I remember following him around and just watching and noticing that he did not use a lot of hype. He didn't promise things he couldn't deliver. And he had a lot of credibility. People tended to believe him when he said things.

The product Ray and his team were selling was the networking system that NDSI had demonstrated at Comdex 82 in Las Vegas. It consisted of a file server with cabling and connections in a star topology that could accommodate up to 24 PCs. The system sold in 1983, called NetWare/S-Net (for Star-Net),[5] had two key selling points: 1) Low-cost sharing of hard disk storage space and peripheral devices like printers and modems and 2) the ability to put both CP/M-based microcomputers and DOS-based IBM PCs on the same network. It did not allow the PCs on the network to talk with each other.

The end users for these systems were typically small or medium-sized businesses that had several stand-alone PCs. By buying a Novell network for a price ranging from $2,000 to $25,000, a company could buy just one printer or storage device that all the PCs could use.

In 1983, Diablo daisywheel printers were a widely used quality printer and the new Diablo 630s sold for $2400 each. Older models still sold for $3600. The HP laser printer was just announced and it too sold for $3600. If a company needed some CP/M-based microcomputers as well as the new IBM PCs, it could let them share the same peripheral devices by putting them on a Novell LAN.

Job One: Sales

Job One in 1983 was to ship product, and Ray used every channel available to get S-Net LANs out the door. He went directly to end users and had systems built to order. Most of his sales efforts were devoted to convincing distributors and resellers that the new Novell could provide LANs that were not only reliable but profitable for them to sell. This was not an easy task, because many distributors had been burned by the products shipped by the old Novell. Ray had to convince them that the manufacturing problems had been fixed, that the product worked, and that Novell would be a company worth dealing with.

Dale described the first Novell customers as "hardy pioneers who are technology junkies, who will try anything once. And if those guys come out of it alive, then you begin to get the attention of a few other people."

When Ray came on in January 1983 sales had virtually dried up, at least in the US. Dale recalled:

> I didn't see any sales really happen to anybody but maybe a few
> from the Middle East. They were the only people who were actu-

---

[5] It has been claimed elsewhere that "S-Net" is a synonym of ShareNet, a usage unknown to this writer.

ally accepting shipments, you know. There were salesmen who were claiming they were making sales but not much of it ever really shipped.

We were basically looking for any way to survive, anything to make a sale. I can remember being frustrated in the early days of Novell that we couldn't sell a vanilla product. [A "vanilla product" is a basic, durable product that appeals to a mass market, like Henry Ford's Model T or vanilla ice cream.] It seemed like every sale we made had some custom piece involved that we had to go and cook just for that shipping.

We weren't in the process of saying, "This is what we've got. Do you want to buy it?" We always said, "What do you want? We'll make it." And that's the attitude that made us survive.

A major obstacle to a vanilla product was the lack of standard PC operating systems. Novell's S-Net LAN operating system ran on the Novell 68000 file server, but the PCs that customers wanted to network might be a DOS-based IBM PC, one using CP/M86 (Digital Research's short-lived competitor to MS-DOS), and/or an older CP/M80-based computer—and different manufacturers would customize their operating systems differently.

So to make NetWare/S-Net work with these different PC operating systems the SuperSet guys had to write a "shell" program that would allow the LAN operating system to interface with the PC operating system of each model of computer.

"There were probably 20 or 30 boxes [PC models] in the early days before there was a big shake-out in the compatibility market," Dale recalled. "A lot of them weren't compatible. And most of them ran some flavor of DOS, but not all of them. And we did a lot of work on those kinds of boxes and on supporting them all. You know, creating a shell for every one of the little monsters. Anybody who wanted one, we'd make it."

The job was to start building an installed base of working Novell LANs. Customer by customer, order by order, the number of S-Net systems shipped each month began to grow. By the summer of 1983 the company was shipping about $300,000 worth of product each month.

Job Two: Burying the Past

While working on building up Novell's strengths Ray also had to discard what hadn't worked at Novell. Some of the problems were self-correcting. Novell had cut a lot of expense in the Time of Six Presidents and none of the survivors were weekly commuters from California, but more needed to be done.

Novell's reincorporation as Novell, Inc., aimed at providing solutions. One was to transform much of the debt financing that had been floated for NDSI into equity financing. Another was to rid Novell of its terminal, printer, and personal computer legacy. After the reincorporation Novell stopped supporting those products and Ray sent Reid to Korea to negotiate a deal to sell the remaining inventory to a businessman there.

Finally, Ray needed to decide what talent he needed to carry Novell forward.

Watching the Players

As Ray threw himself into the business of Novell in the early months of 1983, he began to identify the staff members who were key to the running of the company. Some employees tried to influence Ray in this transition period, with varying degrees of success. Ray was impressed by hard work and results, not experience or talk.

One of the successful ones to petition Ray was Judy. Ray liked Judy. She hadn't had an easy life, yet she was a fighter, determined to better herself. She was willing to work long hours for very little pay. In February 1983, Judy was not quite 40 years old and she was quite attractive. Although Ray was always scrupulously faithful to his wife he enjoyed being around pretty women.

Judy volunteered to serve as Ray's secretary, but Ray said he couldn't justify hiring a secretary just for himself. So she convinced him he needed an office manager and he agreed to let her try.

Judy remembers her interview with Ray.

> I went in, and I had a full-page typed list of my demands. They were things we needed to do marketing-wise. We needed to get a PR company. We needed to create a better environment. The employees needed personnel benefits. All my concerns were for marketing the company and for the personnel, because we were so

battered from this year of just being treated like numbers—so many Presidents passing through and nobody really caring about the product or the individuals.

So I had this list of demands. He was just looking at me like: "We're just starting and you want all this stuff?"

But Ray kept the list and used it to establish goals. "In three months we're going to have this. In six months we're going to have this ...," Judy said. "And we met every goal that we set together."

Just a few weeks after Ray arrived on the scene the more perceptive employees could see who were favored and who were not. Ray spent the most time with his favorites. The four SuperSet guys were obviously crucial, as was Craig, who could articulate a vision of LANing with clarity, sincerity, and enthusiasm.

Ray was also impressed with Harry, Joe's production manager. Orders from the two salespeople (Dave Baumgartner and Reid) had slowed to a trickle and Harry found himself with little to do. On previous jobs Harry had been a salesman, and in a company of 14 employees, everybody pitched in wherever they were needed. So Harry continued to do what he'd been doing since late 1982: Picking up the phone and calling previous customers. "This is Harry Armstrong at Novell's manufacturing plant," he would say. "What can I build for you this month?"

Ray had never seen a manufacturing guy making sales calls before. So although some of the senior managers, like Reid, considered Harry basically inept, Ray thought he was a self-starter. Harry became one of Ray's starting players.

Making the Cuts

Other employees did not make the team. Joe and Rusty immediately sensed that they would not fare well under Ray. As senior managers, they drew relatively large salaries, they were partly responsible for NDSI's failure, and they were used to exercising a level of authority that Ray would not allow. They rightly assumed that Ray had marked them for purging. When Reid tried to put in a good word for Joe with Ray, he got his first lesson in Novell politics.

Reid remembered the incident vividly.

The most reprimanded, I think, I ever got from Noorda was when I went and told him that I thought Maroney was the guy that contributed more to keeping the company moving than anyone on board. If there's any way that he could take a good look at that, I'd help him with whatever information I had. But as the new man, he ought to know that.

Boy, he just ripped me down one side and up the other!

Ray was irritated first with Reid's advice, which he considered stupid, and second with Reid's presumption. Ray wasn't a "new man"—he was the savior, bankroller, and CEO—and he certainly didn't need advice from a member of the management team that had botched up NDSI. Furthermore, he had already made up his mind that Joe was responsible for the manufacturing problems and product returns that had plagued the predecessor company. Novell was Ray's company, and he would make his own decisions.

Reid himself only narrowly escaped the fate of Joe and Rusty; he was the only member of the NDSI management team to survive. "Tell me what you can about this guy Reid Clark," Ray asked Jack Davis. Although Ray was concerned about keeping on a senior member of the NDSI team, in the end he decided to let Reid stay, partly out of charity, partly because of Reid's contacts abroad (the foreign sales generated by Reid accounted for about 30% of Novell's sales in 1983), and mostly because he didn't consider Reid a threat to his authority. Reid was a good Mormon, had a bunch of kids in BYU, and had no ambition to challenge or interfere with Ray.

The decision to keep Reid shows an interesting side to Ray. Ray could be ruthlessly abrupt in dispensing with people for the good of the business, especially people who, in Ray's opinion, could fend for themselves. He could also be generous when the spirit moved him, as it did with Reid.

Another example of his generosity was his reaction towards an employee who worked in a department that was under consideration for layoffs. The employee had muscular dystrophy. "She stays," said Ray, "even if I have to pay her salary myself."

Another high-level employee whom Ray decided he didn't need was Dave Baumgartner, the salesman brought on by Dave Guerrero in the summer of '82. Guerrero had recruited Baumgartner through a headhunter for a fee in the $30,000 range. It didn't take Baumgartner long to figure out he had climbed aboard a sinking ship, and by the time Ray arrived, he was spending several hours a day looking for another job. When Ray came on, he said, "Well, Dave, why don't you quit?" And in a couple of months, Baumgartner was gone.

Joe and Rusty followed soon after and the decks were cleared for Novell's reemergence.

The New Style

One of the first projects Ray gave the green light to when he arrived at Novell was a redesign of the product packaging. Judy recalled that computer companies used very conservative colors in their marketing communications in the early 1980s, in imitation of IBM's look, nicknamed Big Blue (a blue-chip company with a blue logo and packaging).

I went to the first few trade shows and I'd look around and it was just this blue-gray haze, a color—or non-color—through the whole trade show. Everything was the same."

Ray wanted a bright color for the packaging, "Anything but blue," he said. "The opposite of blue ... what about red?"

Judy went to work. She set up a meeting with Dan Ruesch, President of a then-small Salt Lake agency called Tandem Studios.

I said, "I want something that, when you walk in the retail computer store, it's going to stand out on the shelf. When you walk into the trade show floor, you won't be able to do anything else except go straight to our booth because you'll want to see what this color is all about."

I said, "I want something that's red, you know, really bright." So the design company came back with red—a red image. And nobody, *nobody*, in the company liked it at all.

I talked to Ray about it and said, "Let's just try it. No one else is doing it. We'll just use it very subtly. Our corporate look will be really nice and corporate, and we'll just use a little bit of red. But then when we want to make a splash, we can do it because we've got the red. We can use an ounce of it or a gallon of it."

So he bought off on it. He was pretty willing to go along with almost anything to try and see if it would work. ... And I would say within six months from changing to red, we were starting to get attention. I think it was the combination of the color and the whole image change.

The Entrepreneur

Who was this man who handled Novell so differently? Why could he accomplish something with this organization that his five predecessors could not? Part of the answer lies in his background.

The Family

Ray's grandparents, Hendrick and Grace Yff Noorda, were Dutch converts to the Mormon Church. They lived in Landsmeer, a suburb of Amsterdam. In 1894 their eleventh and youngest child, Bertus, was born to them when Hendrick and Grace were both in their 40s. He became Ray Noorda's father.

Hendrick, a laborer by trade, was a devout and active member of the LDS Church. The Netherlands Mission had made numerous converts among the Dutch and several families had emigrated to Utah—their religious homeland in the far reaches of the American West. In the early 1900s Hendrick prayed for spiritual guidance, assembled his sons and daughters, and made plans to claim his destiny with his brethren in Zion.

In 1904 Hendrick and Grace packed their belongings and made the long journey to the Promised Land with all but one of their children. They came by steamer to New York through Ellis Island, then took the Union Pacific to Ogden, Utah.

The large Noorda family was itself a community with stout sons, young wives, and a flock of children, among them nine-year-old Bertus, now Bert. But the Noordas were also embraced by the Dutch Mormons who had preceded them to Utah and by the LDS Church itself. Although 5,000 miles from their native land the Noordas could feel at home in America. Language was no barrier in polyglot Utah, which teemed with European and Asian immigrants. Indeed, among their Dutch neighbors the Noordas could get along quite nicely without uttering a word of English.

Hendrick found work first in the freight department of the Union Pacific Railroad and subsequently as a janitor at a drugstore, the Ogden Wholesale Drug Company. His older sons were also employed in non-professional jobs, as a school custodian, a shift foreman for Utah Power and Light, a railroad inspector, and a baker. When Bert was old enough

Hendrick got him a job at the drugstore as a stock clerk. Bert spent the next 43 years there.

On the first day of spring 1918, Bertus Noorda married Alida Vandenberg, a young woman who had been born in Ogden of Dutch parents. Soon after they were sealed to each other in the LDS Temple in Salt Lake City, Bert was called up for military service.

Ten months after their wedding the couple's first child, Bert Jr., was born. Other children followed: Marie; Raymond John (Ray) on June 19, 1924; and Edna. Alida's parents owned a small rental property next door to their own home in Ogden and they offered this house to their daughter and son-in-law. Ray Noorda grew up as a part of a large extended family that included his maternal and paternal grandparents, numerous aunts and uncles, and dozens of cousins—many of whom lived in the same Ogden neighborhood.

The Early Years

Although Ray's father was a drugstore clerk, the Noordas were in many respects a typical middle class family of the 1920s and 1930s. Bert Noorda was a scoutmaster and an active member of the LDS Church. Though money was tight he was able to provide for his wife and four children even through the days of the Depression. In 1938, when Ray was 14, Bert and Alida purchased their home from Alida's parents. In an era when most Americans were renters the Noordas were property owners.

In a 1988 interview, Ray told a story about his childhood that was probably part apocryphal and part true. It serves the same purpose as the many stories about US Presidents; that is, the story of the youth demonstrates the virtues of the adult.

By the fourth grade Ray "appointed himself CEO of the local playground"[6] in Ogden, Utah. At that time the kids ran their own programs and he was asked to organize a softball team for his own age group. First of all (as he later told the story) he made sure that the team was there. He figured out that they could win 50% of the games if they just had a full team.

---

[6] The phrase appears in Ray's obituary as printed in Britain's *The Independent:* http://www.independent.co.uk/news/obituaries/ray-noorda-422415.html.

Next Ray made sure the best players were there. He called them repeatedly and the night before the game he also phoned their mothers. He even went as far as to pick them up on his bicycle the next morning and wheel them over to the park. That's when he learned how things got done. The experience made such an impression on him that it became a metaphor for his adult management style.

"I'd say more than anything else, it's important to make sure that people get to work and that the best players have extra incentives. Finding the best players has been one of the most important things in the companies I've been in," he explained.

Ray attended Ogden High School, a few blocks from his home. (A year behind him was Brent Scowcroft, who would serve as National Security Affairs Advisor under the first President Bush.) He played on the Ogden High varsity baseball team in his junior and senior years. After graduation in June 1942, he worked briefly as a truck driver for the OUR&D (Ogden Union Railway and Depot Company).

About this time, on a double date he met Lewena Taylor (called "Tye"—pronounced "Tie"), his future wife. Later that year, Ray joined the US Navy. It interrupted their courtship, but they corresponded during the four years that elapsed before they met again.

In fighting World War II, Ray was following the example of his older brother, Bert Jr., a private first class in the Army. On October 14, 1944, Bert was killed in action on Anguar, one of the Palau Islands near the Philippines. Bert left a widow and a son.

After the war, Ray considered his career options. He had learned about electrical devices in the service so from September 1946 till June 1949 he pursued electrical engineering studies at the University of Utah in Salt Lake City. He was graduated with a B.S. degree with High Honors.

He was 25 years old.

General Electric

The Beginning

In 1949 Ray was accepted into General Electric Company's management training program, one of the best in the nation. One August evening in 1950, Ray and Tye eloped and were married in a ceremony in Salt Lake City.

Ever thrifty, Ray and Tye postponed much in the early years of their marriage until they felt more financially secure. One of the things they postponed was children. In 1956, Christopher, their first child, was born; four others followed. Devout Mormons, Ray and Tye raised their children in the LDS Church.

The Career

In his 21 years at GE, Ray progressed from engineer to salesman to founder and manager of the Process Control Division, which used computers to control manufacturing processes. His career required long hours, separations from his family, and frequent relocations. In the 1950s he was needed on a dam project in Tennessee and it was months before he could rejoin his family. When a position in Boston called, the Noordas packed up and moved. In the early '60s Ray and his family lived in Phoenix. Subsequently they moved to southern California when the Process Control Division office opened there.

People who knew Ray sometimes wondered how such an eccentric, freewheeling deal maker could have survived and risen in a large corporation like GE. "The thing that absolutely amazes me," said Ron Eliason, former Chief Financial Officer at Novell, "is that this independent, maverick personality was able to take 21 years of big corporate life. I find that almost hard to believe."

According to Ray, GE gave him his first taste of entrepreneurship and his first opportunities to build businesses.

> GE was an entrepreneurship company, and still is. When I was with the company, I was involved with several start-ups. ... They were started as a new business plan with some level of capability for new people to take the business to a size that was at that time identified as a true 100% profit-and-loss organization with its own management, its own market, its own authority—under restriction, of course—in General Electric to grow as it could.
>
> Saw a whole lot of that and the phases it would typically go through: An engineer would start the idea. A marketer would then recognize the value of that idea and help grow it. And as it developed in strength, typically a manufacturing person would come in to help the business grow, get the cost of manufacturing products down, making sure that the quality was a very fundamental part of

the business. And generally speaking a marketing man might come in and be the manager of that company.

And finally, in our company in General Electric, we used to call it the "milking phase." That means that the business is mature. It may even die because there are technologies perhaps that would supersede it. And so people at the financial level—they're really good at this, they're great "cow milkers"—they came in to make sure that all the costs got under control as you started to harvest the results of this, and that people were motivated heavily towards high productivity. Compete as long as you could but don't count on anything forever. ...

Within General Electric, in the 21 years I was there, I watched about 15 businesses—and participated in some of them—come into growth, develop to maturity level, get into harvest level, [and] go out at the business level or get merged into another department. It's a continuous cycle of entrepreneurship that exists.

Ray and Process Control

Process control is the art and science of controlling a manufacturing process such as making steel, making paper, or even cooking an egg. Ever since the industrial revolution began a lot of workers have earned their living looking at gages and turning valves when the gage readings moved out of tolerance. Process control can be pretty mindless work, so inventors have tried to automate it whenever possible. A thermostat is an example.

In the '60s computer costs were down enough that it was possible in theory to use computers to watch gages and turn valves more economically than people. Ray was one of the pioneers in turning that theory into practice.

Ray started developing process control for automated steel mills and ended his career at GE in their Charlottesville facility as General Manager of Manufacturing Automation Business. As his work changed, his responsibilities changed as well. He moved from technical, to sales, to marketing, and finally to general management.

As he built the Process Control Division, Ray became convinced that he could do for other companies what he was doing for GE. He had the know-how. He had the contacts in the computer industry. He had a little money put by from years of saving. So when an opportunity arose in 1970, Ray left GE to become an entrepreneur.

He was 46 years old, the sole support of his wife and five children ages 5 through 13.

The People

Working for Ray at GE in Phoenix had been a number of people who would later play a role in the Novell story. Jack Davis was a marketing guy who worked as an account rep for GE. Sherrill, Joe, and Reid were also GE Phoenix people.

Among Ray's other employees at GE was an ambitious young man named Jay Kear. Jay entered GE at age 22 in 1959, progressed through a number of technical support and sales positions, and left in 1967 to become Director of marketing for a software company. A year later he landed a job as Vice President of marketing for Digital Industries, and a year after that, in 1969, he was offered a job at General Automation. Jay was then 32 years old.

General Automation

General Automation was founded in 1967 by two former employees of a company called Decision Control, Inc. An engineer named Larry Goshorn and a marketing guy named Burt Yale developed a line of computer products that served as the basis of industrial and commercial automation systems designed to solve automation problems similar to those addressed by the products of GE's Process Control Division. GA sold its systems both directly and to original equipment manufacturers (OEMs) to be included in their systems.

GA products were selling well but expenses were running out of control. By 1970, although the company showed sales of $5 million it was $5 million in the red. Jay Kear suggested they bring his old boss, Ray Noorda, into the company as a consultant to do some trouble-shooting.

"It was an engineer who started the company," said Ray. "He got off track in a couple of cases. He started using too much money. The company got into what I call the Fourth E problem ... and basically had to have some help." Ray identified five stages in the morale of companies: Enthusiasm, Excitement, Exuberance, Euphoria, and Extinction. The Fourth E blinds management and leads to the Fifth E.

"At that time I was leaving General Electric and was invited to come into the company and help out. It was a difficult situation to come into—one that I learned an immense, literally a treasure of, experience from. It was a very good experience for me, even though at the end it seemed as though it was difficult."

Ray left GE and began as a full-time consultant for GA in 1970. Larry Goshorn, the founder and President, was impressed with Ray and decided to bring him on as a company officer, so in May 1971 he was named Executive Vice President of General Automation.

At GE, Ray had had the resources of a vast multinational corporation behind him. At GA, he said, "There was nothing behind me. I had a board but I didn't have any money."

In 1971 General Automation doubled its sales to $10.6 million and for the first time in its history showed a net profit ($3,000) instead of a net loss. By the end of fiscal 1972, sales had increased 51% to $16 million with net income of $1.56 million. From 1972 to 1973 sales doubled again ($16 million to $30.4 million) and the directors made Ray President in December 1973. From 1973 to 1974 sales doubled yet again ($30.4 million to $61.4 million). Those figures made GA the fourth largest minicomputer company in the world.

In Ray's four and a half years at GA, sales increased 1000% and the company had been taken public.

In retrospect, General Automation appears to indeed have been an ideal training ground for the future President of Novell. Typical of the experiences of many young electronics businesses, booming sales created havoc in GA's corporate and physical structure and several major facility expansions were necessary. The closely held company went public in 1971, its fourth year of business. Every year from 1971 through 1974 it acquired other companies and it expanded its international operations, which in 1975 accounted for 29% of total sales.

Rapid sales growth is surely the greatest test of a manager. A flood of money and orders stresses every part of a successful company, and many managers cope simply by throwing money at problems. Others, like Ray, try to focus on key issues and ignore the rest.

One anecdote illustrates the chaos that Ray and the other key people had to wrestle with at General Automation. When Burt Yale, one of GA's founders, had a heart attack and left the company, the international operations he supervised got a little out of control. Ray and Jay invited their old GE colleague Jack Davis to have breakfast with them at the Howard Johnson's in downtown Anaheim. They offered Jack a job putting things right in International. Jack said yes and packed his bags.

"The guys in Europe had been running totally out of control," said Jack. "They had nobody that they had to report to. They were sick and gone. I got over there and found a guy in France, an American expatriate, building a new home. He hadn't been in the office more than half a dozen times in the last six months. He left a message with his secretary to call him if anybody needed him."

But then in 1975 crisis struck hard. A new generation of GA products with a silicon-on-sapphire CPU at their heart never appeared; the technology was fast but turned out not to be commercially feasible. Adding to that problem was a deep recession. Spending nose-dived in the automotive, factory, and electronics markets that were GA's core. Sales sank by $5.5 million (9%) in 1975. Net income, which reached a high of $4.3 million in 1974, plunged to a loss of $4.1 million in 1975. This crisis precipitated a fierce management struggle between Larry Goshorn and his outside directors, who were backing Ray. Ray left the company in October 1975.

Looking back on GA, Ray considered the company typical of entrepreneurial ventures. "The same principle applies every time: A little too much money; a little too much euphoric attitude towards the market opportunity; a little over-expenditure here or there. And before long the company is running out of control, morale is gone, and the incentive for making it improve is dissipated."

Systems Industries

In December 1975, two months after he left General Automation, Ray became a consultant for System Industries, a manufacturer of disk storage systems based in Sunnyvale, California. The company had been founded five years earlier by Edwin V. W. Zschau, whom Ray described as "perhaps the best educated man in the Bay area, a doctorate in both business administration as well as in mathematics and physics". Zschau was Assistant Professor of Management Science at the Stanford University Graduate School of Business from 1964 to 1969. In 1970, with financial backing from three venture capital firms (Brentwood Associates, DSV Associates, and California Northwest

Fund), Zschau set up Systems Industries. In March 1971, the company shipped its first disk storage system.

The central processing units of early minicomputers had very limited memories—a 1969 minicomputer may have had 4,000 bytes of random access memory (RAM) compared to billions of bytes in a 2010 PC. This meant that the supporting storage devices, such as tape drives and the recently developed disk drives, had to carry a lot more of the load in typical data processing. Whole programs were rarely put into RAM at the same time. They would be broken into parts that would "overlay" each other (replace each other in RAM) as they were needed. The parts that weren't being used would be stored on a disk. Software applications such as accounting and word processing programs were routinely handled this way as were the databases containing information. Extensive use of overlaying made disk performance just as important as CPU performance in determining overall system performance.

A disk storage system consisted of a disk controller (printed circuit board); software enhancements (programming commands that worked with the minicomputer operating system); cabling and connecting hardware; and the disk drive. The disk drive might be a removable cartridge or pack or, after 1979, a "Winchester" drive, where the disk is permanently sealed within the drive. (The Winchester name was an allusion to the rifle bullet; the first such drives were called 30-30s while they were being developed at IBM. According to the Smart Computing Encyclopedia online, that was because they featured two spindles with a storage capacity of 30 million characters each.)

Every minicomputer needed at least one disk storage system. In the 1970s a significant number of companies were hooking up additional storage systems to the same computer or to multiple computers, to speed access to data and to provide a system back-up should the primary storage system fail. This concept of "system fault tolerance"—compensating for potential faults in the storage system by creating redundant systems, so that the computer can continue operating even in the event of a component failure—also contributed to the demand for storage systems.

The proliferation of minicomputers in the 1960s had created a growing need for high-performance disk storage systems. Zschau's idea was to bring technological advances in storage systems to the market faster than the competition. When Systems Industries shipped its first product—a system incorporating a new 2.5MB disk cartridge drive—to users of DEC and Data General minicomputers in March 1971, it was in fact several months prior to the release of similar products by DEC and Data General. In 1974 the company shipped storage systems featuring 80MB storage module drives—four years before DEC shipped its similar product.

System Industries started out as a "pilot fish" company swimming around giant minicomputer manufacturers and feeding on their leftovers. DEC and Data General were two of the largest minicomputer manufacturers at the time; they accounted for perhaps half of the US market. System Industries designed its disk storage systems to work with those computers; it also supported military computers designed by Sperry Corp's Univac Division.

Virtually all the company's sales until 1977 were to OEM customers: Manufacturers making computer systems for oil and gas exploration, typesetting operations for newspapers and publishers, office data processing and word processing, engineering operations, military applications, and other process automation markets. System Industries was itself an OEM because it bought its disk drives from other vendors. The only components the company designed and produced itself were disk controllers, cabling and connections, and software.

"Purely by luck," said Ray, "I became acquainted with the company and was invited to come in and see what I could do to help out, because they were shipping about $6 million and losing about $2 million. That's a difficult thing to deal with particularly when there are emotions involved.

"But together we worked the company out of that situation and back into a growth mode. When I left them in 1980 the company was doing about $80 million in annualized sales and profitable enough that the investors decided they could take it public with pride."

For just over a year, December 1975 to January 1977, Ray worked as a consultant to the company. In 1976 he was offered a place on the board of directors. In January 1977, he was named Chief Operating Officer. He was subsequently elected President, then President and Chief Executive Officer.

Following a pattern established at GE and General Automation, Ray simultaneously attacked sales, manufacturing, shipping, and expenses. He set higher quotas and spent hours on the telephone making deals.

He paced the plant and rode the manufacturing people. He looked over the shoulders of the shipping guys to make sure the product got out the door. He cut budgets, personally reviewed expense reports, and worked to stanch the flow of money. He set a productivity goal in terms of dollars of sales per employee. In 1980, the company achieved $131,000 per employee.

Ray also saw that System Industries' focus on OEM sales was a barrier to growth. The OEM market was too small and too dependent on the ultimate end user markets served by a few key customers. If System Industries was to achieve sales in the $100-million range, it would have to sell its products directly to end users. Ray made plans to change the marketing direction of the company, and in 1976 development began on a new product—the 9400 series—that would appeal directly to the minicomputer end user. The plan also called for an expansion into international markets and creation of a service and support business.

At the end of Ray's first year (1976), revenues had doubled from about $6 million to $12.1 million. Instead of a net loss of $2 million, the company showed a net income of $703,000. The 162 employees who worked at System Industries felt proud, and relieved, that the company was finally in the black.

In Ray's second year, System Industries still sold almost exclusively to OEM customers, and it was selling systems that had been developed in 1975 and earlier. Development of the 9400 series—designed to operate with DEC PDP-11 software—was in full swing, with a projected ship date of first quarter 1978. At the end of Ray's second year (1977), revenues were up 35%, from $12.1 million to $16.4 million. Net income was up 70% to $1.2 million.

Ray's third year was a rough one. As the company built a direct sales force in the US and Europe and expanded its customer service capabilities, technical difficulties caused a delay in the development of the new product line. When the 9400 series finally shipped late in the year, it was nine months overdue. Consequently 1978 sales were up just 14% over the previous year to $18.7 million, and the company posted a net loss of $1.4 million.

In Ray's final year and a half with the company (1979–80), the engine he had so carefully tuned finally started humming. The transition to an end-user marketing focus was completed. Sales of the 9400

93

series accounted for nearly half of all system sales and the customer service revenues almost doubled.

The decision was made to phase out an unprofitable subsidiary business, Silonics, that had manufactured an ink-jet printer. System Industries licensed the technology developed by Silonics but no longer manufactured printers. Ray and others decided the company should focus on its primary storage systems business.

Revenues in 1979 were $25 million, up 33.5% over 1978. In 1980, sales increased 51% to $37.9 million. When Ray left the company at the end of July 1980, Systems Industries had an installed base of 11,000 systems and was on track to achieve sales of $63 million in 1981. The company went public in September 1980.

In 1980, Ray received $65,255 in salary from Systems Industries, plus an additional $3,100 in personal benefits. His annualized salary was probably in the $110,000 range (Zschau made $146,899, while two Vice Presidents made $212,782 and $152,076, respectively). Ray seems to have preferred to take most of his compensation in the form of company stock, of which he had conspicuously more than either of the Vice Presidents who drew higher salaries than he. When Ray left System Industries, he had options to purchase 38,250 shares—2.43% of the total shares. Only the founders and the venture capital firms and principals had interests in more shares. Ray's options were worth an estimated $562,656 as of December 1980.

Close Encounter

As mentioned on p. 27 in Chapter One, while Ray was winding down his involvement in System Industries his old colleague Jack Davis arranged a meeting with him. Jack tried and failed to interest Ray in the new business he was trying to start.

> He came to me in the early '80s with a business plan about putting together what ultimately became Novell. I looked at it. I thought it looked like too much too soon and, more important, the things he was planning on making—terminals, printers, and personal computers—were all rapidly becoming commodity items. These are the kinds of things that are sold mostly on cost and very little on features.

If these products were going to have to be sold on cost, then why was he manufacturing in Utah? By the early '80s it was quite clear that electronic commodities should be made offshore.

Why didn't he see this? Because of the early company personalities: He brought in George Canova and Joe Maroney. George was a technical guy; he wanted to build things. Joe was a production man; he wanted to build things even more than George did. None of these people were marketers; they didn't look carefully at the market and the pricing they would need to compete. So in picking his early team Jack more or less locked in his company's destiny as well.

If Jack and George had done their marketing homework they would have realized that the products they were planning to make would become commodities and therefore very price sensitive. They would then have realized that they couldn't follow the inevitable price declines if they were using US labor and production facilities. They would have gone offshore for production and concentrated on other things needed that can't be provided from offshore: Sales, service, and support.

Ray wished Jack luck but bowed out. Jack called George and NDSI was born.

Boschert

In August 1980, Ray joined Boschert, Inc., as Chief Executive Officer. Boschert, like Systems Industries, was a Silicon Valley company based in Sunnyvale, California. Founded by an engineer named Robert Boschert, the company manufactured power supply systems for computers. When Ray joined, the company had about 400 employees.

Computer power supplies are critical to the operation of computers. There is a power supply in every piece of equipment that uses integrated circuits (ICs) and is powered by house current. They are the component that turns 110- or 220-volt AC power from the power plug into the 5- and 12-volt DC power that computer ICs require. (Power supplies aren't needed when batteries are used because batteries provide steady DC power.)

Computer power supplies have a reputation among digital circuit engineers for being "black art": The theory is well known, but the practice is subtle. They are part digital and part analog, and designing good ones isn't a cookbook procedure. Power supplies can range from the bulky looking plug thing that fits into the wall socket and recharges your battery-powered electronics, to the shiny metal box inside your PC, to giants that supply power for big industrial equipment.

Computer power supply equipment is hardware. The manufacture of hardware is a relatively low-margin business in the computer industry and technologically advanced designs rapidly become commodity. Ray's challenge at Boschert was to find a way to reduce manufacturing costs while continuing to develop technologically advanced products.

"I was in the process of moving Boschert's power supply manufacturing offshore," said Ray, "although, I have to admit, I had to do a lot of convincing at Boschert before I got the rest of the organization to see the light."

Ray later described Boschert as "started by an inventor, an engineer—a wonderful man. Very capable in his own right. Skilled at doing what he does best. Not so skilled, as the company began to grow, in setting the right course and keeping it on track in accordance with the expectations of the investors. So I had an opportunity to go in there, as a finder really, and found that there was enough good strength there on which to build a growing company."

The Diamond in the Rough

Ray Discovers the LAN

Less than two and a half years after he joined Boschert, Ray was scouting for new entrepreneurial opportunities. For the 12 years after he left GE he had devoted most of his energies to building up businesses that other people had started. Now he wanted to try his hand at founding his own company.

In 1987 Ray recalled the circumstances that ultimately led him out of Boschert and into Novell.

> I had actually started a business attempting to do some phases of what we are doing here at Novell. My plan was to develop to a typical $50-million to $100-million manufacturing environment [producing] a computer-based system with certain levels of fault

tolerance[7] that would allow me to run 24 hours a day for $250,000 as a system, and I was aimed at doing just that kind of business.

The reason that I had a compelling interest in doing that was that I had run three other companies doing someplace in the $50-million level of business, and to run the business I had to run computer systems which cost about $1 million to maintain any level of security around running the factory without losing time. So I would typically buy two minicomputers, [DEC] VAXes as it turns out, and put them in hot standby so that if one failed the other one could be switched over as quickly as possible—and it usually took not less than two hours—so that I could continue to run the business.

So in my spirit of entrepreneurship at that time, I decided I was not going to run another business that had to pay a million dollars, so I funded and started a company called Reliable Data Systems that was aimed at using a particular technology in a fault tolerant configuration that would allow us to do just that.

And we were headed in that direction when the folks who had financed Novell asked me to come over and take a look at it. And when I saw it, I saw a better way to do it. I saw a short-term and a long-term existence in the business that would provide exactly the same thing that I had started with a different technology in another company. So after a few months, it was clear to me that I had to stop that other business and come over and run this one, because it offered a better opportunity for everybody.

Ray saw something in Novell Data Systems that had not been in Jack Davis' business plan when Jack approached Ray two years earlier: The local area network. The printers, terminals, and computers that Jack had been interested in making, Ray had dismissed as low-margin commodity items. But the LAN intrigued him. Here was a product with a future.

Ray looked at the LAN and saw a business computer system that cost far less than minicomputer systems. Because of its simplicity and low cost a business could buy two of them and achieve fault tolerance. By buying a LAN a customer could preserve his investment in his

---

[7] As we have seen, *fault tolerance* is the term used to describe the ability of a computer system to continue operating even in the event of a component failure, usually achieved by creating parallel or back-up systems.

existing stand-alone PCs, and as a business grew it could simply add more low-cost PCs to the network.

By distributing processing power over a network of intelligent PCs, the LAN overcame the limitations to growth that minicomputer users eventually ran into. In LANs each user has their own "smart" PC which processes information. The more PCs you add to the network, the more powerful the network becomes.

With minicomputers and disk sharing, by contrast, each user taps into the central processing unit of the host computer via "dumb" terminals, and the more users you hook up to the central processor the less performance each user sees. As a growing business added users to its minicomputer system, the computer would take longer to process data and eventually the system would have to be replaced. Ray saw that the LAN could overcome the "planned obsolescence" of the minicomputer.

Another appealing aspect of the LAN was that it harnessed the prevailing technological trends. By 1982 it was clear that there would be a rapid proliferation of personal computers in the 1980s and beyond. Every person or business that owned more than one PC would be a prospect for a LAN.

Finally, the heart of the LAN was a high-margin software product, not a low-margin hardware item, and this appealed to Ray. As software the network operating system was inexpensive to manufacture, difficult for competitors to steal or emulate, and easily revised or customized. Properly handled ShareNet could become for LANs what Digital Research's CP/M had become for microcomputer operating systems: An industry standard.

At the end of November 1982, Ray stopped by the Novell Data Systems booth at Comdex in Las Vegas—a small booth with a wall of the new IBM PCs networked with a wall of older CP/M-based micros. He introduced himself to the attractive blonde in the booth, Judy, and said, "I'm interested in your company."

No Founders

There was one other interesting difference between Novell and the other companies that Ray had worked with. Novell had already cast out its founders—there was no Goshorn, Zschau, or Boschert left at Novell to later contest his success.

This would be Ray's company from the start.

98

The Changing of the Guard:
Novell Data Systems Becomes Novell

In March 1983 the three directors of Novell—Ray, Pete, and Dolf—met for the first official meeting of the board. Dolf was Chairman, a position he would hold until January 1986, when Ray became Chairman. After reports on the progress of the company, the first order of business was the election of company officers. Ray was officially installed as President and CEO, and Harry Armstrong was elected Vice President. Scott Loveless, a Utah attorney, was elected Assistant Secretary. The other officers were all Safeguard people: Ray Kraftson was Secretary, Bill Gillan was Treasurer, and Gerald Wilk was Assistant Vice President. The officers were elected for a term of one year.

Ray's choice of Harry as Vice President indicates the importance of his role relative to the roles of others in the company. Harry was personally responsible not just for the manufacturing and shipping but also for many of the sales that kept NDSI's head above water. In contrast, Craig was still Director of Marketing at this point and would not be elected Vice President until 17 months later, in August 1984.

Much has been made of Ray's willingness to entrust great responsibility to little people. Part of the Noorda legend is his ability to discern among the mob those individuals of genius and talent, the diamonds in the rough. In interviews and speeches Ray made a point of encouraging this idea. "Finding the best players has been one of the most important things in the companies I've been in," he said to an interviewer in 1988.

As mentioned (p. 79) at the beginning of this chapter, Ray went to the trenches for his players.

By May 1983, Ray had, as suspected, found that people like Craig and Judy, plus some of the programmers, knew far more about the company than those who were managing it. Needless to say, management was "streamlined".

SuperSet, Harry, and Craig formed the core management team, although "management" was a somewhat ambitious description of what these six individuals actually did. Ray had picked them not for their managerial skills—because they had never demonstrated any—but for their ability to make things happen. They were all "do-ers." In any case there were no employees to manage. If something needed to be done, it was up to them to personally handle it.

Among the support employees were Judy (whose job now was to help manage the office and to dress up the Novell booth at trade shows), her husband Reid, Diane, and Lorraine. Other employees were hired about this time, some of whom had previously worked for NDSI. Kelly Spencer was hired in March to help Harry in the plant. Jim Bills, who had headed Technical Service in the NDSI days, rejoined in June. David Owen, an engineer who had worked for NDSI for a year, rejoined in July.

Although Ray cared little for titles, the differences in rank do reflect the relative standing of each individual in the company.

Harry was Vice President of Sales.[8] Craig was Director of Marketing. Dave was Director of Engineering. Kelly was Materials Manager. Jim was Director of Technical Services. Judy, at first Manager of Corporate Communications, was made Director of Corporate Communications.

The individuals Ray picked to fill the key roles in the new Novell were, without exception, relatively young and inexperienced people. All except for Harry (age 40) were under 30. The four members of SuperSet were recent graduates of the "Y" and Craig was a college drop-out. They shared similar qualities: A burning faith in the destiny of NetWare and Novell; a willingness to commit themselves totally to their work—to eat, sleep, and dream Novell; an ability and desire to make things happen without waiting for direction; and an absolute personal loyalty to Ray.

Ray's critics attribute different motives to his choice of managers. They see him not as a great liberator of human potential but rather as a CEO who would not brook the independent ideas of experienced professionals. In elevating people with no career histories to key management positions, he guaranteed their loyalty and their good behavior. They were his creatures: He made them and if necessary he could break them.

---

[8] In Novell's Form S-1 filed with the SEC at the beginning of December 1984), Harry Armstrong is listed as Director of Operations and Sales from January 1983 to November 1983, when he was elected Vice President. However, the Delaware franchise report submitted by Novell in March 1983 lists Harry as Vice President. Further complicating the record are the frequent statements made by Ray and others in various interviews that Harry was Production Manager when Ray arrived in January 1983.

Following the Money: The Incentive Story

Another important agenda item at the March 1983 meeting was approval of the stock incentive plan. The plan used a combination of stock grants and stock options to "incent" key employees. Eight employees would be allowed to buy a total 26,500 shares for a nickel per share ($1,325 total). Although the plan was adopted in March, Ray apparently waited about six weeks before making the actual distributions to employees.

In March, Jack Messman bought 20,000 shares at a nickel per share ($1,000), and eight other Novell employees bought a total 371,000 shares at the same price ($18,550). In July, Jack bought another 280,000 shares also at that price ($14,000).

At initial capitalization, Ray had invested $125,000 for 200,000 shares, or $.625 per share. Safeguard "invested" assets worth $1,015,381 and received 350,000 shares of convertible preferred stock, the equivalent of $2.90 a share. In October 1984, Safeguard converted these shares to 4.9 million shares of Novell common stock.

Ray made sure that all his employees had a generous stake in the new company. True, the shares were worthless at the time they were issued, but it was clear to all that if they could make Novell a success they could do very well for themselves.

The most important people Ray had to please were the four Super-Set guys who had created NetWare. Drew, Dale, Kyle, and Mark were not employees of Novell but outside consultants. In exchange for the rights to NetWare and continuing work for Novell each of the four was allowed to buy 11,875 shares at a nickel per share ($593.75). The shares were to vest over four installments from May 1983 to January 1986. In addition, each member of SuperSet was to be paid a salary. In the fiscal year ended October 1984 the four SuperSet members received a total of $248,200.

Dale recalled the contract negotiations as another example of Ray's "win-win" philosophy.

> He doubled SuperSet's equity position in Novell when he came on board. We had already negotiated a position with Safeguard, and we had a position in Novell based on our value and so on.

When Ray came in, he doubled it. He said, "You guys, I need you to be here and I need to keep your attention a long time, and that isn't enough."

Other employees and consultants were given the right to buy a total 56,500 shares of Novell for an average exercise price of $2.42 per share ($136,600). The employees put up a cash total of $5,700 for their shares and the company lent them the balance of $130,900.

Different employees were given different opportunities to purchase stock. Harry received 5,000 shares plus options that would vest in annual increments over the next four years. Reid received 3,000 shares plus options to purchase 4,000 more over the next four years. Since Judy and Reid were a couple, Judy received no shares of her own. (Remember, this was the '80s. In Utah, in Utah Valley.)

In December 1983, Novell sold the SuperSet consultants an additional 30,000 shares at $.29 per share.

Following the Money Further: Some Loans Are Made

By the summer of 1983 the new Novell was taking its first tentative steps forward as a company. Ray had his key people in place, properly incented, and had eliminated those employees he didn't want. He had addressed his problems in manufacturing and the list of successful installations was growing almost weekly. He had a new name and marketing image for the company and the flagship product. He had a vision of a future LAN industry that would grow from the file server model developed by Novell.

In June an incident occurred that illustrates an aspect of Ray's involvement in the computer industry. As Novell struggled on its upward climb to profitability Ray approved a loan of up to $200,000, made by Novell, to Gateway Communications, Inc., a company in which Ray owned a substantial interest and served as director. The loan was apparently designed to improve Gateway's financial standing; Gateway actually borrowed only $20,000 of the $200,000 available to it.

The loan was paid back a year later but it shows how Ray could use one company to serve another. As President and CEO, Ray's energies were focused on Novell but he continued to take an interest in other high tech companies as an investor, director, founder, and where appropriate, strategic partner. Ray's involvement in other companies was an asset to Novell in many cases, although his critics suggest that certain deals may have been more to Ray's benefit than Novell's.

As the orders for S-Net LANs grew, the company needed additional capital to build and ship the systems. In November, Ray made a personal loan to Novell of $125,000. By March 1984 he had loaned an additional $25,000. Safeguard also made a series of loans to the fledgling company which by the end of 1983 totaled some $800,000.

The Company Prospers

At Novell's Comdex booth in Las Vegas in November '83, the mood was confident, determined, and optimistic in contrast to the fey but ultimately pessimistic mood of a year before.

By January 1984 at the end of its first year of business the new Novell had a pulse and seemed likely to survive. From zero sales in January 1983 the company had somehow managed to bring in $3.8 million. True, there was still a year-end loss of almost $1 million, but if the income continued to grow as projected the company would be in the black in fiscal 1984. Foreign shipments contributed significantly to first year sales—30%, in fact—and this was largely due to Reid's efforts. On January 13, 1984, Novell's stock split four for one.

On New Year's Day, 1984, most Novell employees felt good about the progress made in 1983 and the work that lay before them. There was, however, at least one casualty from the rebirth of Novell. That was the marriage of Reid and Judy Clark. In light of the role Judy came to play in the company it is a casualty worth mentioning.

According to Reid, Novell presented a vast new set of opportunities and possibilities for Judy and she wanted to be free to pursue them. "She just got to a point where she didn't want to have to report where she was going or what she was doing. What she wanted at that moment was not to have a husband. She saw a wholly different lifestyle for herself. So I said, 'Well, if that's what you want, then we can arrange that.' Because everything else had changed, you know, she had stopped going to church, taken off her garments."

Adult Mormons, which includes anyone married in a Mormon temple, wear special underclothes called temple garments. For a married Mormon to stop wearing garments is an indication of apostasy.

"There was a split in terms of what she was doing in her lifestyle," Reid went on.

By the end of the year, they were divorced.

Following the Technology: In Pursuit of the PC-Compatible Marketplace

I came here to drain a swamp but I spend all my time wrestling alligators.

—Anonymous

In 1982, Engineering was tied up wrestling the enormous alligators of quality problems, personal computer problems, and getting the LAN delivered. The continual battering had left them quite conservative and focused. When the IBM PC was introduced few engineers showed any interest. They had no time to see that the IBM PC was the key to draining their swamp.

SuperSet, on the other hand, was quite interested. They were independents and their contribution was software, to which they still felt some proprietary attachments. They could see Novell's problems as clearly as anyone, and if Novell sank beneath the waves they wanted to have another market for their work.

All through 1982 they actively explored alternatives. Some involved marketing, such as selling a game they designed to performance-test the network (the origin of Snipes) and discreetly inquiring who else might be interested in network operating system technology.

They also explored technology alternatives, including the IBM PC. As mentioned in Chapter Two (p. 65), Drew got one of the first PCs in Utah Valley. He could see that it would be easy to network as a workstation. It had an open bus structure and a well-documented BIOS that would make designing a network board easy. So in 1982 and 1983 Drew campaigned, with Craig's help, to include the PC as one of the kinds of workstations Novell would support.

The PC was fine as a workstation but as a file server it was marginal because it had no standard hard disk. Then in 1983 the IBM PCXT was introduced, a PC with a standard hard disk installed, and that obstacle was removed. The PC-compatible file server was now technologically practical and supporting PC-compatibles as file servers became a marketing question.

However, the PCXT was underpowered compared to Novell's proprietary 68B file server and the 8088 CPU couldn't process as fast as the 68000. The PCXT supported smaller-capacity disks—5MB and 10MB compared to the 40MB available on the 68B. Would such a file server sell? Finally, even if it would sell would it cut into the much more profitable business of selling 68B file servers? Those cost a few thousand dollars when an operating system for a PC-compatible sold for a few hundred.

Craig and Drew argued that a PC-compatible file server would not only sell, it would sell much better than the 68Bs because the PCXT was an open system. There would be dozens of companies and thousands of people trying to sell PC-compatible file servers with dozens of kinds of networking boards installed. If Novell could service that market with a "glue product" it would be a much larger market than that of selling just 68B file servers with Novell boards for the PCs.

But it was a tough choice. It went against the grain of what Engineering perceived their mission to be: Circuit-designing engineers aren't going to have much to do in a company devoted to producing floppy disks and manuals. They are going to perceive that they can add a lot more value to the company by redesigning the file server or designing a new network interface card (NIC).

In the end, the circuit designers adapted to the glue product concept and remained useful by designing drivers for the NICs and by dealing with the many kinds of hard disk drives and disk drive controllers that came to be attached to the PC-compatibles.

Novell's open systems approach to marketing NetWare eventually became famous. But the path to it was not obvious in 1983. It took a lot of inspired salesmanship both within and outside Novell.

From the Outside

When viewed from the outside, 1983 was a year of no change for Novell. Novell hadn't grown in people, the people hadn't changed much, the LAN product hadn't changed much, the sales were only $3.5 million. There was absolutely no sign that a billion-dollar company was in the making.

The only surprising news was that Novell was still alive at all and that the chaos of the Time of Six Presidents had ended abruptly with Ray's arrival.

But in 1983 the foundation was built: The key elements of NetWare were resolved technically and now the battle would move to marketing this wonderful technology. The task ahead would be to prove that NetWare wasn't just another over-engineered product, with lots of nice features that no one needed.

In 1983 the team was forged and its goal was defined: 1984 would be, in the eyes of Novell's founders, the Year of the LAN.

CHAPTER FOUR
Crossing the High Sierras

Tunneling through Granite

In January 1984, after a year of Ray's management, Novell had still to overcome some major obstacles to growth. These obstacles—differentiating the product, creating hardware independence, establishing sales channels, winning support from independent software application developers, and obtaining capital—had loomed large before Novell since the earliest days.

To recall an image from the Old West, the job was like that faced by the Central Pacific Railroad in the early 1860s, as the company blasted tunnels through the granite peaks of the Sierra Nevadas, clearing the route for the western half of the nation's first transcontinental railway. Compared to the Union Pacific, building across flat prairie, their progress looked glacial; but it was just as real.

Ray and his team had been chipping away at the barriers for a year with some effect and would continue to do so through 1984 and well into 1985, when the light appeared at the end of the proverbial tunnel. Until the obstacles were cleared the whole project remained too dicey for all but the most adventurous speculators to have any serious interest in.

We're Different, and Much Better

One of the biggest obstacles to Novell's growth was communicating how NetWare differed from the other LAN solutions in the market—and why that difference made NetWare better. There were perhaps 20 companies selling LAN systems besides Novell.

The key to differentiating NetWare was a semantic and conceptual distinction that Novell worked hard to get the marketplace to accept:

107

File server vs. disk server. NetWare used a file server approach, Novell's people said, while other LANs used a disk server approach. The file server approach was the superior technology and the wave of the future, Novell maintained, while the more traditional disk server solution contained inherent flaws that would ultimately make dinosaurs of LAN systems that utilized it.

As established in Chapter One (see "Disk Server versus File Server", p. 53), Novell's claims were true. Let's review why, in a little more technical detail.

A disk server chops up a shared hard disk into separate "volumes" so that each PC on the network has its own piece of the hard disk. Each PC manages its own directories and files in its volume. Some of the flaws in the disk server approach are:

- It is an inefficient use of the hard disk space.
- One PC on the network cannot share the files in another PC's volume.
- Because each PC manages its own disk-space allocation, data integrity is a problem.
- The network operating system frequently cannot accommodate the addition of advanced network features.

Although disk server technology developed to the point where some of these flaws were overcome or compensated for, Novell argued that it was still an inherently inferior solution to the problem of managing LANs.

By contrast, NetWare's file server technology relieved the networked PCs of all hard disk management responsibilities. The file server provided central control of data file management, improving security and the ability of different PCs on the LAN to share information in the same directory without interfering with each other. The file server approach, Novell maintained, was the more sophisticated approach, the more elegant solution, and a distinct technological advance—the first "milestone" in the history of local area networks. (In the earliest childhood of the company Novell employees had a sense they were making history.)

The problem was getting the marketplace to buy this distinction. Novell's competitors claimed that their disk servers were file servers. If confronted with the technological differences, the competition claimed that their disk servers were simpler, more cost-effective, and more reliable than Novell's file servers, and that in actual practice, most businesses would never need the advanced data sharing capabilities that NetWare claimed it could support.

Although SuperSet had articulated this distinction between disk server and file server as early as 1982, two years later they were still fighting to have the concept—and the terminology—understood and accepted.

Why Did Novell Develop File Server Technology?

Two historical accidents allowed Novell to be the first with file server technology. One was the long gestation period for the network operating system (NOS or just OS) that happened while Novell was undergoing the trauma of 1982. During the Time of Six Presidents discussed in Chapter Two above, as much as Novell wanted to launch the LAN quickly it was not in a position to do so. This gave the SuperSet people a chance to promote the merits of the file server concept within Novell before the OS design was frozen.

The second was that the Novell file server was equipped with the Motorola 68000–family processor rather than an Intel 80xx–family processor like that being used in most competitive machines. The Motorola chips of that era had more horsepower than comparable Intel chips so the server had more processing power. File server technology required more power than disk server technology so Marketing was behind this as another way of differentiating the Novell product.

Other Barriers to Growth

Another major obstacle to company growth was the lack of standard hardware and software in the PC and LAN market. Amidst the petty fiefdoms of an immature marketplace, how would tiny Novell rise to a position of leadership? The strategy for overcoming this was a noble if somewhat chancy vision that would require enormous energy to implement (as will be seen starting on p. 112 below): Hardware independence.

Yet another barrier was the lack of sales channels to bring NetWare to the customers who would ultimately buy and use the LAN. Sales channels are how a product gets from a provider to a user. Opening channels was and still is a huge task; when you have a totally new product, figuring out who will become a sales channel is as much of a challenge as finding out who will be a customer. Besides sales to distributors, resellers, and systems integrators, Ray was working on deals with retail computer stores and with original equipment manufacturers (OEMs).

Novell's growth was also limited by the dearth of software application programs—word processing, databases, accounting spreadsheet programs, and so on—that took advantage of the NetWare LAN environment.

In the early '80s most PC applications were designed for use on individual PCs and some were copy-protected. Some of the simpler applications for single users, for example word processing and spreadsheet programs, could be used without too much trouble on a network. But the high-end applications, such as databases and programming tools, needed to be customized first, because data would be corrupted if more than one user on a network tried to use the application at the same time.

There were also questions of cost, licensing, and convenience. LAN users wanted to install one version of the application on the file server that all PCs on the network could access, but that was not always possible. Until software programs adapted to NetWare LANs became widely available, users were limited in the multi-user kinds of things they could do with their Novell networks.

Finally, money was a problem. Like every rapidly growing business, Novell had an ongoing need for capital infusions. Cash was needed to pay for the parts and overhead necessary to fill ever-growing orders. This cash could be tied up for months before payment was received for the shipments. Until Novell attained a critical mass of orders, it would need regular additions of capital from outside sources.

Where Angels Fear to Tread

It was not as though Ray and his team had started in 1983 with a careful plan to solve their marketing, development, and financing problems. The employees just threw themselves at the job of moving product with all the energy and enthusiasm of excited amateurs—that's why Ray had picked them. The mission of growing Novell and the industry was clear, but little else was obvious in the way of strategy or tactics. They were all grunts—if the day's progress through the granite was measured by inches instead of by miles, that was all right. They didn't know how impossible their task was.

Judy reflected on the early days: "We were just naive enough to know that we had a good product. I wasn't afraid of the competition. I wasn't afraid of IBM or Microsoft or 3Com. Who were they? They're just people. You know, they had a lot of money, but so what? If we were telling the truth and we had a really good product and people needed it, then I could communicate it to them."

The years from 1983 to 1985 were the years of steady, dogged labor when the groundwork was laid for Novell's future spectacular growth. 1983 was a year of transition from NDSI to the new Ray Noorda company. In 1984 the patterns of work crystallized into policies, programs, and more formal initiatives. In 1985 Ray and his people could see the results of their efforts and the company was primed for a sales explosion.

Educating the Marketplace

To overcome Obstacle 1, differentiating NetWare from its competitors, Novell worked on educating the marketplace—as opposed to merely advertising in the marketplace. SuperSet and Craig were the principal sources of educational information. They explained "file server" versus "disk server" to distributors, resellers, and direct customers. They explained it to software developers. They explained it to other computer companies who were possible strategic partners. They explained it to the press. But for all their efforts, in 1983 and early '84 the industry as a whole still did not acknowledge the superiority of the file server approach.

"*File server* was the most difficult thing in the world to communicate," recalled Judy, "and we never could get the point across. We would say, 'Yes, we're a file server and this is why we're a file server, and they're not—they are a disk server.' And so we'd get this all straightened out with the editor, and then he would go talk to somebody else, another company. ... And they would say, 'Yes, we have a file server [too].' And so then the editor would [write], 'Yes, these two products are file servers.' And they were completely different kinds of products."

Then one day in September 1984 the heavens opened and the revelation was handed down to the mortals below. Dale explained:

111

The big break for Novell was when IBM endorsed Microsoft's PC LAN v1.0, an early [file-server-based] LAN product. Until that point, Novell was fighting an incessant battle with 20 other small manufacturers about whether file server or disk server technology was a better technology.

When IBM did that, all of a sudden the 20 other companies who had been trying to sell disk servers withered up and blew away. Almost all of those, those that didn't go bankrupt, within a couple of months came and started buying Novell stuff and selling it, because IBM had now spoken. The giant had said: "We will have file servers. We will not have disk servers."

So Novell found itself on the side of the angels, or even the gods.

Hardware Independence

Mother Necessity Inspires Again

Hardware independence is a software's ability to function with many kinds of hardware. In a general way, the idea of hardware independence had been around for a long time. That NetWare had it was a consequence of the file server model developed by SuperSet.

But the Novell that Ray bought into in 1983 was a systems manufacturing company—a company that produced primarily hardware with software bundled in, and pretty much all in a self-contained environment. Nearly all of the income in 1983 was from sales of the NetWare/S-Net system and related hardware components.

This was the fashion of the time. In the 1960s and '70s, IBM and other computer manufacturers had established proprietary computer systems designed to lock in customers. They tried to be the single vendor for all the customer's equipment, supply, and service needs. As the customer's needs changed, the single vendor would lead him down well-established migration paths to bigger and better systems. Compatibility with other systems was discouraged.

This single-vendor model inherited from the mainframe and minicomputer worlds was the goal of virtually all of the early LAN companies; they all sought to provide a total solution to the customer's needs.

Novell at the beginning of 1983 wasn't a strong company, and it was just one of many companies offering proprietary LAN systems and networking products for personal computers. Novell offered a system that included a file server computer, network interface cards, cabling and connections, hard disk subsystems, and the NetWare Operating System. (Novell did not sell PC workstations.) As a manufacturer of yet another proprietary LAN, Novell faced an uphill battle against Corvus, whose Omninet already dominated the emerging LAN market of the early '80s.

Whatever slim chance Novell had of carving a dominant niche in the hardware end of networking personal computers sank forever in 1982's stormy sea of red ink and crisis.

Loading the Shotgun

In the course of doing business in 1983, Ray and his team soon realized that by limiting the sale of NetWare to LANs based on Novell file servers they were limiting the growth of the company. If NetWare was ever to become an industry standard, it would need the kind of mass distribution that could only be achieved through licensing: To gain the "critical mass" of installations, NetWare would have to be bundled with other LAN systems besides Novell's S-Net system.

The choice was between "rifle shot" marketing, where NetWare would be carried to the market in a single slug (S-Net), and "shotgun" marketing, where NetWare would be carried to market in a shower of vehicles made by many hardware makers and marketers. To make a massive impact in a short time, Novell decided to load the shotgun.

Craig recalled how this vision came to him.

As soon as Ray joined the company, I was going to move from Marketing into Sales. Ray convinced me that I should stay and be Director of Marketing.

It was sometime in early 1983, I think, that the [IBM PC]XT was announced.

Drew and I both felt that the competitors were Corvus, Orchid, and a new company called 3Com. PC-Net [from Orchid Technologies] was probably growing faster than all of them at the time. Drew and I both thought the XT would be a terrific server and that we should start being as hardware-independent as we could— not drop the hardware yet, just become hardware-independent. Ray was supportive of it and allowed us to buy the equipment to do that.

One of the questions we were struggling with at the time was: What network [system] should this hardware-independent version of NetWare run on? We hadn't come up with being network–hardware independent, we'd only come up with targeting NetWare on the XT.

The question kept coming up that we needed to pick a medium to run on. Should we build a product that's compatible with the Novell 68000 box or should we find someone else's network adapter? The choices we were struggling with were: Should we do Corvus? Should we do 3Com Ethernet? Should we do Orchid PC-Net? Should we do ARCnet? Those were the four big choices at the time. Or should we do our own?

I sat down and listed all the companies that were these companies' vendors—Orchid had the biggest list, I think 3Com was next. The other thing was that Ray was a big investor in this company in southern California called Gateway Communications and they had yet another network called G-Net with no network operating system on it. Because Gateway was willing to cooperate with Novell at the time, that was the first we started working on.

But I can remember very clearly when I finally came up with the answer in my head about which network we should support. And the answer was: All of them!

I was driving to the airport and I pulled over and drew a box that had all these different network cards in it and all the companies that were supporting the networks attached to them. So it had an Omninet, an Ethernet, and an ARCnet line, and a G-Net, but there was no one but us at that time.

I took it back to Drew and said, "I want this box. I want an XT to have all these cards in it and have them look the same."

He said, "I can't do it." (Of course, several years later, he did.)

I said, "Well, okay, we'll pretend like we did." [So for the time being there had to be a different box—a different file server—for each network brand.]

We went out and started creating. I think that was the other major event that caused a significant turn in the mentality of the company. Coming up with the notion that all of the hardware, including the server and the network adapter, was irrelevant to us. That we would do all of them.

We had a lot of resistance to that at the company.

Making a Networkable Computer in 1983

The key to an easily networkable personal computer in 1983 was whether or not it had a well-documented expansion bus. An expansion bus is a socket or series of sockets on the main computer circuit board (the mother board) to which other circuit boards (daughter boards) can be attached to expand the computer's capabilities. This is the idea of modular design applied to personal computers.

The first generation personal computers were built for hobbyists, with an expansion bus on the mother board. The uses to which these early computers would be put were so varied that the designers needed to make them easy to customize. Game playing, voice recognition, appliance control, and serious number crunching were a few of the many uses the hobbyist users of the early '80s found for personal computers. The easy way to customize was to add different boards, so the early makers always put in a place where many different kinds of boards could be added—the expansion bus.

An expansion bus can be a single socket—as it was on the Macintosh SE—or it can be many. The most prolific were the late '70s era IMSAIs and Cromemcos which had 19 and 21 slots respectively. These were so modular, in fact, that the mother board consisted of nothing but expansion slots—all the RAM, all the I/O, and even the CPU came on daughter cards.

But modularity adds expense and size to products. By 1982 some of the next generation CP/M-based computers that were coming out were integrated—they had everything on the mother board and no expansion bus. These new machines cost less and looked more stylish, but they couldn't accept a networking card.

The IBM PC followed the Apple II tradition and stayed modular. This made the PC exciting to people like Drew who wanted to do more with a computer than just connect it to a printer and a modem.

Novell's Original Network: The S-Net

Novell's S-Net hardware was a product of its times. Engineers and marketers had discussed other alternatives but S-Net seemed best suited.

In 1981–82 there were no networking standards. The computer magazine articles of the day were still discussing the theoretical virtues of baseband versus broadband (modulated versus unmodulated) signal transmission, and various physical networking topologies such as linear bus and star, because there were few real networks to discuss.

Novell considered Ethernet, but in those days it was much too expensive—over $1,000 per connection—and "thin" Ethernet hadn't been developed, so the only way to connect was with bulky converter boxes connecting equally bulky quarter-inch-thick coaxial cable.

ARCnet was also explored and rejected because of its cost.

The end result of this elimination process was S-Net, an in-house design. S-Net used a star topology with all the workstations connecting directly to the file server. It used an RS-422 electrical protocol that was inexpensive to design and build, because it was carried over dual twisted pair cable (alias 4-wire phone cable).

S-Net was attractive for its simplicity. All the cables had only two devices on them. This meant there was no need for a sophisticated communications protocol[9] that had to provide for addressing different stations on the wire. The file server knew which workstation it was talking to simply by knowing which communications port the signal came from.

S-Net was yet another quick and inexpensive choice in the head-long rush to get the LAN to the market. It was a good choice at the time, when LANs were self-contained systems of half a dozen work-stations devoted to sharing hard disks and printers, and little more. S-Net would serve less well as LANs embraced larger networks and connectivity to many other kinds of data processing systems.

Evolving beyond S-Net

The New "Open" PC World

As the LAN concept evolved to include making larger networks and interconnecting many networks, other needs appeared that would be better served by other architectures. Novell had a hard choice to face: How was it going to expand its market beyond S-Net?

---

[9] The Internet's protocol suite (TCP/IP, for Transmission Control Protocol and Internet Protocol) is an example of the sort of sophisticated protocol that was avoided, along with the army of programmers that would have been necessary to produce it.

The decision to market the software component apart from Novell's hardware required a leap of faith. For one thing, all the company's money came from sales of the S-Net system, which was mostly hardware, and other hardware items like network interface cards (NICs). The only thing really unique about S-Net was the software operating system. If other companies could buy NetWare, wouldn't that kill off Novell's lucrative hardware sales—and therefore Novell? Wouldn't Novell be shooting itself in the foot by OEMing NetWare?

One of the most passionate and articulate advocates of unbundling the NetWare operating system from the S-Net product was Craig. In working with PCs of the late '70s, he had seen how their manufacturers could use third parties to leverage sales of their products, like the Apple II and the IBM PC.

The Apple II did very well in the pre-IBM PC world because it was a very open system. The design specs for its bus and monitor program were well known, so third parties could come in and build boards to their heart's content. In that period you could do more things with an Apple II than you could with a CP/M machine, even though there might be more power in the CP/M machine. Variety was definitely the Apple II forte and that's why it sold so well.

When Apple came out with the Apple III they closed up the bus. And when they shipped the Lisa they kept it closed. And when they came out with the Macintosh it was still closed. The people swelling the ranks of the growing Apple Computer Corp. fell in love with their sexy new graphic and mouse-oriented operating system and lost track of the importance of an open hardware system.

But Phil Estridge, who pioneered IBM's PC business, did not. As IBM rushed to bring its entry into the personal computer marketplace he talked to a lot of ComputerLand retailers and other people. One of the things that became very clear to him was that the open bus was an important selling tool. Technologically the successor to the Apple II was the IBM PC, not the Macintosh, because both were open systems. Third parties who had worked and developed on Apple II looked for the next machine to go on to, and most often they went to the IBM PC rather than the Apple III or the Lisa or the Mac because none of those were open systems.

Craig brought this open systems vision to Novell: When you're playing in the PC world the ability to let other people play with you is of paramount importance. This was also SuperSet's vision, and Ray picked up on it quickly.

Novell's weak position in 1983 reinforced the concept—leveraging sales of your product off the backs of your competitors was the only practical way for a small company to attain market acceptance in a short period of time. A year in the high tech computer industry is like a decade in more traditional industries, and if a company fails to make an impact on its market quickly its hour may pass, dooming it to second-rate status or extinction as its competitors gobble up market share. Craig called the game of strategic alliances "corporate jujitsu": The successful player would turn the force of its opponents to its own advantage. In the years to come Ray and Craig would prove themselves masters of corporate jujitsu.

An Evolution Begins

In 1983 Novell began to evolve from thinking of itself as a LAN systems company (hardware/software) to thinking of itself as a LAN *operating system* (software) company. It would continue to manufacture and sell hardware as a way of promoting the software—and as a way of surviving, because software sales were nonexistent in 1983—but the strategy for growth would focus on the software that ran the network hardware.

Dale described the reasoning that led Ray to take Novell down the software track from 1982 to '84.

> The hardware independence business came about because there was an incredible proliferation of small companies who were selling lots and lots of hardware solutions and Novell was just one in a crowd.
>
> The thing that made us a little different was that we owned our own software. And it ran better than most of the other software offerings that people were making right then.
>
> Corvus, Nestar, TeleVideo—there was a huge number of them, and a big number of these people ended up becoming Novell OEMs. Most of those people started as Novell competitors. There were 30 or 40 different companies who were all trying to push PC networking solutions. Most of them had proprietary network hardware, had proprietary board plug-ins, and proprietary software.

And that's why we went hardware independent. We looked at it and said, "You know, our hardware is not really that cost-effective. Let's face it, guys, we've got some problems. But if we could leverage off our software then every time one of our competitors makes a sale we get a little money. That will keep us alive."

Evangelization

By the end of 1983, Novell was trying to market the NetWare Operating System independently of its S-Net LAN. This effort entailed:

- Trying to get other LAN companies to OEM NetWare.
- Porting NetWare to the hardware of other LAN companies so that the customers or resellers of other LAN hardware could install NetWare themselves.

("Porting" means moving software from one computer architecture to another. A small part of that process is making a communications "port" attaching the two systems so that files can be transferred.)

With help from Ray and SuperSet, Craig was the principal evangelist for NetWare. ("Evangelist" is a term applied by Apple Computer in the '80s to its marketing and developer relations people. Their job was not merely to sell and persuade but to spread the gospel.) The effort really got underway in 1984.

Support for this concept was far from universal within Novell. Jim Bills pointed out as late as 1986 that "Novell makes more money selling its hardware than it does its software. If we're going to keep growing we can't abandon the hardware until the software can carry the load."

Harry concurred. "It's a good concept, but it can't happen too quickly."

And there were a lot of engineers who felt it was a good idea as long as they could keep improving and releasing new versions of S-Net and the 68B file server.

If Novell was a bit unsure about unbundling NetWare software from its hardware, its competitors were even more skeptical. Judy remembered how resistant the companies were to OEMing NetWare.

And by that time we had figured out that the only way to really be successful was to be in every distribution channel and to be on everybody's hardware product. And so we had put together this campaign that ... internally it was called Project Piranha because we were just going to eat up everything. And it was to port the software over to everybody else's hardware.

I had gone on trips with the two of them [Ray and Craig] to try to explain to these people what the product was: That it was a file server, not a disk server, and that it could work on everybody's hardware. ... If they would just dedicate some manpower to it, then they could do it. Then they could have NetWare on their products too!

It was just like talking to a wall. Everybody was so territorial and protecting everything they had already come up with. They didn't want to cooperate. It was a really immature industry, and no one could see how big it could really be.

Other companies didn't see how they would benefit by helping to proliferate Novell's LAN operating system. In classic computer industry style, they were still trying to deliver a total solution. And it was by no means clear to anyone at that point that NetWare was a superior technology or one that would win wide market acceptance.

The industry's lack of interest in Novell did not deter Craig; he proselytized relentlessly.

In April 1984, after weeks of negotiations, Novell lined up its first OEM customer, based in Atlanta, Georgia. Shortly after, a second agreement was made with Gateway Communications, the company Ray owned a piece of. Others followed. Judy remembered:

We went from one and then two, you know, it was really slowly on the third one, and then we had six. It was thrilling. You know, there are certain moments in the history of Novell where you're struggling, struggling, struggling—and all of a sudden you have six OEMs! ... That was a big, big break.

The next six OEM customers were Sperry Corporation, Quadram Corporation, TeleVideo Systems, Texas Instruments, North Star Computers, and Santa Clara Systems. The breakthrough had come through a combination of diligent work and the felicitous support of IBM for the file server technology of the PC LAN v1.0. As Dale noted, after the IBM announcement NetWare looked a lot better to Novell's larger competitors who had placed losing bets on the doomed disk server operating systems.

NetWare Anywhere

A wide open channel strategy was a natural complement to Ray's emphasis on hardware independence. Novell was a company in a hurry. If it was to succeed in its bid to dominate the market, it would have to push its products out through every available channel.

Judy remembered the drive to get NetWare available anywhere and everywhere.

> Starting at the same time, we started hammering away at every single distribution channel. Because we felt that if we could get NetWare into everybody's hands and everyone selling it, then everybody would have it, then that would increase the market share.

> That was definitely very, very key to the success of Novell—of being in all these distribution channels. You could get NetWare anywhere. That was the slogan that we had internally: "NetWare Anywhere".

In 1984, Novell opened four sales offices: Three in the United States (California, Virginia, and Texas) and one in Germany. Ray and Harry continued to establish relations with resellers and distributors in the US and abroad. By the end of 1984, Novell had 15 US distributors and 15 foreign distributors.

Ray also tried to get national computer retail stores to carry Net-Ware. In 1984, he succeeded in obtaining agreements with two chains, Businessland and ValCom.

From January 1983 through 1984, about 80% of Novell's sales were made to distributors and dealers. By the end of 1984, however, Novell had opened up channels through OEMs and retail chains in addition to making direct sales to major accounts. Two years later, by the end of 1986, only 59% of the company's sales came from distributors, but by the end of 1988 distributors still accounted for 55% of sales.

Balancing multiple channels is a fine art. Novell got away with courting multiple channels in the early days because no one knew what a PC-based network was—it had no pre-defined "slot" in the many channels for distributing computer equipment. It wasn't "obviously":

- A computer retailer sales item
- A value added reseller item
- Something to be handled by distributors

- Something that should be bundled with LAN hardware
- Something that should be offered as an accessory to a mini-computer system

Rather, it could be any of the above. So a lot of different kinds of businesses were willing to try reselling NetWare.

But there was one channel that all these others knew conflicted with their channel. That was the "selling direct" channel: Novell company representatives contacting end users directly and trying to sell product without using middlepeople.

Anywhere but Direct, That Is

Selling is an expensive process. Half the price of a typical product sold off a retail shelf goes to pay for the selling process. This means that there is always a temptation, by selling direct, to internalize the sales effort and collect that revenue as profit rather than hand it off to another organization as a cost.

One obstacle to selling direct is that building a sales force is expensive. Salespeople won't work for peanuts. If they're making peanuts, they'll move. It takes time to recruit and train good salespeople, which adds cost, and they like impressive surroundings so they can impress customers, which adds more cost. And these are upfront costs—the kind hardest on a fast-growing company.

Distributors are important to the sales channels because they are adept at taking a trained and in-place sales force and redirecting it rapidly from one product to another. They off-load part of the burden of maintaining a sales force from the manufacturer.

Direct sales is not only expensive to establish, it makes a statement to the other channels. Many of those channels, for good reason, see direct sales as such a hazard that they won't cooperate if a manufacturer is "going direct". They see those direct salespeople as cutting into or skimming the cream off their business.

Still, with half the price of a product going to the selling process, Ray was not immune to the continuing temptation to internalize more of that revenue stream. The issue of selling direct remained controversial. It is the heart of the NetWare Centers controversy that gets covered in Chapter Seven.

Courting Software Developers

Another strategic initiative begun in 1984 was to persuade independent software developers to write NetWare-compatible application programs. Ray and the team came up with the DIO ("Do It Once") NetWare Affiliates Program. The idea was that developers could save themselves a lot of trouble by supporting NetWare. By "doing it once" (writing a NetWare-compatible program), developers would in effect support all the popular LAN hardware systems, because NetWare was hardware independent. Novell would give third-party developers the tools and information they needed to write for NetWare.

However, developers were concerned that LANs would cause their sales to drop, because single users would stop buying individual copies of software and share one copy with many users on their LAN. To allay these concerns, Novell created NetWare/MUSLS (Multi-User Software Licensing System) for NetWare-compatible LAN applications. MUSLS provided copy protection to help prevent piracy and usage restriction mechanisms that controlled the number of network users who could access a program.

In February of 1984, Ray and company attended Softcon in New Orleans, a trade show where software developers could exhibit their products. Novell did not exhibit but had a hospitality suite. Developers were invited to come to the suite to hear about the DIO Program. Judy recalled:

> There were 30 companies ... none of the big companies came. There were all these little tiny developers—really obscure companies. They were just anxious to get their software running on anybody's hardware and compatible with any kind of operating system. If anybody would listen to them, they were thrilled.
>
> Some of them, they came in suspicious and wanted to know why we were going to give them this software and hardware and what did they have to do for it. And then they went away understanding the value in it. We had a great response.

One of the developers that came to the hospitality suite was SoftCraft, a little company out of Austin, Texas, owned by Doug and Nancy Woodward. SoftCraft was pushing a database program called Btrieve. The Woodwards understood Novell's vision of the LAN industry and enthusiastically agreed to support NetWare. Their relation with Novell grew closer over the years and in 1987 SoftCraft was acquired by its former partner.

Another early developer to become a NetWare Affiliate was Cosmos Incorporated, a company based in Seattle and devoted to moving the Pick operating system environment to the personal computer world. After working with Novell for several months, Steve Kruse, Director of Marketing for Cosmos, praised the DIO Program:

> Novell's approach to the LAN market has been interesting and in some ways revolutionary. They have not only shown that the real key to local area networking is software, but Novell has made the market much easier for vendors to enter. I like being able to do the development work once and have my package running immediately on all the major LAN systems.

By the end of 1984, about 100 software development companies were participating in the DIO Program, and on its 1984 Form S-1 filed with the SEC Novell estimated that as many as 1,000 multi-user application programs were NetWare-compatible. (In the first issue of *LAN Times*, for fall 1984, the number of applications is more conservatively estimated at 500.)

Getting Finances in Place

In addition to the strategic marketing and development issues with which Ray and his people contended in 1984 there was the problem of capital. But what a difference sales growth, profits, and credibility made to solving it! In addition to the $800,000 it loaned to Novell in 1983, Safeguard loaned the company an additional $450,000 in 1984. Although Ray contributed an additional $25,000 in March 1984, by June Novell was strong enough to pay him back the total $150,000 he had lent the company since the previous November.

In the fall of 1984, Ray met with Ron Eliason, a Vice President of First Security Bank in Salt Lake City, to discuss a line of credit. The manager of First Security's Orem branch had called Ron to tell him that Novell seemed to be turning around and might be in the market for a loan. Ray reviewed Ron's proposal and a proposal submitted by Zions Bank, and he decided to go with First Security. This was the beginning of Ron's relation with Novell; less than a year later Ray would hire him as Chief Financial Officer.

The First Security line of credit relieved the cash crunches that periodically pinched the growing company.

When Novell was incorporated, its fiscal year was to have concluded on the last Saturday in January. This virtually guaranteed a weak fourth quarter, however, because orders tended to drop off during the holidays between Thanksgiving and New Year's. So in October 1984, management decided to change Novell's fiscal year so that it ended on the last Saturday in October.

At the end of October 1984, everyone felt good about the company's performance, though it would take a few weeks to run the final numbers. For the first time in the history of Novell, clear back to the founding of NDSI, the company was in the black.

When the final tally did come in, even Ray was surprised. In the 12 months ended October 27, 1984, Novell had sales of $10.8 million—an increase of 182% over the previous year's sales of $3.8 million. (Due to the change in fiscal year end, the quarter from November 1983 through January 1984 was included in both the 1983 results and the 1984 results. Even so, in the nine months from February through October 1984, Novell's sales were $9.3 million.)

Better still was the bottom line: A profit of $958,700 compared to the 1983 loss of $996,800. And the company had an $800,000 backlog of orders.

The Personnel Pieces Fall into Place

Besides wrestling with the enormous strategic issues facing Novell, Ray had to deal with the myriad operational issues that beset a growing company. For example, even though most employees put in so many hours that they practically lived where they worked, there was a physical limit to what they could accomplish. More bodies were needed. Between January 1983 and December 1984, 83 new employees were hired, and most of those came aboard in 1984. Judy helped with the hiring and administration at first, but by 1984 a full-time Human Resources person was needed. John Thompson was brought on.

Safeguard Scientifics wanted to keep a close eye on operations, and they insisted on having their own people fill the key positions of Chief Financial Officer and Secretary. Bill Gillan, the CFO, and Ray Kraftson, the Secretary, accomplished their duties from Safeguard's offices in Pennsylvania and commuted to Orem as necessary. Corporate filings, insurance, stock incentive plans, and other similar operational matters were also handled by Safeguard. In exchange for Safeguard's providing these and other administrative services, Novell agreed to pay 0.75% of its net sales. The payment for 1984 came to $64,200.

By the summer of 1984, Ray thought it was time to reward the performance of some his key people by making some promotions. At the quarterly meeting of Novell's board of directors in August 1984, Craig was elected Vice President of Marketing and Dave Owen was elected Vice President of Engineering. During 1984, Craig and Owen and other valued employees received salary increases and additional stock. Considering the prior experience of these individuals and the still precarious financial situation of the company, Ray was generous. At year end, for example, Harry's base salary was $48,000, Craig's was $50,000, Owen's was in the neighborhood of $40,000, and Ray himself drew a base of $90,000. With commissions based on sales results added in, Harry received a total $72,666 and Craig $62,550 for their work in 1984. This was more than double their 1982 compensation from NDSI, and in Orem it went a long way.

In July 1984, SuperSet was allowed to buy a total 140,000 shares for a dollar per share, of which 3% ($4,000) was paid in cash.

Another employee whom Ray rewarded in 1984 was Judy. After her divorce from Reid, Judy went to Ray and asked for the founder's stock that he had failed to give her in the spring of 1983. Ray agreed that she deserved it and Judy received her stake in Novell.

Judy reinvented herself after her divorce. She retained her married name of Clark, but to distance herself from her association with Reid she added an "e" to the end: Clarke. She also started referring to herself as "Judith" instead of "Judy"—it was more in keeping with her new image. "Judith A. Clarke": It had a nice ring to it, appropriately serious and corporate. Her co-workers were instructed never to refer to her as "Judy" in public.

The Technology Pieces Fall into Place: Advanced NetWare

By November 1984, most of the pieces of the Novell that would later dominate the LAN industry were in place.

The company was profitable and had a diverse product line.

It had clarified its marketing and development strategy: Novell was a software company whose products freed users of the limitations of proprietary hardware systems. All users needed was the NetWare operating system and they could use whatever hardware they wanted.

Most importantly, as a result of IBM's PC LAN announcement, NetWare's file server technology was finally recognized as the superior solution to the problem of networking PCs.

But one important piece was still to come: Advanced NetWare.

Before Advanced NetWare

As Ray and Craig worked to win industry support of NetWare, SuperSet labored to make hardware independence a reality.

Achieving it created a steadily increasing drain on SuperSet's development time and energy, and by 1984 the drain was enormous. The job of creating shells in NetWare to support different kinds of PCs, different PC operating systems, and different types of network cards occupied SuperSet from 1982 until well into 1984. With Project Piranha in 1984 (see p. 119), NetWare server side had to be ported to all the major network hardware, not just the client shells.

And while they plowed through the hard ground of compatibility problems, the SuperSet guys were also working on a new version of NetWare. The new version, called Advanced NetWare, simplified adapting client and server software to various hardware platforms, allowed users to add multiple servers to their LANs and to connect previously separated LANs together via "bridges". (Bridges, routers, and gateways are three different ways of connecting different kinds of networks together. The terminology was not standardized in the '80s, so Novell had different meanings for the terms than, say, Cisco does today.)

Novell's product line at the end of 1984 showed how far the company had come from offering just the S-Net system of 1983—and how prolific SuperSet had been.

There were two major product lines: 1) complete LAN systems, where software was bundled with hardware in packages that sold for $2,000 to $25,000, depending on the package, and 2) separately sold LAN software, including the NetWare Operating System, network communication software, and program generator languages used with making NetWare-compatible applications. Individual copies of Net-Ware cost about $1,500 each; the other programs cost significantly less.

Novell sold four different kinds of LAN systems, three of which were OEM products.

- NetWare/S-Net. This was the system that saved Novell in 1983. It used the NetWare/68 operating system on the proprietary file server that Novell manufactured using Motorola MC68000 microprocessors. Configured in a star topology, S-Net supported up to 24 PCs of different types, up to 500 megabytes of storage, and up to 5 shared printers. You could use over 9 different kinds of PCs on the S-Net, including all the IBM PCs, certain IBM compatibles, the Texas Instruments Personal Computer, the Victor 9000, and the DEC Rainbow.

- NetWare/Omninet. This was one of three kinds of NetWare/86 systems with LAN hardware purchased from other companies and packaged together with the NetWare/86 version of the Net-Ware Operating System. They supported PC-compatibles as file servers using the Intel 8086 or 8088 microprocessor. Novell bought the Omninet hardware from Corvus Systems, Inc.

- NetWare/G-Net, another NetWare/86 system. Novell bought the hardware from Gateway Communications, Inc.

- NetWare/ARCnet, the third OEM NetWare/86 system. Novell bought the ARCnet-PC network interface cards from Standard Microsystems Corp.

Variations of each NetWare/86 system used the IBM PCXT, IBM PCAT, or IBM clones as file servers. Each of these could support up to 50 PC workstations, 252 megabytes of disk storage, and 3 shared printers. The file servers could be either dedicated file servers or combination file server/workstations (non-dedicated file servers).

Advanced NetWare

Two Problems

Advanced NetWare solved a couple of looming technology problems that SuperSet, in particular, saw coming.

The first problem was a growing product line of custom-developed NetWare versions—in essence, a new OS for each new piece of server hardware and network board.

The second problem was that each of these LANs was standalone: It did not "talk" to other LANs or other networks.

Advanced NetWare addressed both of these.

To solve the problem—the growing complexity of too many servers and LAN boards—Advanced NetWare changed the architecture of basic NetWare. The OS was divided into an unchanging "core" that was linked to "drivers"; the drivers handled dealing with the peripherals that would be installed on the server and/or on the "clients", the PCs that were networked with it. At first these drivers dealt only with different LAN boards. Later they also dealt with the disk controllers of high-capacity disk drives. (Printers were handled separately.)

This linking occurred at installation time. The person installing was asked which LAN boards were installed in the server or client "box". The installer program then asked for appropriate floppy disks to be put into the disk drive, from which drivers were uploaded onto the user's system.

This linking process was revolutionary to NetWare. It allowed the list of usable LAN boards to be updated rapidly by simply developing new driver floppy disks *and it allowed the PC to support more than one board at a time*—up to four.

This also opened the door to solving the second problem, letting NetWare LANs be connected to LANs, LANs to host computers, and LANs to remote PCs. With Advanced NetWare, bridges between networks were possible, so networks of ARCnet and Ethernet could be attached together (and were at Novell).

Since this same architecture of core-and-drivers could be used in the client PCs as well as server PCs, it opened the door to using clients as bridges as well as servers, which opened the door to even more interconnectivity. (Note that bridges in this early Novell terminology acted more like what are now called routers.)

NetWare/86, in the last of the basic and first of the Advanced versions, could operate on no fewer than 12 different LAN hardware systems. These systems offered different topologies, transmission speeds, communication media, and protocols. Some were broadband systems; others were baseband (single-channel) systems.

Below is a list of the 12 different LAN systems that SuperSet succeeded in porting NetWare to in 1983 and 1984. The list shows how fragmented the LAN marketplace was in 1984, how monumental a task it was to realize the goal of hardware independence, and how important the Advanced NetWare concept was going to be for further growth:

Novell Name	OEM	LAN Type
NetWare/D	Davong Systems	MultiLink
NetWare/E	3Com Corporation	EtherLink (Ethernet)
NetWare/G	Gateway Communications	G-Net
NetWare/N	Nestar Systems	PLAN 2000
NetWare/O	Corvus Systems	Omninet
NetWare/P	Proteon	proNET
NetWare/PC	Orchid Technology	PCNet
NetWare/PCN	IBM Corporation	PC Network
NetWare/ SMARCNET	Standard Microsystems	ARCnet
NetWare/ ISLAN	3M Company, Interactive Systems Division	PC
NetWare/WD	Western Digital Corp.	PC-LAN
NetWare/UB	Ungermann-Bass	Net/One

NetWare was also sold in various modified forms to OEM customers who would then sell NetWare as part of their LAN systems. No significant income was generated in 1984 from the OEM customers Novell had lined up, but in subsequent years OEM sales would account for a significant percentage of total sales.

Other Products

Besides NetWare, Novell sold other software products such as communications software, electronic mail, and interpreter programs. Communications software included gateway products to connect PCs through their NetWare LANs to mini or mainframe systems. NetWare/ EMS was an electronic mail service. Various runtime and interpreter programs allowed application programs written in popular programming languages to operate without modification on NetWare.

Novell customers also bought various hardware components and equipment from the company. For example, users who added PCs or storage devices to their networks might buy additional network interface cards, disk subsystems, cabling and connectors, S-Net LAN boards, network server memory, or other components from Novell. Such equipment sales accounted for a relatively small—but nevertheless important—percentage of total income. In the early years, every dollar was important.

The Evolution of Advanced NetWare

By the middle of '84 it was SuperSet's turn to wrestle with alligators. They had been so successful at proselytizing other companies that they now had developed dozens of drivers for various network interface cards (NICs). They were about to get overwhelmed with the dreaded bugaboo of all successful software programs, software maintenance: If you develop it and sell it, then you've gotta fix it when it goes wrong and when things change. If Novell sold a dozen different kinds of NetWare then it was going to have to maintain a dozen different kinds.

There was another problem with the custom NetWare trend: Cost to the resellers. There was no way a reseller or distributor could stock a dozen different kinds of NetWare profitably.

This wasn't a new problem and SuperSet applied themselves to the established solution: Make Advanced NetWare modular and design it so that the custom parts could be "linked" into a single uniform whole.

This linking idea had one other benefit: There was no reason to stop at linking just one driver into the whole—two, three, or even four could be linked. Up to four different kinds of NICs could be supported in the same box. Advanced NetWare became the tangible result of Craig's vision of a year earlier when all the boards were supported from a single box. The linking was designed to allow all the boards to talk to the computer and to each other. Having two different boards talk with each other was called "bridging" by SuperSet. With Advanced NetWare, bridging between different kinds of hardware was supported for the first time in NetWare.

This linking also took some of the development burden off Novell. Other companies, such as the hardware designers themselves, could design drivers for NetWare. They would put a floppy disk in with the NIC boards they sold and instruct their users to insert it at the appropriate time during installation.

With this linking, Advanced NetWare was a powerful breakthrough that saved Novell Engineering from getting bogged down in the task of supporting dozens of LAN boards. But it had drawbacks, too. Advanced NetWare shot the floppy disk total in a NetWare package to over thirty and added diskaerobics[10] to the battery of skills needed to accomplish a successful NetWare installation. NetWare became something much more easily installed from one file server to another rather than from the floppy-disk set.

Advanced NetWare allowed NetWare to become comprehensive, but some of the complexity it unloaded from Novell engineering it threw to the reseller's installers. Installing became a complex task, and NetWare started its evolution from being a simple extension of a personal computer operating system to becoming a complex minicomputer-like operating system that required minicomputer-like technical support.

Parting the Waters: NetBIOS and DOS 3.1

Creating Standards

In 1981 the personal computer industry cried out for a standard ... and IBM produced the IBM PC. IBM asked for help from Microsoft and Microsoft produced MS-DOS. Many buyers cheered and bought; many manufacturers wailed and gnashed their teeth; the industry churned and grew immensely. A standard was made.

In 1983 the LAN industry cried out for a standard ... and IBM produced PC LAN Program featuring NetBIOS. IBM asked for help from Microsoft and Microsoft produced MS-DOS 3.1 to replace MS-DOS 3.0. Many buyers cheered and bought; many manufacturers wailed and gnashed their teeth; the industry churned and grew immensely. A standard was made.

NetBIOS was a standard communications driver program IBM produced as part of PC LAN Program. It defined a standard way to talk

---

[10] "Diskaerobics" is a Roger-coined word for an activity made obsolete by later storage technology. It was the exercise of inserting floppy disks in and out, in and out, of the disk drive—preferably under the driving beat of something emanating from a Walkman. Symptoms of diskaerobics overindulgence: Glazed look, frayed temper, calloused finger tips, and "disco elbow".

with a LAN board. MS-DOS 3.1 added "hooks" to the operating system that defined standard places to make networking "calls".

A *hook* is a piece of code that is not complete in itself but that provides a convenient place to add features later. It's the software analogue of a hardware expansion bus.

A *call* is a command in a program that brings in a feature from another piece of code. For instance, when a word processing program is ready to display a character on a screen it calls the video display function from the operating system and hands it the character. The word processing program itself contains no code to display characters on the screen. It counts on the operating system to carry out that function.

In the case of networks, the MS-DOS calls meant that network programmers would no longer have to pry apart the MS-DOS operating system and fit their network calls into the system in various customized ways; they could all use the same standardized framework. Applications programmers wouldn't have to be detectives and figure out how their applications would interact with these various customized ways of calling a network. They could count on network commands responding in a standardized way.

SuperSet had already pried MS-DOS apart, so for them this new feature offered little technological improvement, but for the sales side of networking this was manna from marketing heaven. IBM had spoken; and in the '80s when IBM spoke, a standard was created.

It *Was* Manna … if Novell Took Advantage of It

The reflexive impulse when somebody else brings something new onto the market is to say, "Ours is better, why are you considering that product?"

Novell could have done that; over the years it's been shown that NetWare did have some distinct feature and performance advantages over IBM/Microsoft's various offerings. Adding to that temptation was the fact that PC LAN Program, IBM's first offering, was a lightweight item. (It lasted only about six months as a serious LAN operating system contender before being replaced by Microsoft's MS-Net.) Novell could have trampled all over it and "won" the argument about which operating system was better. But would doing so have sold more NetWare? Probably not.

Instead, thanks to the open systems orientation that Craig brought to Novell, and Ray's sensitivity to the importance of what it means when IBM moves, a different solution was developed: The "jujitsu" or "join 'em" solution.

Novell declared that it was supporting the NetBIOS and MS-DOS 3.1 standards, and that these standards were good because they would help the industry grow. Novell took this jujitsu one step further: Novell pointed out that IBM had decided that file service was the right way to handle a LAN operating system and that Novell had been doing file service for two years now. This was jujitsu indeed! Novell customers could have their cake and eat it too: They could use Novell equipment, still be IBM-compatible, and get the technology that IBM had blessed in a package that worked better than IBM's offering.

Building a Company Mission

By the end of fiscal 1984, Ray and his team had articulated a lofty mission for Novell: To make the LAN industry grow faster with Novell than it would without Novell. They came up with a slogan: "Dedicated to Serve All LANkind."

The following article from a Novell company publication is reprinted in its entirety because it reiterates all of the key messages in Novell's marketing communications at that time.

NOVELL CEO ON COMPANY ROLE IN INDUSTRY

Novell CEO, Raymond J. Noorda, was interviewed recently concerning his company's current role in the dynamic computer industry. Mr. Noorda, whose career began with a business automation division of General Electric, expressed his views:

"Novell's mission is to cause a substantial increase in the growth of LANs—as much as 25% over current industry projections."

Noorda explained, "This can only be done by bringing end users together with software technology which provides a standard operating system for all popular LANs—including but not restricted to hardware provided by one vendor."

Having recognized early the coming desktop computer revolution, Mr. Noorda involved himself and his growing company in local area networking. While some potential LAN users debate

134

the need for standards in networking, Mr. Noorda expanded, "No-vell has seen the emerging world of LANs differently. As a result, we created NetWare—an operating system specifically designed for LANs supplied by other manufacturers. We feel that a LAN is only as good as the software that manages it. Our company's 'top down' approach provides a uniform interface for the user and appli-cation regardless of the physical connections between devices. NetWare creates a system that lets personal computers perform at a mini/mainframe level. With NetWare the data flow is managed efficiently along with the security, dependability and performance found in former data processing, MIS [management information system] days."

Noorda added that this was with the added benefits and features found in today's advanced PC technology. "By preserving the control and ease of use of the PC, NetWare gives the best of both worlds."

When asked about other problems that NetWare solved for its users, the Utah executive replied, "NetWare promotes compati-bility among different kinds of personal computers and operating systems. The customer is then left to choose the computers and software that best suits his company's needs." He noted that Net-Ware is compatible with the IBM PC Network. "Applications written for the IBM PC Network run unchanged on Novell's Net-Ware—only much faster."

Noorda mentioned that another strong point of NetWare was that it allowed control and management of data while maintaining the individuality of personal computer use. "And that's done right because it's a file server."

When questioned as to whether some potential LAN users were interested in LANs because local area networking would protect existing corporate investments in hardware, software, data and training, Noorda nodded agreement. "Besides that, NetWare will help create company information systems that are efficient, but also flexible, while at the same time staying on the edge of changing LAN technology."

Noorda, whose company has doubled its work force in the last year, concluded, "Our commitment at Novell is to make LANs function as they are intended. We've created an operating system that provides a standard across all local area networks. By imple-menting that standard, leading software suppliers can easily create multi-user PC software that runs on *all* popular LANs. At Novell we create systems that open up new areas of practical application for PC local area networks. That's our commitment. The success of LANs ensures ours."

Comdex 84

The crowning event of 1984 was Novell's presence at Comdex in Las Vegas (November 14 through 18). At Comdex, Novell rolled out its newly minted products and philosophy. It was also the first major demonstration of the innovative marketing communications that would establish Novell's image and make Judith a LAN industry celebrity.

Novell's most daring undertaking was to create a LAN that would network about 20 exhibitors scattered in different areas of the Convention Center. Novell had help from 3M Company's Interactive Systems Division, a new NetWare OEM customer, but for both companies the Comdex LAN was an enormous project fraught with risk. If the LAN worked, it would gain a lot of attention for Novell. If the network failed, Novell would be embarrassed before the industry partners it had worked hard to line up. And it would be impossible for Novell to hide its failure from the show attendees, because all of the company's promotional materials at its booth were designed to showcase the Comdex LAN.

At that time, the sprawling trade show was still contained within the walls of the Las Vegas Convention Center. (In subsequent years it would spill out to occupy more than seven hotels and other exhibition spaces.) The Las Vegas Convention Center is a gargantuan building, each side nearly a quarter mile long, and it comfortably houses dozens of booths that are two stories high. To lay the network cable through the building was a physically demanding task. Then connections had to be made linking the cable to each of the participating booths. And the entire project had to be set up and operational in just 72 hours.

The purpose of the Comdex LAN was to demonstrate Advanced NetWare. Visitors to the show were invited to play MUT, a multi-user trivia game, on various different brands of PCs located in various booths and locations throughout the convention center. The program engaged multiple users in a race to answer multiple-choice trivia questions. Speed, accuracy, and a person's score relative to the other players determined the winners. Ten prizes were awarded to the top 10 players on each day of the five-day show. The top three players each day received cash prizes ($100, $50, and $25) and all 10 winners received Novell T-shirts.

A typical question was: "What did Benjamin Franklin advocate as the US National Symbol?" The choices were:

a. The bald eagle

b. The flying burrito

c. The turkey

d. The Frisbee

People loved it. MUT was a smashing success. It demonstrated some key features of Advanced NetWare, such as Master Edit, a program that edited the configuration and game information on a real-time basis without disturbing the game. And it brought people into the Novell booth.

When visitors showed up at the Novell booth, they were engaged by a number of different attractions. In one corner of the booth, five PCs were set up, each one containing the same 10-minute interactive LAN seminar on diskette. Nearby a large bookcase displayed packages of NetWare-compatible software applications, and next to the bookcase was an area where independent software vendors actually demonstrated their products. At the other end of the booth was a PC running the trivia game beside a television showing *The Novell Story*, a 10-minute video explaining Novell and NetWare. At another PC station, an e-mail program (developed by MAI/Basic Four) allowed visitors to send messages to other exhibitors on the network. At the center of the booth was a display showing demonstrations of Advanced NetWare. At the booth's information desk, visitors could pick up a copy of a little eight-page newsletter called *LAN Times*.

All the elements of Novell's marketing strategy were represented in its Comdex booth. The Comdex LAN, trivia game, and e-mail program demonstrated the concept of hardware independence. The large number of independent software developers who were demonstrating their products at Novell's booth sent a message that numerous applications were compatible with NetWare and that Novell was eager to form alliances with other players in the industry. The educational video, the interactive diskette, and *LAN Times* showed Novell's strategy of educating the industry.

The booth was an example of Judith's flair for marketing communications. Although the ideas for the booth were contributed by many members of the management team, including SuperSet, Ray, and Craig, the execution fell mostly to Judith. The combination of video, LAN demonstration, trivia game, newsletter, bookcase, and educational seminars led by live people was more than just clever—it was devastatingly effective. The booth was a high-powered marketing communications device to match Novell's high-powered marketing strategy.

The *LAN Times* newsletter distributed at Comdex was a seed that would ultimately grow into a multi-million-dollar industry magazine. The first issue was a rather crude affair, replete with typographical errors and produced in great haste on a low budget. It contained short articles on Novell's Comdex activities, on Novell's OEM partners, and on Novell's strategy and philosophy. A one-page advertisement called "LAN Report 1", aimed at independent software developers, described the Multiple User Software Licensing System (MUSLS). But for all its simplicity, the *LAN Times* was a popular item at the show and Judith resolved to do a few more issues.

On the first day of Comdex, Novell held a press conference. About 150 people were invited to hear Ray Noorda talk and to find out about Advanced NetWare. A fair number of people showed up, including many editors. Ever since IBM announced the file server–based PC Network Program in September, people were taking a second look at Novell and NetWare.

In addressing the audience, Ray focused on three key messages: 1) The IBM announcement had delivered the *coup de grace* to the LAN manufacturers who relied on disk server technology; 2) the Net-Ware Operating System offered, in effect, a standard solution to the problem of networking different proprietary LAN systems (and, incidentally, could be purchased as an OEM product); and 3) by writing applications for NetWare, software developers could access not just Novell LANs but the entire LAN market. Novell was in a position to rescue all those LAN manufacturers and software developers who had bet on the wrong pony.

The following are excerpts from the version of Ray's speech printed in the *LAN Times* newsletter. The article was prepared in advance of the press conference, before Ray had actually delivered his speech, hence the mix of past and future tenses.

Mr. Noorda commented that he has changed Novell's 1984 slogan from "NetWare, Dedicated to SERVE all LANkind" to "NetWare, Dedicated to SAVE all LANkind." Ray Noorda will announce a plan that will enable LAN vendors to standardize their networks so that they are IBM compatible and will run much faster with increased functionality, flexibility, and security.

Mr. Noorda stated, "Our commitment at Novell is to make LANs function as everyone intended them to with network operating systems that deliver optimum performance. We've created an operating system that provides a standard across all local area networks. And by implementing that standard, leading software suppliers can easily create multiuser PC software that runs on all popular LANs. At Novell we create systems that open up new areas of practical application for PC LANs. Because LANs are here to stay."

By the end of 1984, Novell was shipping about $1.3 million per month.

PART TWO
Novell Emerges, 1984–88

The Technical Thread

CHAPTER FIVE
The PC-Based LAN Revolution Begins

Early Technical Goals for NetWare

In 1984, the broad strokes of NetWare were in place, but a lot of soldiering still remained to make those strokes reality. It was time to provide more than hard disk and print sharing services. It was time to bring reliability—system fault tolerance (SFT) reliability—into the picture.

And there was new hardware to arrange into the NetWare picture. 1984 was the year IBM's 80286-based PCAT (PC Advanced Technology) and Apple's Macintosh were introduced.

The Opportunity, and Challenge, of the PCAT

When the machines were first introduced, SuperSet, Craig, and others at Novell dreamed of harnessing PCATs' enhanced computing power for file servers. The 286 (as the 80286 was called) could address 16MB of RAM where its PC/PCXT predecessor, the 8088, could only address 1MB. But the big difference was running in "protected mode". This was not just bigger and faster, it was a new way of running a CPU chip. There were new commands available designed specifically for multi-tasking, which file servers do a lot of. NetWare/286 products realized the dream of utilizing all this breakthrough possibility.

Using a 286 as a 286 was called native mode, also called protected mode—"protected" because the RAM was protected during multi-tasking from having different tasks use the same RAM. MS-DOS used the 286's emulation or "real" mode—real mode because the CPU's addressing referred to real memory locations rather than the virtual memory locations that were used in the aforementioned protected mode.

145

OS/2, IBM/Microsoft's operating system that would use any Intel CPU in protected mode, was announced at the PCAT's introduction but suffered one of the worst cases of sliding delivery in personal computer history. It was years away from finally appearing and the first PC-compatible OS to fully embrace protected mode would be Windows 95, which came nearly a decade later.

Craig, Novell's Vice President of Marketing, explained in a Fall 1985 *LAN Times* article by Michael Durr, titled "Advanced NetWare/286 Makes Most of IBM AT".

> "No one had released a product in conjunction with DOS that took advantage of the protected mode of the AT. We wanted to be able to take advantage of the additional addressable memory and the performance and features it would provide for a network server."

> And take advantage of them it does. Advanced NetWare/286 can address all the RAM you can stuff in an AT and, by using some of the AT clones that have more slots, you can push it up to its limit of 16MB. It can also handle up to 2GB [gigabytes; one GB = 1 billion bytes] of mass storage as well as perform multitasking operations. If that's not enough, this extra memory, power and storage allows a network running Advanced NetWare/286 to handle up to 128 users per server, five printers per server and two intelligent disk coprocessors (which allow you to use up to 32 hard disks).

> ...

> "Advanced NetWare/286 takes full advantage of the extended features of the 80286," says Burton. "What that buys you is more users, more disk space, and better performance."

Novell may have considered its jewels to be its software, but there was still hardware required to make those jewels shine. NetWare 286 was one of the first products to use a 286 CPU as a 286 rather than just as a faster 8088 CPU the way MS-DOS did.

Because so few applications used the protected mode of the 286 in those early years, there was little drive to standardize those parts of the hardware design or the BIOS design that dealt with protected mode. (BIOS is the software that operates between the CPU and the OS.) And once again, a standard was lacking. Genuine IBM PCATs and PCAT clones acted quite differently from each other when used as NetWare 286 file servers. This presented Novell with a challenge: Would the

146

company support only genuine IBM PCATs as 286 file servers or would they support others as well?

Craig wrestled with this problem in the Fall 1985 *LAN Times* as well, again in an article by Durr, this one called "Novell Announces Family of Expandable Server Products".

> "Unlike Advanced NetWare/86, it has not been easy to support third-party drives under Advanced NetWare/286 and SFT Net-Ware/286, both of which run in the 80286's protected mode." Burton was quick to point out this is not an indication that Novell is beginning to reverse its field and close its architecture to third-party products.
>
> "Closing the door is ugly and we're not doing that," he says. "But when you move into the protected mode on the 80286, writing multitasking, fault-tolerant drivers is not simple.
>
> "The only reason we don't currently support other drives with the NetWare/286 systems is because of the complexity. We plan to break out the code for companies that want to fit in that protected mode environment so they can write their own drivers.
>
> . . .
>
> "We don't want to be in the position of making people choose between IBM and us. We want to be able to say that we offer an excellent family of servers, but whatever hardware you choose, Novell offers a better solution to your networking needs."

Craig felt that similar explanations needed to be made for the new NS286B file server.

The NS286B file server and its accompanying Advanced Net-Ware/286 operating system were proprietary (i.e., Novell-owned and -marketed) products that were less accessible to third-party companies. In these products openness was sacrificed in order to achieve higher performance. Yet Novell remained committed to the idea of open systems. If NetWare was to proliferate and the LAN industry flourish, Novell had to let other companies play in its backyard. The corporate jujitsu had to continue. From 1985 forward, Novell began to distinguish the terms "open system" and "proprietary system" as compatible, not mutually exclusive, terms. Although NetWare was proprietary, it remained an open system accessible to third parties.

Novell announced support for other servers by starting a certification program. One of the first non-IBM computers certified was Compaq. Even at this embryonic stage Compaq could see a bright

147

future for networks and they wanted to be involved. This testing and support of 286 products started a dramatic increase in the size of Novell's testing and support divisions.

Novell marketing also supported an alternative plan. They OEMed PCAT clones from Samsung and Micro V in Korea to make sure that clone alternatives to the IBM PCAT were available and, of course, to pick up a bit more of the revenue stream that went into building a network. These clones became the 286A and 286B Novell file servers.

They were also sold as the basis of complete Novell LAN systems and LAN systems marketed by other companies. New disk subsystems, add-on drives, gateways, and the NetWare Disk Coprocessor Board (DCB) rounded out the new line of hardware offerings.

There was one other effect: The 286 chip was an Intel product that finally passed the 68000 in performance, so the 68B file server could at last be put to rest.

The Genesis of SFT NetWare

In 1985, the focus of development was System Fault Tolerant (SFT) NetWare, a product Novell described as the second milestone in the history of LANs. System fault tolerance refers to the ability of the NetWare operating system to continue functioning even in the presence of faults or failures in parts of the network. SFT was billed as a milestone achievement because it allowed LANs to accommodate greater numbers of PCs networked in more complicated configurations and still maintain good reliability. And obviously if LANs were ever to be taken seriously by the business customer, they had to work reliably with a minimum of downtime and provide security against accidental data loss.

SFT, as applied to NetWare LANs, was born in a conversation between Drew and Roger in December 1981. As mentioned on p. 65 above, Drew said he first appreciated the importance of the concept as he explained the philosophy of NetWare to Roger. After subsequent discussions with other members of SuperSet, Craig, and others, SFT became a goal of the NetWare development team.

The idea was also appealing to Ray. Before he started looking at Novell in the fall of 1982, Ray had founded a company whose purpose was to develop an inexpensive way to create fault tolerance in minicomputer systems. In a sense it was the notion of inexpensive, fault tolerant LANs that attracted him to Novell.

148

In the Fall 1985 *LAN Times* article announcing "System Fault Tolerant NetWare", Mike Durr described the market need the new products were designed to meet.

> The traditional way to have fault tolerance is to use redundant (duplicate) components. In the mainframe world this may mean installing two mainframes, with the second computer available to take over if the first computer fails.
>
> Minicomputer vendors have come up with another solution that involves building special, fault tolerant computers. Such a machine is equipped with redundant components such as processors, circuits, or power supplies. The machine is highly resistant to system failure. But it is expensive—as much as $100,000 to $300,000 per mini.

SFT NetWare LANs were marketed as a data processing environment that offered inexpensive fault tolerance.

SuperSet designed SFT NetWare as an extension of the Advanced NetWare operating system. Three levels were to be offered.

Level I. The directory and file allocation table were automatically backed up on two duplicate areas of the network hard disk. (Previously, this data was stored in only one area of the disk.) A feature called Hot Fix detected bad areas of a deteriorating disk and automatically stored data elsewhere in a good section of the disk.

Level II. Disk mirroring and disk duplexing were available. Both options used duplicate or redundant system components to achieve extra protection—if the first disk failed, the second would take over with no data loss. In disk mirroring, the second disk is an exact reflection of the first disk. In disk duplexing, the entire disk subsystem (including disk controller, power supply, and cabling) is duplicated.

Level III. The entire file server was duplicated, not just components. The file server hardware was interconnected by a high-speed bus and a parity checking feature made sure both servers were sharing the same information.

Another feature of SFT NetWare under development in 1985 was the NetWare Transaction Tracking System (TTS). This feature, offered with SFT NetWare Levels II and III, also helped protect the integrity of the LAN database in the event of system failure. As explained in the *LAN Times*:

When a database is being updated, if part of the system fails the update may be only partially completed. When this occurs, the database is often corrupted and all of the data in the database is lost.

TTS prevents this kind of data loss by monitoring each transaction (update) as it takes place. If the transaction fails to be fully completed, TTS will automatically roll back to the point prior to the beginning of the transaction. The integrity of the database is thereby maintained.

SFT NetWare with NetWare TTS was indeed a milestone for Novell and the LAN industry. It was a step that had to happen if LANs were ever to be used for the mission-critical business applications then being handled only by mainframes and minicomputers.

E-mail

Embryonic E-mail

Another dream product that became a reality in 1985 was an electronic mail system (EMS) that ran on NetWare.

From the earliest days when LANs were still in embryo, SuperSet, Craig, and others had ruminated on how the new LAN technology might be used. There were many answers to the question "What is it good for?" including sharing of peripheral devices, lowering costs, etc. But the most exciting application by far was the idea of distributed processing, where various users dispersed across a network can distribute parts of a job and work as a team to create a single project. To achieve distributed processing (which was as much a change in how people worked together as in the way they used computers), users would have to be able to share common databases via the LAN. Being a good platform for this was the goal of SFT NetWare.

Users would also need to be able to talk to each other via electronic mail (now universally called e-mail).

Among the powerbrokers at Novell—at this time Ray, SuperSet, Harry, Dave Owen, and Craig—everyone agreed that adding an electronic mail system to NetWare was a good marketing strategy. The idea of a paperless office was a hot one in the computer industry that year, even in corporate MIS departments. E-mail systems were available on host-based networks; they would be even more useful on LANs. Another consideration was relative ease of design. Here was a popular application that could be simply and cheaply distributed with every LAN sold. It was an easy add-on application that would enhance the functionality of the network.

SuperSet cooked up a NetWare Electronic Mail System (EMS) designed to send messages between workstations on a single network. EMS was a good basic "intercom" style mail system but it lacked features for doing much message processing or for sending messages outside the LAN environment. But it was a start at e-mail, and from February 1985 it was included for free in every shipment of NetWare.

Meanwhile Craig started looking for something better while the engineers dreamed of designing something better.

The Birth of MHS

As time went on, e-mail evolved from a neat add-on into one of a LAN's important features, which led to friction within Novell that centered around MHS (Message Handling Service).

Engineering wanted to develop an e-mail product, but Craig wanted a mail system that would fit the glue product philosophy—something that would interconnect various e-mail systems.

Craig researched and came up with a product he liked being developed by a company called Action Technologies. Action had developed their e-mail product, The Coordinator, with group dynamics in mind. They had built in an innovative message threading concept and added a superstructure over that threading designed to help people see projects through to completion.

Craig was lukewarm to the message threading, cold on the superstructure, but very hot on the "engine" that did the actual moving of messages from mail server to mail server and from mail server to workstation. What he wanted Action to do was split out that engine and make it another glue product—a standard that would spread through the industry.

Action wanted to work with Novell, but they weren't as excited about giving away the family jewels as Craig was in getting them. In fact they were much more excited about their innovative work-aiding superstructure than they were about the mundane e-mail engine. This difference in opinion about what was important led to chronic friction between Novell and Action, which escalated to career-breaking crisis in 1989. (For the conclusion of this thrilling story, see "The Action

151

Technologies Contract", p. 226 in Chapter Eight. See also Action's mention under "The Tale of the Missing Press Conference", p. 160 below.)

Background: What's Happening in 1986

1986 was the year that the total processing power of PCs in use surpassed the total processing power of mainframes in use. Personal computers were not only here to stay but they were becoming a big part of the American business scene. The personal computer revolution was at hand.

In 1986, thanks to Advanced NetWare and Microsoft's MS-Net, personal computers were not only being used in business, they were being wired together. The average size of a PC LAN had grown to twelve, and thanks to Advanced NetWare bridging, the maximum potential size was now hundreds of machines. By comparison, the average network of 1984 was about three machines and the maximum potential size was between 24 (for S-Net) and 128 (for ARCnet and Ethernet).

Apple Macintosh and IBM PC compatibles were both still hot contenders for the average person's PC dollars. (Windows was not viable yet, so Apple had not yet been driven into just the education and publishing niches.)

Ethernet cards were still comparatively expensive (about $300 each) and Fast Ethernet was not available, so ARCnet was the card of choice for NetWare networks. IBM's Token Ring was coming (and generating a lot of talk) and there were still a plethora of other hardware networking technologies in use.

Hard disks were using the 5″ "form factor" (shape and size) and 3.5″ floppies were now becoming standard on PCs.

"Letter-quality" dot-matrix printers in many forms were kings of the roost in the printer world and daisywheels were headed for the typewriter niche. Epson's market dominance was slipping. Hewlett-Packard was having a rough time but it had introduced the LaserJet line of laser printers. HP proudly announced there would be good times coming, but at the time the announcement looked like another case of hope springing eternal. (As you may know, this time the hope was justified.)

Meeting the Challenges

The Business Challenge

When you asked a typical Novell employee in 1986 who the competition was, the answer was 3Com, Orchid, or one of the other LAN board makers of that era. When you asked Ray, the answer was "the minicomputer companies", such as General Automation or General Systems or even DEC, then the 2nd largest computer company after IBM.

To compete with those minicomputer companies, Novell products had to talk to their products. The minicomputers stored the valuable company information of businesses that Novell wanted to sell LANs to. If PC LANs were to take over market share from minicomputers and their terminals, the PCs had to be able to access the information on the minicomputers. From this realization came the "stack company" concept.

The Technology Challenge

Ray saw that the business challenge was taking on the minis. Craig's vision was to meet that challenge by Novell becoming a stack company.

"Stack" was short for communications protocol stacks, another concept that Craig embraced. A stack is a series of rules or protocols that describe how the various components of any network system—mainframe, mini, or PC—are going to talk to each other. This communicating task is complex enough that a networking system will be using between four and six protocols that coordinate with each other. Some examples of communications protocols are the Internet's TCP/IP (Transmission Control Protocol/Internet Protocol), Novell's IPX (Internetwork Packet Exchange), Apple's AppleTalk, and the NCP (Network Control Program) part of IBM's SNA (System Network Architecture).

What Craig meant was that Novell would develop the technology to allow workstations and file servers to talk in these "alien" protocols and allow file servers to support requests for file service given in these alien tongues. When this was accomplished, then NetWare LANs could accept minicomputers as just another device on the network and the minicomputer could accept workstations as just more terminals requesting service. Once that happened, the low cost of LAN networks compared to minicomputer networks would suck the lifeblood out of the minicomputer business.

When Craig did a survey of what it was going to take to have PCs communicate with minicomputer environments, he quickly encountered a "software fortress" situation; it was clear that minicomputer companies were going to move towards having PCs connect to their networks at a glacial pace. But Craig saw this as an opportunity.

He saw that PCs could support minicomputer protocols as easily, or more easily, than minicomputers could support PC protocols. He saw that the NetWare Everywhere concept could be extended to communications protocols, to the great benefit of Novell.

Early in 1985 Craig started outlining the environments that Novell would be moving to support.

Workstation Environments	Communications Protocols	Server/Disk Environments
MS-DOS	IPX	MS-DOS/Windows
Windows	TCP/IP	UNIX
Macintosh	SNA/3270	Macintosh
	AppleTalk	

The goal was to make NetWare the glue that would join these diverse environments together so that files and data could move between them. NetWare was to become a glue product.

The Evolution of Computer Networking and Protocol Stacks

Computer networking began in the '60s, before there were even minicomputer companies. It was driven by the then-new concepts of timesharing and CRTs (cathode-ray tubes—terminals with keyboards and TV-like screens). Before timesharing, mainframe computers were batch processors—you fed them punch cards or a paper tape and they worked on just one job at a time. But if a collection of Teletype printers or CRTs were going to work with a mainframe computer, a communication network was needed to connect them.

154

As each mainframe manufacturer got into timesharing and CRTs they came up with their own proprietary network design, and each was very custom. The most famous and enduring was IBM's 3270 network design. (A trivia point: The 3270 was a fallout technology of the Space Race—IBM was contracted by NASA.)

As computer networks were being designed in the US, the European standards organization, ISO, was coming up with the OSI (Open Systems Interconnect) Model—something well known to network aficionados and one of the origins of the term "protocol stack". It was this ISO OSI model that outlined the concept of communications protocol stacks as they are known today.

In the '70s minicomputers were developed. These computers needed to network, too. But in the early '70s some protocols were developed that were non-proprietary, or open. An example was TCP/IP, which was sponsored by a government agency, DARPA (Defense Advanced Research Projects Agency), and was available for any computer maker to use. Universities were the first civilian users to embrace TCP/IP. The minicomputer companies used a mix of proprietary protocols such as DECnet and open protocols such as TCP/IP.

As LANs developed in the '80s, they were faced with the same proprietary-or-open networking choices. But by the '80s even more open standards were available.

Ironically, the first Novell LANs did not need a communication protocol stack—with the S-Net system all the communication was point-to-point between the workstations and the server, and SuperSet cobbled together their own homebrew communications system. But as soon as plans to support other LAN boards solidified, NetWare needed to support a formal communication protocol that could work with many kinds of boards and work in a multi-point environment where many computers would share the same communications line.

SuperSet investigated several possibilities, including TCP/IP, and selected ... their own version! It was based on a protocol developed at Xerox PARC (Palo Alto Research Center) called XNS (Xerox network services). The Novell version was called IPX (for inter-network packet exchange). Unlike the minicomputer companies that preceded them, Novell decided to make IPX an open protocol, and as Novell prospered IPX prospered. For many years it was the protocol of choice for LAN-based multiplayer games along with many other applications.

The Evolution of Open Systems Software

In the world of mainframes in the '50s, the concept of standardizing software was hardly recognized even within a company's own line of products. It was a nice idea but hardly necessary.

When minicomputers burst on the scene in the '70s, there was some trend towards standardizing but it was not strong—each mini-computer company was content to reside behind the walls of its own "software fortress". And the mainframe companies now had considerable investments in their own software technologies so they weren't about to open up, either.

When personal computers gained in popularity in the mid-'80s, something different happened: Customers demanded that third-party software run on their computers. The earliest version of that demand expressed itself at trade shows of the mid-'80s when customers would make the rounds of new computer offerings and ask. "Can this run Lotus 123 [*the* popular spreadsheet package] and Flight Simulator [a game]?" These packages were notoriously fussy about how the computer's architecture was set up, so if a computer could run these it could run most of the software library available for PC-compatibles at the time.

In the personal computer arena open systems became a reality rather than lip service.

This customer pressure for open systems was steady and in some areas produced results even in the minicomputer world. Those areas developing around UNIX, TCP/IP, and in particular the education environments were becoming open.

Other Developments

The Rise of CompuServe

Large scale computer networks for public use were being pioneered in 1986 and CompuServe was one of the pioneers. Novell saw Compu-Serve as valuable for their e-mail system and for their forum system (forerunner of chat rooms and blogs). The forum system was an ideal way to handle technical support issues—one person could ask a question and dozens to hundreds of interested people could see the answer.

This saved dozens to hundreds of phone calls to tech support. Novell's tech support on CompuServe forums was called NetWire.

(Epilog: CompuServe was the Internet of the '80s, and could have become the Internet of our day if it had been more aggressive in expanding its presence. Instead it was bought by H&R Block and run in a conservative fashion. Instead of leading it was swept up by the Internet tide. America Online—AOL—bypassed CompuServe by hitching itself to the rising Internet technical boom and the dot-com business boom. Nevertheless, between the mid-'80s and the early '90s, CompuServe was king.)

A Path Not Taken: Job Server

Novell did not pursue all the possible technology paths of LANs. And some paths were pursued in fits and starts, often as labors of love nourished in the Engineering Department.

One of those was the Job Server concept: Partitioning a big computational task into smaller, more manageable chunks and then handing those small chunks off to workstations to "crunch". When the workstation finished a chunk it would hand results back and ask for a new chunk. The server that handed out chunks and arranged finished results was called the Job Server.

During Christmas–New Years' vacation of 1986 a bunch of Novell engineers came back into the office to show off a massive demonstration of this Job Server concept. They arranged for one hundred workstations to share the problem of calculating how to display a piece of a Mandelbrot graph. Chaos theory was the hot science item of 1986 and a Mandelbrot was the symbol of it.

The demonstration worked flawlessly, but it was not enough to fire the imaginations of the powers-that-be at Novell, so Job Service was not pursued as a NetWare feature.

But that was not the end of the Job Service concept. It has showed up again and again in the networking world. Twelve years after the Novell Christmas demo one of its most widespread implementations was the SETI@Home project, in which volunteers install a screen saver program on their workstations. Whenever workstations are not busy, the screen saver has them analyze chunks of radio signals for signs of intelligent communications and feed their results back to the SETI@Home Job Server.

Contrasting Marketing Plans

MS-Net, Microsoft's replacement for their first LAN offering, had considerably more success than its predecessor, and it was marketed quite differently from how Novell handled NetWare.

Microsoft's MS-Net was a "core" without drivers, licensed to OEMs for them to add drivers to match their product line. They could and would add embellishments to make "their" version of MS-Net more attractive than other versions of MS-Net.

This approach had some benefits.

- It was attractive to those managers who wanted to differentiate their company's products more, who wanted to set up their versions of the minicomputer software fortresses. To them, the opportunity to embellish meant an opportunity to lock in customers.
- It took much of the effort of developing drivers out of Microsoft Engineering and laid it in the manufacturer's lap.

It also had some disadvantages.

- Locking in customers was swimming against the tide of the open systems movement that was strong in the PC world at that time.
- Moreover, the quality of the driver software and the embellishments depended on the software skills of the hardware manufacturer, and these were not uniformly good.

TeleVideo was one of the first companies to sign on with Microsoft's MS-Net program. They were enthusiastic and competent. So competent, in fact, that they were helping Microsoft redesign the core so that the hooks were easier for other companies to work with. In spite of their help, MS-Net remained for many years a touchy product.

Sales and Trade Shows

The Dream Starts to Come True

Although development was proceeding apace on the new software and hardware offerings, most of these products were not available for shipping during fiscal 1985. Yet the company managed to triple its income, from $11 million in 1984 to $33 million in 1985, on sales of products developed in 1983 and 1984. Where the company was shipping about $900,000 worth of product a month as of June 1984, by September 1985 over $4.2 million per month was shipping.

The number of installations also tripled in 1985, from less than 9,000 to an estimated 30,000 by year end. In a Spring 1986 *LAN Times* article by Maxilyn Capell, Marlowe Ashton (Ray's executive assistant) calculated Novell's total number of nodes or users at about 200,000. This used a figure from *Future Computing* magazine, which estimated 6 users per LAN.

Comdex 86: Novell Becomes a "Two-Story Booth" Company

After the Milestone II celebration in New York (covered on p. 178 in Chapter Six), Novell geared up for the fall Comdex 86 in Las Vegas. The Comdex 86 show was memorable to Roger because Novell had become a "two-story booth" company.

Trade shows have always been exciting for me. They are the "county fairs" of industry where people gather to socialize and strut their stuff.

I remember in 1979 first gazing down on the Consumer Electronic Show from the wide stairs leading from the North Hall to the East Hall. The sight took my breath away; I don't know how long I stood there. The East Hall itself enclosed a space larger than anything I'd seen since visiting the GE turbine plant in Schenectady as a teenager, and it was filled from end to end with the outlandish architecture of trade show booths—visually screaming at me to come explore the exotic delights they held. There were pennants, balloons, and giant signs everywhere. The Japanese electronic giants had built massive fortresses of wood panels and chromed plastic fifty feet on a side. RCA had a giant pyramid filled with TVs. Someone else had a forty-foot tall inflated animal.

The effect was a visual smorgasbord more stimulating and more immediate than any I've seen anywhere else. Art museums, great buildings, natural wonders. They all seemed restrained compared to what I saw there.

"Here is an architect's delight," I mused. "These designs are purely for show. There's a lot of money available. And they aren't permanent so the building codes they are constrained by must be minimal."

Most impressive of all were the two story–high booths. On top of those booths, inside this cavernous space, you would see people gazing out high above the churning crowds. I envied those booths and wondered if I ever would be part of a company so prosperous and so image-oriented that it would sport a two-story booth.

In 1986 at Comdex I smiled quietly when I remembered that moment. Novell, the company that had struggled even to attend Comdex in 1982, the company I was part of once again, was sporting a two-story booth.

At Fall Comdex 86 Novell was finally gaining enough notoriety to be respectable. The open systems strategy Craig had been pursuing for three years was moving into high gear. Players of all sizes were getting interested. Where in 1983 Craig had been interesting to niche firms such as Ryan/McFarland, Micro Focus, and SoftCraft, he was now negotiating with the mainstream corporations of the day: Ashton-Tate, Oracle, and IBM.

Craig was presenting to these companies the concept of providing open standards, as Novell had done, so that the LAN industry could grow. Novell in turn would support those standards.

The Tale of the Missing Press Conference

Craig's goal was to promote the open systems approach beyond Novell's walls. He felt that Novell was not the only company that would benefit from pursuing an open systems approach. Two of the companies with top management receptive to Craig's ideas were Action Technologies and Ashton-Tate.

Craig envisioned Action becoming the "Microsoft of e-mail transport systems". As explained above (p. 151), he wanted to see Action enhance their The Coordinator "postman engine" and pull it loose from the "front end" so that many different companies could use it. The alternative was to wait for X.400 and X.500 standards to be thrashed out and developed. Craig saw this as taking a long time and producing a product too complex and too expensive to be well-suited to a LAN market primarily using PC-compatible workstations attached to PC-compatible file servers. He wanted something simpler and sooner and he felt that Action's postman engine could be the starting point for that.

In Ashton-Tate Craig saw a "Microsoft of database engines" and the timing was perfect. Ashton-Tate was about to announce their support of the new SQL standard for database engine commands. This language had originated in the IBM mainframe world a few years earlier and in 1986 it was about to migrate down to the personal computer world. Novell was interested.

Database engines were a vital tool needed to allow LAN applications to migrate from being essentially single-user to becoming multi-user in the form that minicomputer and mainframe applications are multi-user. Novell had bought SoftCraft for their expertise in dealing with database engines. But if Novell was to be true to the spirit of open systems then Novell had to work with many database engines, not just one.

Craig talked to Ed Esber, President of Ashton-Tate, about his open systems ideas. He offered a deal: Novell would support Ashton-Tate's SQL product if Ashton-Tate would publish the details of the command language so that third parties could also use it. This would save the world from having to bear with each SQL developer developing his or her own command set. Ed agreed and a press conference was scheduled for Comdex 86.

Then began yet another of those little non-linearities that was to lead to a major change in the course of an industry—as the fluttering of a butterfly wing is said to precipitate a hurricane on another continent.

The final negotiations took place between Ray and Ed in Ed's office. As they concluded the afternoon before the joint press conference was to be held, Ed was called out of the office and Ray was there alone. The phone rang and Ray answered it. It was a writer for one of the trade publications trying to reach Ed. He was surprised when Ray unthinkingly answered the phone. He thought this tidbit was interesting enough that he mentioned it on a subsequent call that afternoon to Bill Gates, CEO of Microsoft, then as now based in Redmond, Washington.

Bill thought this was interesting enough to investigate too, and in a few hours he had tracked down what the meeting was about. At two o'clock in the morning before the press conference, he called Ed in his hotel room at Comdex to remind him who Ashton-Tate was licensing SQL Server from: Sybase, a company that Microsoft had just purchased—and that if Ed wanted to hear from Bill's lawyers, he should go ahead and announce that he was offering other companies the command language he was licensing from a Microsoft subsidiary.

The press announcement was called off with no explanation and SQL server commands have remained fragmented ever since.

Other than the mystery of an announcement that was called off, Comdex once again went smoothly and Novell continued to gain in notoriety. But now Ray had one more reason to pursue the "that person from Redmond" thinking that would shape Novell strategy in the early '90s.

The State of Play

By 1986 the groundwork had been laid for the next couple of years of Novell effort. Novell would become a stack company and Novell would promote NetWare Everywhere as both a distribution slogan and as a tool for communicating between PCs, various minicomputer protocols, and open system software.

It was Novell's success in pursuing these visions that drove it to become 70% of the installed LAN base in the late '80s and early '90s. The late '80s were all The Year of the LAN for Novell.

The Cultural Thread

CHAPTER SIX
Corporate Culture

The Cycle of Life at Novell

The Quarterly Cycle

There is a rhythm to the business of a computer company, a pumping action not unlike the cycle of a four-stroke internal-combustion engine. The movements of the piston—intake, compression (aka pressure), power, and exhaust—correspond to the fiscal quarters.

At the beginning of each quarter, product sales and shipments are relatively thin, employees are less tense, and fewer man-hours are logged. As the quarter progresses, the volume of business gradually builds. In the last month of the quarter, the pressure is on to achieve quarterly sales and shipment goals. The entire organization strains under the effort—employee nerves throb raw as overtime accumulates and sleep is sacrificed on the altar of enterprise. The phone lines buzz around the clock as deals are cut with distributors and other customers in order to get product out the door. The frenzy peaks in the final days, and in the last 72 hours the entire company is running at the proverbial 110%—beyond maximum effort. When the engine's fuel finally ignites and the deadline passes, there is exhaustion, collapse, and in Novell's case the satisfaction of having achieved or surpassed the goals. Like some huge snake, the market slithers away to digest the enormous meal of product it has just consumed.

The next workday morning a new quarter dawns and the cycle begins again.

As the quarter advanced and the fight for sales and shipments was increasing joined, Ray always led his troops personally into battle. In the last month of each quarter, he focused on sales and shipments to the exclusion of everything else. He spent hours on the phone—at every moment of the day and week—talking with customers and distributors, making deals, giving discounts in exchange for large orders, flooding the market with NetWare. He would arrive at the office at 5:00 or 6:00 AM to catch the East Coast customers and work the phones nonstop till 8:00 or 9:00 at night, only quitting when the last customer in the last corner of California went home for the night.

At the points in the day when he was unable to reach his prospects over the phone, Ray visited the areas of Novell responsible for getting product out. Judith reminisced about the early days in 1983, '84, and '85 when Ray, dressed in jeans, would appear in the warehouse and personally prepare the red boxes of NetWare for shipment.

"It was like a party," she said. "We were all there, late into the night, filling the boxes with Styrofoam peanuts, shrink-wrapping, getting the product out the door."

Just as each quarter had its own cycle of business, so was an annual cycle of business discernible. Novell's fiscal year originally coincided with the calendar year. But much to Ray's annoyance, the year-end holidays from Thanksgiving through New Year's usually led to a slow-down in sales; a fiscal year ending in December meant a weak fourth quarter. So as previously mentioned (p. 125), in 1984 Ray decided to change it so that the first quarter ran from November through the last Saturday in January. This structured Novell's cycle so that each quarter would end on a relatively strong month: January, April, July, and October.

The Trade Show Cycle

Novell also marched to other beats besides the rhythm of the fiscal year. There was a movable feast of product introductions. Trade shows provided an opportunity to come face-to-face with customers, analysts, and the trade press. Trade shows are also a forum where companies make announcements about their latest technological breakthroughs, alliances with other companies, and strategic direction.

In the early years, the major show for Novell was Comdex, generally held in Atlanta in May and in Las Vegas (its original site) in November. As the personal computer industry grew, a host of other shows were introduced: PC Expo, held in June in New York City, and shows in different regions of the country. Many targeted different vertical markets; for example, the Federal Office Supply Exposition, or FOSE, held in Washington DC for the government market. By the mid-1980s
166

it was possible for a company supplying personal computer peripherals to exhibit at more than one show per month.

Like other computer companies, Novell planned most of its strategic announcements to coincide with industry trade shows. Craig would work with Ray and SuperSet on the theme and announcements for the show, while Judith handled the logistics of the booth, special events, and the presentation of the message. Craig and Judith and their staffs did most of the actual work for each trade show.

Mounting an exhibition for a major show is a huge undertaking. In a small company, or even a medium-size one like Novell was then, it will suck weeks of resources from the Marketing, Communications, Engineering, and Management departments. At Novell, detailed planning of a show exhibit usually began three or four months in advance of the event.

However, space for a show is often purchased a full year in advance, so show salespeople try to get commitments from current exhibitors for next year's space. Of course location of the booth is the paramount consideration, and this decision is influenced by the location of a company's competitors and allies. Space for special events outside the show must also be purchased far in advance of the actual show date, lest competitors buy up the choice locations in town. Spectacular special events have included a Beach Boys concert in Las Vegas and renting Disneyland for a night in Anaheim.

Coming of Age Financially

What a Difference Two Years Makes

January 1985: On a cold morning precisely like this in 1983, Ray had pulled into the same parking lot and entered the same Orem office building. The old Novell was still recognizable in the fixtures and many of the faces among the staff. But how the future had changed!

The giant south parking lot was now filled comfortably with the cars of employees. Survival was no longer an issue—at least it was no longer a preoccupation. Still ridiculously puny with only $10 million in 1984 income, the company was nevertheless profitable, and Ray could see by annualizing the current monthly sales that 1985 would bring significant growth—even a doubling of income was possible.

The staff was in place and properly incented, the access to capital was assured, and the products were moving.

The portents were all favorable. IBM had pronounced the benediction over file server technology, and there was no more eloquent articulation of file server technology than NetWare. The waters had parted for Novell, then crashed down upon the horses and chariots of its competitors, sweeping all (or most) away.

Most importantly, Ray and his team had defined a vision not only for Novell but—what audacity!—for the entire computer industry. This was a vision of world domination. In its way, the idea was every bit as preposterous as history's other long shots: That a small town on the Tiber might rule the world; that eighteenth-century Frenchmen might vote for the execution of their king; that a tramp might rise from a Vienna flophouse to rule the German nation and throw the world into war.

The vision was that PC-based local area networks would supplant minicomputers and mainframes in many office functions.

There was a feeling among those at the office on these cold January mornings that Novell had placed its claim on the future. Now the task loomed large before them, and with pick, pan, and shovel, they set forth to extract the ore.

Novell Becomes a Public Company

Safeguard's Dream Finally Comes True

One sign of the company's bright prospects was Safeguard Scientific's decision to create a public market for its shares of Novell. After four and a half roller coaster years—where much of the ride had been a relentless downward plummet—the white-knuckled Safeguard principals felt they could finally relax their grip somewhat. They guessed Novell was finally on track to some level of success and that the market would bid up the value of their remaining holdings.

They were right. On January 17, 1985, Safeguard sold its interest for a considerable profit. Its initial public offering (IPO) in the OTC marketplace of 2.15 million Novell shares immediately sold at $2.50 per share, and in a few months the market bid the price up to $18 per share. (Novell is listed daily in the NASDAQ list under the symbol NOVL.) Although Novell did not receive the proceeds from this public offering, Safeguard got a good return on their investment and the Novell employees saw their stock holdings increase more than seven times in value.

As explained above (pp. 13, 15, and 42), Safeguard had been investing in Novell since 1980 to accomplish two things: To invest profitably in high technology and to gain a product they could offer as an automated enhancement to their One Write system.

With the IPO, they had as planned spun off a high technology company from their investment. It may not have been as smooth or as fast as they wished, but thanks to Ray's intervention they weren't writing off millions either.

Safeguard also got the automated accounting upgrade they wanted, but in an indirect way. The explosion of the PC-compatible standard had grown the personal computer industry and provided a hardware standard that was well suited to become the platform for the computerized upgrade to One Write that Dolf and Pete were looking for when they first backed Jack Davis. This hardware platform was amply provided with service and accessories; all Safeguard had to add was software, marketing, and support—things they would have had to add even if Novell were providing the hardware.

Ray Takes Advantage

The IPO was also significant in that it reduced Safeguard's power over Novell and Ray. At the beginning of 1983, two of Novell's three directors and two of its six officers were Safeguard people. Over the next four years, Ray would work to dilute and eliminate Safeguard's influence over the company.

The offering also gave Novell a higher profile in the PC industry and awakened interest in the financial community. Six analysts began to follow the company. These analysts were more curious than convinced—they had no clear idea of what LANs were, how they differed from other networking solutions, or what niche they might carve in the computer marketplace. Indeed, in this and subsequent years, as growing numbers of analysts were attracted to the company, Novell had to spend considerable time and energy proselytizing for LANs and educating the financial community about the significance of the technology it was creating.

In 1985 the idea of a "LAN industry" was so impossibly ambitious that it provoked laughter. Most industry observers considered LANs a boutique or niche market at best, serving mostly small mom-and-pop type companies—the low end of the computer market. One of the early analysts at Smith Barney assigned to follow Novell dismissed LANs as a mere fad. Yet in 1985 who could prove him wrong? Ray used to say at that time, "We don't even have an industry; we have to build an industry." Ray even welcomed competition. "If we have some competition, the whole thing will expand and we'll sell more."

Even the leadership of Novell had doubts about the ultimate potential of its products. When Ray hired Ron Eliason in July 1985, to become Chief Financial Officer at the end of the year, Ray said he expected to develop Novell into a company with annual sales in the $100 million range and then leave to start something else. He told Ron he would take him along in the new venture, providing yet another opportunity to make a fast fortune.

Ron himself had his own doubts. "I just couldn't imagine when I joined the company that they could ever sell enough networks to make this a big company," he said. "I used to run numbers about 'how many pieces of networking software do you have to sell to get this much revenue?' I just couldn't see it because, I thought, it's not like selling WordPerfect. Each machine needs WordPerfect; each machine needs DOS. But in a network, you can put 10 or 50 or 100 people on that piece of software. Of course, I've been totally surprised."

The Culture of Growth

Novell had more than cycles. It had astounding growth. The '80s were a time when several companies sprang from nothing to billions of dollars in annual sales. Besides Novell, such companies included Microsoft and Compaq Computer. In all these companies not only did sales grow, employee numbers grew as well.

I don't need to take up space here summarizing Microsoft's amazing history.

Compaq was founded in 1982, was the largest startup company of its time, for many years was the largest maker of PC-compatibles, grew enough to buy DEC in 1998 when that minicomputer company was on the rocks, then imploded in the face of competitors such as Dell and sold out to HP in 2002.

Here are some stories about how Novell did its growing.

Growing Beyond the Founders

The rapid growth in both income and installed base caused equally rapid changes in the company's personnel. One of the major changes was raw growth: More employees and managers were hired. The number of Novell employees more than doubled, from about 97 at the end of 1984 to about 236 by the end of 1985, with some 200 based in Orem.

Banker on Board

As mentioned above (p. 124), Ron Eliason's connection with Novell began in the fall of 1984 when he was a Vice President, based in Salt Lake City, of First Security Bank (which became part of Wells Fargo in 2000). Eliason recalled:

> The branch manager in Orem said, "Why don't you go visit Novell; I think they're turning around." So I went down and called on Ray Noorda and found out he was working for a line of credit and Zion's Bank currently had the line, and they [Novell] subsequently went back and met with Bill Gillan, the controller, and we extended a line of credit and Zion's did, and Novell preferred what First Security offered and we got the business.

> Some months after that, I was aware that Ray was looking for a CFO to replace Bill Gillan. I had taken Ray out to dinner at the Underground Restaurant in Provo, when he was first looking for the CFO, and volunteered my services and gave him my resume. That's when they hired Dick Eales as CFO.

Eales had been the CFO of the Penn Central Corporation's Energy Group from about 1979 to 1984. His involvement with Novell began in January 1984, when he worked as a financial consultant to Safeguard and Novell. In November 1984, he became Novell's CFO, although he continued to spend as much as half of his time working as a consultant to Safeguard and its affiliates.

According to Eliason, the replacement of Eales as CFO was made possible by Safeguard's sale of its Novell holdings.

Ray wanted a CFO, but at that time, Safeguard owned 52% of the company. And Safeguard wanted to put their own guy in, and so they hired Dick Eales, who was based in Philadelphia. He commuted from Philadelphia to Orem for about a year. After the public offering in January 1985, Safeguard no longer owned 52%, so Ray figured he could do what he wanted.

Eliason recalled that Ray hired him the same way he had hired Jack Davis at General Automation years before: At an early morning meeting.

About July 5, 1985, Ray called me at 7:00 in the morning and said, "Why don't you stop by before you go up to Salt Lake City?" And so I did, and that's when he offered me the job to take Dick Eales's place. It was August 5th when I joined the company, and it was planned that Dick Eales would leave at the end of December. He did, and I became CFO.

I remember Dick Eales' telling me as we had this five months of overlap, "Ray likes to do things quick and dirty"—that was his terminology. Which meant that he won't give you any help and he likes to do things as quickly with as few resources as possible and kind of wing it, and that turned out to be exactly true.

The Path Taken Too Late

Another key person brought on in April 1985 was Richard King. Richard's is a classic story of once-in-a-lifetime opportunity narrowly missed, like the person who loses a winning lottery ticket, or Gary Kildall of Digital Research (makers of CP/M) allowing Gates and Microsoft to get IBM's main contract for licensing a PC disk-operating system (DOS).

It seems that Richard had the opportunity to become a member of SuperSet. In 1981, he received a BS degree in computer science from BYU. He used to hang out with Drew, Kyle, Dale, and Mark when they were still undergraduates at the Y. Richard was invited to join SuperSet when they incorporated and were doing contract work for Novell Data Systems, but Richard declined because he had landed a regular job—with a salary in the low 20s and benefits—in BYU's computer science department. Richard was married and had a couple of kids, so he decided he was better off playing it safe.

At the time it seemed like the right thing to do. Who could have guessed that so many multimillionaires would leap from the loins of the failing company?

In 1985, Richard's old SuperSet buddies finally convinced him that Novell was going places and he ought to come along for the ride. He was hired in April as Manager of Software Development. A year later, he was promoted to Vice President of Software Development and his department had grown to 22 employees.

Additional Ways of Growing

The personal computer industry of the mid-'80s was new enough that there were not enough industry experts to go around. Finding a resume that said "Five years experience in the personal computer industry" was like finding a needle in a haystack. In the Provo-Orem area, people from all walks of life were now getting hired into Novell and its sister high tech growth company, WordPerfect, but this was not enough. People conduits were set up.

One conduit was from the declining minicomputer industry to Novell. As minicomputer companies began to feel the heat of competition from the still viable mainframes above them and the new PCs and PC-based LANs below them, their growth suffered and they reorganized or (a term that became popular in the '90s) downsized. Many of the people they laid off moved into the growing PC and LAN companies.

David Bradford was recruited by a different route. He had been running a retail computer store in the Bay area. David was hired as company Secretary and staff legal counsel October 1985, reporting to Ron.

Acquiring Personnel

Besides recruiting, the other tool Ray used to grow Novell personnel was acquisitions—he would buy a company to get its good people. This was a strong tool for getting people, but like any strong tool, it could be misused. The hazard of adding people through acquisition was that they would bring their culture from the acquired company into Novell relatively intact, even if that culture had been a losing one in the marketplace.

It was from acquisitions that the eclipsing of the Utah-centric management of Novell occurred. Most of the companies acquired had their top management in northern California. As Novell grew by acquisition, it became like many high tech companies—an organization with top management in Silicon Valley and much productivity taking place in hinterland areas in the US or overseas. In the case of Novell, Utah became the main hinterland. As we will see ("Culture Clash", p. 187 below), this created a problem of having different cultures understand each other and cooperate successfully.

The Relationship between SuperSet and Novell

About the same time their old friend Richard arrived at Novell, SuperSet's role as guardian of the NetWare code began to change. As the product line was expanded in 1985 to include electronic mail, gateways, and other features peripheral to NetWare, the company hired outside firms or set up separate in-house engineering units to develop these add-ons. Eventually, as SuperSet focused its attention on developing new versions of NetWare—such as SFT NetWare 286, which began development in November 1984—sorcerer's apprentices were brought in to take over responsibility for certain parts of the code from the SuperSet wizards.

As Dale described it in 1990:

There was a substantial change in the ownership [of NetWare]. Most of the utilities that ran on the workstations were pulled out of SuperSet. Until that time, we were doing almost all of it. We gave away all of those things like archive servers, communications servers, all of that stuff basically moved out when Richard King came.

And so we concentrated on a much smaller set of codes. When a piece of code gets to the point where we need to get rid of it or want to get rid of it, or Novell wants to lighten our burden and focus us on something else, then typically they will nominate a sorcerer's apprentice who will come and work under us for as long as it takes for them to become comfortable with the code. And that's still what happens.

Early sorcerer's apprentices were Howard Davis and Kevin Kingdon, both of whom picked up chunks of the NetWare operating system.

NetBIOS-related code and all of the LAN card drivers were also handed off in the 1985 period.

Different parts of the code were given away at different times from 1985 onward.

Early in 1987, development began on "Portable NetWare" a version of NetWare that could be "ported" to a host of different operating systems, such as UNIX. Introduced in February 1989, Portable NetWare could run on various minicomputer systems, effectively marrying the PC LAN world and the minicomputer world. In 1987, SuperSet turned over the keys to the NetWare kingdom to the Portable NetWare development team. In that 1990 interview, Dale recalled:

There was a really big convocation of wizards, and a big gift when Portable NetWare was set up. When Portable NetWare was set up, for the first time Novell set up an entire SWAT team of programmers to come in and learn how the entire operating system worked. And at that point, Drew and Kyle and I gave away the understanding for the entire operating system of NetWare itself. And that team took that understanding and then went out and made Portable NetWare so it would work like the existing NetWare.

Then that was the cloning of the whole understanding of architecture, the philosophy, the code of the operating system, when that project spun off. Then Novell took some of the people out of that, then cross-fertilized back into the engineering group and took over NetWare 286. So that SuperSet no longer deals with NetWare 286 at all.

It's now to the point where it's a stable, mature product handled by other engineers. And a lot of new development is handled by Novell engineers who are not SuperSet.

Right now, what goes on inside SuperSet is mostly new operating systems work. NetWare 386 is a prime example of that project over the last couple of years. And also new communications technology, beyond TCP/IP.

For a long time, NetWare had been our toy. We got to call all the technical shots. And that had to quit happening. It just doesn't work over the long haul when the company gets big. The guys who are making the products cannot also be the guys who are doing all the specifying on the product, because either one is a full-time job.

As Novell grew, SuperSet also began to lose touch with the business aspects of Novell. Some of them missed that small company feeling. As Dale said:

> We were no longer writing the sales materials and making some calls on customers and getting the weekly reports on what shipments had been made and having our finger in all of the hardware and everything else like we had done for years. That was a lot of fun. You know what's going on instantly in all areas of the company. And so when you lose touch with some of those things, it's kind of sad.

Education and Marketing

Starting the Education Machine

Earlier (p. 88), we mentioned Ray's five E's, tracking the stages of company morale. Another of his "letter maxims" was the three S's—Service, Software, and Support.

Since his days running Boschert Industries just before coming to Novell, Ray had felt that East Asian competition was going to keep profit margins in data processing hardware too low to be interesting. An American company was going to make better margins on the three S's. Novell Education was spawned to bring tangibility to the first and third S's, service and support. (The two words were usually used together and never carefully distinguished.) If huge masses of people were going to use NetWare, huge masses of technicians would need to know how to support it.

NICI

An important Novell Education event in 1985 was the organization of user groups—local clubs of NetWare owners or network managers who met to discuss ways of enhancing the functionality of their LANs. In June, an executive committee of power users convened to create an international organization tentatively referred to as NetWare In Common International (NICI). The list of those committee members shows that NetWare had already found supporters in some large organizations: Laurie Antonell from Merrill Lynch in New York City; Dennis Eccleston from the New York Power Authority in White Plains, N.Y.; Jeff

Farris from Southland Corp. in Dallas; Tom Frantz from Policy Management Systems Corp. in Columbia, S.C.; Aaron Greenberg from the US House Information Systems, Washington DC; and Larry Thomas from Security Pacific Automation Co. in Los Angeles.

Groups in Toronto, New York, Chicago, and Houston were among the first to organize.

Novell committed financial and staff support to the fledgling user groups. Reid was named Manager of Users Group Relations, and T. Allen Lambert, a BYU graduate completing his doctoral thesis at Cornell, was hired as a consultant to act as a liaison between Novell and the user groups.

Both Reid and Allen reported to Judith, then Director of Corporate Communications. Reid was now working under his ex-wife, who was a Director-level manager. If he had nourished any hope of a career at Ray's Novell, this change in assignments brought him round to reality. Not only was he not wanted as an executive, it seemed he wasn't even wanted as an employee. His new job was basically an invitation to resign. But Reid stayed on for two years to collect on his founder stock options.

Dealer Education

From August to November 1985, Novell held traveling seminars in six major US cities. The first Dealer Authorization Program was also rolled out, with authorization given to resellers who had received product training and who had a demonstration LAN on-site.

In November, Novell's Corporate Communications began to distribute weekly information packages to resellers. Called LAN Information News Kits—or LINK mailings—these packages contained product announcements and updates, technical bulletins, third-party information, and any other literature that might be useful to resellers.

"Its main purpose is to let everybody know what we're doing," said Judith. "Our products are so complex and we move so fast, they can't keep up with us. We were getting six months ahead of our resellers."

Technical Education

Novell offered classes to certify technicians as well as dealers. Certified Netware Engineer (CNE) certificates were awarded, and Roger's was one of the first. This teaching and certifying activity grew steadily in student count, classes offered, and kinds of certificates awarded. By the '90s there were over a hundred thousand CNEs.

Growing the Marketing Team's Size and Scope

Judith was ably served by her staff of writers and promotions people.

Planning for the trade shows, press conferences, and special events like the SFT announcement (see below) was handled by Anita Reece, Novell's promotions manager. Maxilyn Capell, public relations manager, was also editor-in-chief of *LAN Times*. Several other writers contributed articles to the tabloid and to other company projects. Whether they belonged to Corporate Communications, Product Documentation, Education, Customer Service, Marketing, or even Engineering, these writers helped articulate the Novell's philosophy to the budding LAN industry.

Writers on staff by the end of 1985 included Elizabeth Lowder, Barbara Hume, Jennifer Johnson, Mike Durr, Jamie Lewis, and David Doering. Additional writers, including Ed Liebing, Mike Hurcwitz, and Roger White, joined early in 1986.

Milestone II: SFT

The "Milestone II" celebration in New York City for SFT 1, the first System Fault Tolerant NetWare, was one of those events that helped establish Novell's reputation as the host of great parties. (Milestone I had been LANs and had not been feted.) When planning the celebration, Judith and her people figured 300 guests would constitute a good turnout. Yet over 700 resellers, distributors, users, third-party allies, media people, and other industry luminaries were invited to spend an evening with Novell at the Marriott Marquis Hotel in Times Square, then only recently opened. A champagne reception was followed by a speech by Ray, a presentation of the fault tolerance concept, and dinner. After dinner, a standup comic warmed up the audience for the headline entertainment—a concert by Ray Charles.

In his speech, Ray told the crowd, "We are an excited company."

He spoke of the four P's of Novell's success: Perspective, Performance, Products, and People.

Regarding perspective, Ray reminded those assembled of how tenuous Novell's hold on success was. Compared to the real players in the computer industry, Novell was just a mouse scurrying about at the feet of elephants, and it had to be careful not to get squashed.

As for performance, he mentioned Novell's commitment to doing what it said it was going to do—in terms of financial results, product development, and service.

Products obviously were key, and Ray paid tribute to both the skill of the engineers and the vision of the visionaries, like SuperSet, Harry, and Craig.

Finally, Ray spoke of the importance of people—of finding them, motivating them, and giving them the opportunity to succeed.

Ray concluded by calling the Milestone II celebration "a night of euphoria". "I allow for euphoria once every six months," he said, downplaying the danger of his fourth E leading to his fifth, Extinction.

The Networld Idea

Ray and Judith sat next to each other on the flight back to Utah. Judith recalled:

> Ray and I were talking about how it went and what we thought the follow-up program was going to be. And he says, "So, what are you going to do next, Judith?"
>
> I said, "What I think we need to do is some kind of vendor fair where it's just networking and nothing else."
>
> There had been a show held in London. It was one of the first networking shows, but the audience was really sparse. Ray said, "Well, we don't want to be like that show. Nobody goes to it because there's not that much interest in networking."
>
> I said, "Yeah, but we can make it really exciting and interesting, and it's only going to cost about $500,000."
>
> He said, "No way! No, no, no, no, no, no, no!"

Of course Ray eventually agreed to sponsor the networking show. Judith called it "Networld" and scheduled it for the fall of 1986. As Judith, Anita, and the rest of the staff worked to launch the show, they never imagined it would evolve into the multi-million-dollar international trade show it became. (It is now called Networld + Interop.)

Judith later described the genesis of her idea for a trade show specifically devoted to networking. She was influenced by the lack of focus at Comdex and by the strategy of a small software show, Softcon, which Novell participated in at New Orleans.

I had been frustrated trying to get the attention of the press. You would go through the media at that time and there would be a small section on networking—maybe a page or an article. And of course it was my whole world and Novell's whole world, and we could see the growth, and we could see all these vendors that were coming to us for support and all the OEMs and all the distribution channels that had built up. It was really getting big.

But you'd go to Comdex, and there would be a networking booth way over here and another one way over there. They were just so far apart and lost in between the exhibits of office furniture and paper and computers and everything else there was at Comdex.

So I really liked the look of Softcon because it was all about software. They divided the show into groups where they had accounting software, entertainment software—all these sections of the show. I thought, "If we could do just networking, everybody could see how much momentum there is, how many companies there are, and how many people are interested in it."

Novell's planning for Networld began in earnest in 1986.

Suffering amid Success

The fall of 1985 was a period of intense activity for Novell. The Advanced NetWare/86 products began to ship, a special event was held to introduce SFT NetWare (see above), and the usual frenzy accompanied the end of the quarter and the preparations for Comdex.

Judith's Corporate Communications department was generating an enormous quantity of work during this time. Besides the planning for the SFT event and Comdex, Judith's people were working on a corporate video, *The Realities of Life*; getting out weekly LINK mailings; and publishing *LAN Times*, three issues of which were published in 1985. By the end of the year, *LAN Times* was a 40-page tabloid with a press run of 30,000. Fifty free copies were sent to each distributor and four to each reseller, in addition to a small subscriber list and trade show distribution.

Judith supervised the production of this work in the shadow of a personal tragedy. In June 1985, she was relaxing at her Orem condominium with two of her sons. Craig dropped by to visit, riding a minibike. Judith's youngest son borrowed the bike to take a spin around the block. He was hit by a car and killed.

She buried her son in a new cemetery high on the mountainside above Provo. The solitary grave is marked by a headstone and a small stone bench, and the spot affords a serenely beautiful view of Utah Lake and the valley below.

Judith's friends and colleagues say her son's death was a staggering blow; her grief visibly affected her for over a year. Always a hard worker who put in long hours, Judith began to spend even more time at the office. It was not unusual to find her working close to midnight and even later.

Making Novell "Bricks and Mortar"

In the summer of 1985, Novell enlarged its world headquarters by remodeling another building a block away from its original offices at 1170 North Industrial Park Drive in Orem. The new 22,000-square-foot facility (at 748 North 1340 West, the former Ogden's Carpet building) brought Novell's total space in Utah to 41,000 square feet. Engineering, corporate communications, and marketing moved into the new "Ogden" building, leaving sales, accounting, customer service, product education, and manufacturing in the original "1170" site.

At the ribbon-cutting ceremony in August, Ray announced that the enlarged quarters were only temporary and that Novell would be constructing a new plant in Utah within the next year. This was a welcome decision, because the growing company was gobbling up adjacent commercial space at a fast pace.

The new headquarters building was Ron's first assignment. He surveyed employees to find out their preferences as to location, and they were practically unanimous in choosing Orem, where most of them lived. However, as Ron and the other executives studied possible locations, they chose a site in Provo, the sister city continuous with (and, to an outsider, indistinguishable from) Orem.

The site for the new world headquarters was a remote and fairly desolate area of swampy land at the southernmost section of Provo (the opposite edge from Orem), just barely within the city limits. There were a few light manufacturing companies there, a couple of motels, an Elk's Lodge, a city golf course, and the town dump. This area, optimistically referred to as the East Bay Business Center, would be Novell's new home. Ron was allowed to hire a facility and materials management professional, Boyd Worthington, to help plan the project.

In the six months after Boyd was hired and before the new building was ready, August 1985 to January 1986, the company expanded from two buildings to seven, all former warehouses.

"Our biggest challenge is to adapt these various warehouses to serve as offices," said Boyd.

On October 31, 1985, a groundbreaking ceremony was held at the new site. Seven or eight of Novell's managers, including Craig, Ron, and Judith, wielded shovels as Provo Mayor Jim Ferguson watched. The Boyer Company, a major Utah real estate developer and construction firm, was awarded the contract to build the $5-million 90,000-square-foot facility.

In announcing the choice of the site, Ray said, "Our future growth will be considerable. I am convinced that we can achieve our targets in growth and employment in this location." Ray estimated the company would provide 600 to 800 additional jobs in Utah by 1989, for a total Utah work force of 800 to 1,000. As it turned out, Novell attained this employment level in 1987, two years ahead of schedule, and ever since Novell has been one of the largest job creators in Utah. (There is good reason why "Uncle Ray" is a hero within Utah.)

Just a few months after the groundbreaking, Ron and Boyd were already planning an addition to the new headquarters building. Boyd said, "My guess is that as soon as we walk in the doors we'll fill the building. We'll probably need to go to an immediate Phase Two. We really need 90,000 square feet right now, and before the new place is done we still have nine months of growth." Ron estimated that at least 200,000 square feet would be needed by 1988.

Lack of work space was a problem at Novell for at least five years, from 1984 until Phase III was completed in 1989. Employees often had to share cubicles, and at various points in 1986 and 1987 temporary offices were created in trailers out in the parking lots. Sandy Searles, Manager of Product Education, was quoted in a 1986 *LAN Times* article:

> Growth and finding enough space was a problem even two years ago [May 1984]. When I was interviewed I was asked if I would mind not having a desk, or even if I would mind working out of my car. Now I've hired two people to work in an unused closet. This place is a palace [compared] to what we've had in the

past. We've made 10 moves in two years. Every time we thought we had finally made it, but even today we've run out of room.

As Novell expanded its home office, it also expanded its field locations. In the summer of 1985, a Silicon Valley/Western Regional Office was opened in Mountain View, CA; a regional sales office in Düsseldorf, West Germany; and a training and service office in Vienna, VA, close to Washington, DC. The regional offices were used to provide technical support, sales support, and training to customers.

The Düsseldorf office was Novell's third European location in 1985. The other two were a technical services office in Frankfurt and an office in Maidenhead, near London, used for both sales and tech support. Twenty of Novell's 41 international distributors were based in Europe, and European sales accounted for about 19% ($6 million) of Novell's 1985 revenues.

More on all this in the "International" section (pp. 198–205) of Chapter Seven.

... and West Is West

Here is a dramatic example of the importance of culture to a business.

In April 1989 the announcement of a merger (which eventually fell through) between Novell and Lotus Development Corp. caused a sensation in the entire computer industry. The trade press gave it front page/special section treatment, and scores of analysts and industry pundits were interviewed for their reaction and predictions. Virtually everyone agreed that a major problem in the merger would be the clash of corporate cultures, as the yokels from Provo got down to business with the yuppies from Cambridge.

It seems odd to the uninitiated that culture should be an issue. Is Utah really so different from Massachusetts? Is life at Novell so unlike life at other computer companies? And if Novell's culture is unique, how important a factor has it been in the company's meteoric success?

In the early days, from its beginnings up until the late 1980s, most people in the computer industry correctly thought of Novell as a Utah company managed by Mormons. As the company grew through acquisition, both the reality and the public perception of Novell's nature changed. Yet in some ways the perception changed more than the reality. Novell in the 1990s still retained many of the characteristics that distinguished it in its first decade.

Novell grew up in Utah. Most of its employees were Mormon Utahns. As one might expect, this regional and cultural influence shaped the way the corporation went about its business.

Utah in a Nutshell

Utah is a large, very scenic state located on the western side of the Rocky Mountains. It occupies an area almost the size of New England, yet only 2.2 million people reside there, versus the 14 million or so in New England. Most of the year, even in the winter, the weather is sunny and pleasant. Its climate is semi-arid and much of it is a high desert. Provo and Orem are about 4500 feet above sea level, with urban rainfall about 16 inches a year including an average 5 feet of snow (accounting for about 5 inches of the so-called rainfall). Of course it gets a lot deeper in the nearby mountains, providing an awe-inspiring view especially for first-time visitors.

Tourists come to Utah for the skiing (and now snowboarding) in the winter—state license plates boast "The Greatest Snow on Earth"— and for the spectacular scenery and recreational areas in the summer. The state is home to 5 national parks, 7 national forests, and 41 state parks. Thousands of square miles of public land, more than 40% of the state, is managed by the US Bureau of Land Management (BLM).

Besides the mountains and the canyonlands, Utah's most distinctive natural feature is the Great Salt Lake, a vast inland sea (salty because it has no outlet) some 100 miles long and 50 miles wide, but averaging only 25 feet deep.

These facts were of some interest to Novell's US customers. Although international customers seldom had trouble locating Utah, Americans in other parts of the country were sometimes deplorably misinformed. Some thought Utah was near Iowa, others placed it in the Northwest, and more than one believed it was somewhere in Canada.

The Utah Territory was colonized in 1847 by the Mormons, the followers of their recently killed prophet and church founder, Joseph Smith. This group had been persecuted everywhere it put down roots— from New York State, to Ohio, to Missouri, to Illinois. After Smith's murder by an angry mob in 1846, the Mormons commenced their great thousand-mile trek to Zion, their promised land, by walking through

184

roadless wilderness. They arrived in the valley of the Great Salt Lake in July of the following year, under the leadership of Brigham Young, the new church president. The Kingdom of Deseret, as it was called in the early years, flourished. By the time the nation's first transcontinental railroad was completed 22 years later in 1869, over 80,000 people were living in the territory. (A final symbolic golden railway spike was driven at Promontory, Utah.)

Utahns are proud of their pioneer history, and for most this history is also the history of their church, officially known as The Church of Jesus Christ of Latter-day Saints, informally referred to as the LDS Church. According to the *Salt Lake Tribune*, about 62% of Utahns are Mormon.[11] Their faith teaches strong devotion to family, strong devotion to community, and strong devotion to the Church. They believe that spiritual progress can be made by living in accordance with Church teachings. They are also urged to work towards continual self-improvement.

Like members of other faiths, Mormons are inclined to think of themselves as a people chosen and blessed by God. Indeed, Church doctrine holds that the early Native Americans were descended from the lost tribes of Israel, and the LDS Church uses many of the terms and symbols associated with the Jews: "Zion" in reference to Utah, the six-pointed star, and "Gentile" in reference to non-Mormons. (It is jokingly but accurately said that only in Utah can a Jew be a Gentile.)

They are active proselytizers. Between high school and college, many young Mormon men and women leave home to go on a one- or two-year "mission" for the Church where they seek converts and spread the good news of their faith. Many Mormon Utahns speak a second language more or less fluently as a result of their missionary training. Since the LDS Church has a lay clergy, an active Mormon may hold various positions within the Church hierarchy and may even rise to positions of Church leadership while working full time.

Over six million people around the world belonged to the LDS Church in the 1980s, and the largest Mormon population lived in the western United States, especially in Utah, Nevada, Arizona, Idaho, and California. The prototypical Utah Mormon has or comes from a large family, goes to hours of Sunday services at the "ward" (the equivalent of a parish), and may devote one or two additional days a week to Church work or some other community service. He or she is likely to be well-educated, politically conservative, respectful of authority, an avid sports fan, accustomed to working in groups and committees, and closely involved in the affairs of the ward and community. Mormons abjure the use of tobacco, alcohol, and coffee. Utahns in general, including many Mormons, enjoy athletics and other outdoor activities.

Although Utah's population boasts a wide variety of ethnic groups, including many people of Greek, Chinese, Japanese, Italian, Irish, Dutch, Afro-American, and Native American descent, the vast majority are of English, Scottish, or Scandinavian ancestry. This makes for a rather homogeneous-looking population—lots of tall, blond, blue-eyed people.

Life in Utah was a bit more placid and laid-back in the '80s and '90s than it was in more populous areas of the country. There were virtually no traffic jams—not by East or West Coast standards, anyway. Salesclerks were mostly courteous; at grocery stores they would not only bag your groceries but take them out to your car as well (and at least some supermarkets still offer to do so in the early 21st century). Real estate prices were low and gas was cheap. Cities were clean of litter, and are still comparatively so. The airport was very easy to negotiate; Utah was only a two-hour flight from almost any point in the US west of the Mississippi.

Utahns tend to be offended by direct, openly aggressive, or impatient behavior. Conversely, people who move to Utah from out of state are sometimes annoyed at the slower pace of life and business. And those individuals who do not share the values of the majority are sometimes made to feel unwelcome.

About 80% of Utahns live and work on "the Wasatch front", an urban area some 100 miles long including Ogden in the north and Provo in the south (Salt Lake City is in between). Novell, founded in Orem and relocated to Provo, is situated in Utah County. Because the population there has been over 90% Mormon, locals sometimes refer to it facetiously as "Happy Valley".

Culture Clash

Attitudes

To a large extent, especially in the early years, the culture of Novell reflected the culture of Utah. Most Novell employees were Utah Mormons. When people from other parts of the country—customers, analysts, members of the press, and employees at field offices and at acquired subsidiary companies—came into contact with employees in Utah, a learning experience was often in store for both parties.

Novell employees outside of Utah had a tendency to regard the employees at company headquarters as rustic, benighted, in thrall to a strange religion, and inefficient if not downright incompetent. At trade shows or other corporate events these non-Mormon out-of-staters would often get together for drinks at the end of the day and swap headquarters horror stories: Problems that had been ignored, situations that had been poorly handled, bizarre executive behavior or decisions, steps taken to save money that ended up costing money, flagrant waste, employees who continued to receive paychecks for weeks or months after they had resigned or been terminated, headquarters employees who had lied in order to evade responsibility, and on and on. Although the horror stories were for the most part true, the laughter that attended the recounting of them derived from a sense of isolation—geographic, political, and cultural—that field employees felt in their relations with the home office.

Utah employees sometimes picked up on this "outsider" attitude. Their first reaction was usually shock or disbelief because, like most people, they believed they lived in the best place and all other places were an inferior second choice. Some Utahns believe their way of life is pretty much the norm across the nation and are genuinely unaware of the diversity of ideas and cultures that also define America, but many other Utahns have experienced diversity, have lived and worked elsewhere, and are in every sense citizens of the world. So the second reaction to this condescending attitude of some outsiders was anger: "Where do you get off … !" Many headquarters employees looked down on the field employees—especially those who worked in the acquired subsidiaries—as pushy, abrasive, sinful, obnoxious invaders.

Such a clash of cultures occurs whenever people from different areas interact. The Dutch think their Belgian neighbors are rather dull-

187

witted. New Yorkers think the worst drivers come from New Jersey. The East Coast jokes about the West Coast and vice-versa. Yet the disparity in cultures is much greater between Utah and other areas of the country. Someone from Chicago would have an easier time adjusting to Los Angeles than to Provo.

Some flexibility, on both sides, was required in acclimating new employees from out of state to the pervasive Mormon influence at corporate headquarters.

A Case Study

Consider the case of one non-Mormon employee who was recruited to Novell from the East Coast in 1988. On moving to Provo, she was asked numerous times by both neighbors and coworkers the inevitable question: "Are you LDS?" Upon answering no, she was immediately reassured, "Of course it doesn't matter; I was simply curious." But of course she soon realized that religion does matter in Utah—in ways it matters nowhere else in the country.

Later, in employee orientation, this new recruit learned how to use The Coordinator, Novell's electronic mail system at that time. The class was asked to send messages to each other. What message did our girl receive? "Do as you should. Read the Book of Mormon every day and live right."

By now she was wondering what kind of company she had joined.

Soon after her hire, she attended one of the monthly MEMBERS[12] meetings in the cafeteria, where Ray gave hugs to new employees and briefed everyone on how well Novell was doing. Engulfed in a sea of blond heads, she was struck by the lack of ethnic diversity and by the youth of those assembled—the company was run by kids! After some comments by Ray and some irreverent wisecracks by Craig, the pep rally concluded with the cutting of several huge sheet cakes from Provo Bakery, all slathered thick with sugary icing. As the acres of cake were devoured, it occurred to her that sweets might be the Novell intoxicant of choice.

---

[12] See "MEMBERS Meeting", p. 194 below.

A Misunderstanding

The Salt Lake City advertising firm, Fotheringham & Associates, was hired to design a Novell publication. After this was announced, an engineer sent a memo to Judith complaining of the choice of agency.

"It has come to my attention that we have retained the services of an agency called Fathering Haven," the engineer wrote. "I think we should strongly consider asking this agency to change its name as a condition of doing business with us. I think Fathering Haven is an insult, and I'm sure our Father in Heaven would consider it insulting also."

He was serious.

The Prism of the Prisoner's Dilemma

One reason the "Are you LDS?" question is important in Utah is that it sets a framework for future relationships—whether to expect Cooperation or Defection, in the sense of the mathematical concept called the Prisoner's Dilemma.

First published in 1950 by scientists working for RAND Corporation, the concept has caught on and there are now a number of variations on the original Prisoner's Dilemma. As I discuss in Chapter Nine of *Evolution and Thought* (Author House: 2010), in many kinds of day-to-day transactions, two choices are being made: The first choice is how to structure a deal. The second is whether to cooperate or defect on the deal after it has been agreed to.

In the mutual cooperation environment, protections against betrayal are minimal, the deal can be made quickly, and it can be changed quickly if the surrounding circumstances change. This deal structure works best when there is mutual trust, an agreed goal, and the parties expect an ongoing relationship.

In Utah at least, the question "Are you LDS?" is not so much a question of religious belief as a question of "How should I treat you in terms of cooperating and defecting?" If you say "No" then it will take a while longer to establish a double-cooperator relationship with a Mormon.

The dark side of this is that Utah is renowned as the fraud capital of the US. If you answer "Yes" then the typical Mormon lets some of his or her guard down. He or she expects that if you recommend an action, you will have the interests of both sides in mind when you make that recommendation.

Chairman Ray

Ray's Management Style

Beyond the religious and regional influences, corporate culture at Novell was shaped by its management. Despite some token statements made by Ray to the contrary, Novell, Inc., was always Ray's company. To an unusual degree, his personal decisions, policies, and behavior affected how Novell managers and employees behaved. It is almost impossible to overestimate his influence.

People who have worked for Ray say he was a poor manager of people who nevertheless managed to run his companies successfully. He was the sort of manager who is well-suited to running entrepreneurial enterprises: Bright, perceptive, hard-working, able to motivate people one-on-one, obsessive about making sales and controlling costs, "married" to his business.

From his managerial strengths flowed his weaknesses: Irascibility when confronted with fools, a quickness to judge that sometimes led him to the wrong conclusions, an inability to delegate appropriately and a tendency to work himself beyond the limits of his effectiveness, neglect of his management team, a tendency to embrace false economies, and a lack of interest in anything beyond the business.

Ray's standard operating procedure was to mull over problems and situations, sometimes for weeks or months. He might seek advice on parts of the problem from various individuals in one-on-one meetings. When an opportunity to solve the problem presented itself, Ray tended to leap at it, and he might commit all his "troops" or resources to it. He was willing to make the entire organization stop and turn on a dime. That's what Dick meant when he told Ron (p. 172) that Ray liked to do things quick and dirty.

Ray's Frugality

Ray's frugality is legendary and had a direct effect on Novell's corporate culture. His concern about expenses, both corporate and

190

personal, transcended mere thrift; he was almost pathologically cheap. Some of the best "Ray stories" relate to money.

After Novell went public, he reduced his salary to a figure between $30,000 and $40,000 per year, making him by far and away the lowest paid CEO among corporations of Novell's size. For years, he drove an older model pickup truck; he only gave it up when it broke down on his way to the airport and he missed a plane. He was delighted when he turned 65 because he qualified for senior citizen discounts on airfare. At Novell, he had a reputation as an inveterate food moocher with internal radar to help him locate cookies and popcorn. Once in New York he arrived late for an analysts' conference. Not wanting to spend the money for a cab, he took the subway and got lost. Imagine: Hundreds of millions of dollars lost in the New York Subway system!

He imposed this somewhat warped sense of economy on Novell. No one would have dreamed of flying first class—it would have been grounds for dismissal! All Novell employees, from executives to clerical workers, had to share rooms when traveling on company business. (Ray not only wanted to save money; he also wanted to make sure employees weren't hiding out in their rooms instead of making contacts.) From time to time, Ray would personally review expense reports. A personal telephone call, a room service charge, or, God forbid, a pay movie could mean the end of a career. Once Ray decided you were a spender, a seeker of comfort, you were finished.

Many of Ray's attempts at thrift might have worked if consistently applied, but he frequently stepped over dollars to pick up quarters. For example, he insisted on personally approving the list of employees who would attend trade shows, so that only those who were absolutely necessary would be there. Well and good. But due to his hectic schedule, he invariably approved the list at the very last minute, so Novell was unable to take advantage of discounted advance-purchase airfares. Where Ray saved perhaps $100,000 per year by forcing employees to share rooms, he wasted perhaps $500,000 per year by purchasing airline tickets at the eleventh hour.

Another example was the printing the company bought. In 1988 Novell spent an estimated $23 million, nearly 10% of its total revenue or five times its R&D budget, in printing manuals, marketing communications pieces, and corporate communications projects. Most of this printing was marked up between 10 and 30% by various advertising and design agencies. By hiring a print buyer to negotiate volume discounts and impose some discipline in this area, annual savings of $3 million and more might have been possible. Yet when a print buyer was finally hired, management support was only grudgingly provided for this function, and when the print buyer quit the position was essentially eliminated, just 18 months after it had been created.

Then too there were the costly acquisitions. Although Ray nickeled and dimed in operations, in several acquisitions he was willing to pay more than market share because he was impatient to conclude the deal. Indeed, Ray's frugality seems incongruous with his entrepreneurial spirit, his willingness to risk everything. How could such a penny-pincher be such a high roller?

Building a Management Team

Ray's most destructive shortcoming as a CEO was his failure to create a cohesive, cooperative management team. His style was such that he set executive against executive, created rivalry for personal promotion and company resources, and in general created a highly politicized environment at Novell. Many employees feel this political maneuvering engendered by Ray sapped morale, undermined productivity, and wasted both money and talent.

Politics were always present at Novell—what company *is* free of conflict and partisan activity? Or would seek to be? For conflict is desirable as long as the outcome is constructive. Yet at certain points in Novell's history, political conflict became so intense that work stopped and initiative was paralyzed.

Until Ray started acquiring other companies in late 1985 and 1986, his management team was relatively stable and cooperative. Such conflicts as occurred had led to positive results. But as the company grew and more outsiders were introduced, the political game became ugly and desperate, leading to resignations, layoffs, and bad feelings among those who were forced out and those who survived. Between 1985 and 1990, Ray went through 32 Vice Presidents.

Ray's style that so politicized the company was his habit of meeting one-on-one with his executives to discuss situations and make decisions. These decisions were then presented as *faits accomplis* to the rest of the management team at weekly staff meetings. In the early years, the staff was small enough that Ray's style was annoying but not destructive, and staff meetings were held pretty regularly. In the period from 1986 to 1988, the press of business was such that the "weekly" staff meetings often fell by the wayside and were held only sporadically. Politically oriented maneuvering increased during this period.

One-on-one decision-making led executives to compete for Ray's attention, and many of those reporting directly to him felt the last person to "get to Ray" was the person whose agenda would prevail. In this situation, people cease to cooperate in a search for the right decision but rather seek to curry favor personally with the boss. Debate is replaced by sycophantism. Innovators are replaced by yes men. Talented contributors are replaced by poseurs.

An interesting question is whether Ray deliberately set his managers against each other or whether he unintentionally allowed politics to flourish as he focused on the sales end of his business. Among his direct reports opinion was divided, and the answer probably lies somewhere in between. As a man in a hurry, he intervened wherever he thought he was most needed. He micromanaged the critical functions and refrained from managing less critical areas. To some executives he gave, through default, absolute power over their domains, even where it may have been unwise to do so. If they messed up, he got rid of them.

Was this *sturm und drang* necessary? Was this turmoil an inevitable result of growth through acquisition, or might it have been handled better? Whatever the answer, it hardly matters. Politics at Novell under Ray, and the damage and waste it caused, were completely overshadowed by the company's stupendous success.

Contemporary Evidence

Catching Ray

From *Novell Network*, Jan/Feb '86, pp. 18–19

15 Proven Ways to Catch Ray Noorda

By his secretary

Catch the same plane.

Make a trail of nut mix from his office to yours.

Disguise yourself as Craig Burton.

Sit in his chair and wait. And wait. And wait.

Disguise yourself as a quarter horse.

Hide in his Suburban and wait for him to go to the "other" building.

Keep sweets in your candy jar and cement it to your desk top.

Disguise yourself as a nut mix.

Trip him in the halls and talk very fast.

Disguise yourself as his 3-year-old red-haired granddaughter.

Steal his phone and run to your office; wait 15 seconds.

Pick him up at the airport—all of them.

Disguise yourself as his Golden Retriever and wait for your nightly walk.

Grab his brown travel bag as he's running out the door to catch a plane. You'll have one minute to speak before rigor mortis sets in.

Page him and tell him his wife is on Call Park. (Make sure you speak with a high pitch when he answers.)

Ray's Maxims

From *Novell Network*, Oct '86, p. 2.

On the small document are 12 maximums [sic] Noorda has carried in his wallet for 15 years. They are:

The value of time.

The success of perseverance.

Do not be discouraged, no matter what the problems seem to be.

Get great pleasure out of your work. If one doesn't get pleasure out of his work, boy, that is bad.

The dignity of simplicity. Too many people want to dress up things beyond their worth and really destroy what worth they have.

The worth of character.

The power of kindness.

You must set the standard.

The obligation, duty, and wisdom of economy.

The virtue of patience. There is nothing in this world that is more important right now than patience.

The improvement of talent.

The sincere and real joy of originating something.

MEMBERS Meeting

Back in the days when the company consisted of about 20 employees, Novell personnel used to get together about once a month for a potluck lunch, celebration of the month's birthdays, introduction of new employees, and the chance to hear Ray talk about how the company was doing.

As time passed, things changed some, especially the company. And when the company reached the magic number of 85 employees, someone suggested that maybe the thing was getting a little out of hand with all the food and work people were putting into the meeting.

So Novell held a final, company-wide Mexican potluck, after which the meeting was reorganized into a different format. The potluck turned into a cake and milk affair and with the move to the Ogden Building was divided into two separate gatherings.

Judith and Communications Coordinator Dianna Solberg then devised the name MEMBERS, an acronym for Monthly Employees' Meeting Before Enjoying Ray's Speech. (But at least one Life After Novell member guesses an unofficial "Barely" for the B.)

From *Novell Network*, Apr '86, p. 17

MARCH 86 MEMBERS MEETING

The meeting started with a whistle. Putting his fingers in his mouth, President Ray Noorda did a loud "wolf whistle", proclaiming that the noise was the "Call of the LAN".

Then Noorda proceeded to conduct business as usual for the Novell monthly members meeting. The March Members' Meeting was slightly unusual, however, in that it was held March 25, a Tuesday. Members' Meetings are traditionally held on Fridays.

748 North Members Meeting

In introducing the new workers in both buildings, Noorda alluded to a family theme. This all started with new employee Doug Crookston in the 748 North Building. Doug is related to Jenny Crookston, who works for Novell's Sales Department.

After that, Noorda said that all of the relatives belonged on his right and all of the non-relatives to his left. This amused the group of employees.

After the announcement of new employees, Noorda noticed that there were a disproportionate number of new employees from the Communications Department. (Communications announced six new employees at the meeting.) He asked the group, "Does anyone have a feel for what is the fastest-growing department here at Novell?"

Maxilyn Capell [the PR manager] jumped in and responded, "Marketing, because all of the women are pregnant!" Right now there are at least three pregnant women in Marketing.

Then Noorda led the group in a chorus of "Happy Birthday" and introduced a guest to the members meeting. Ken Perkins from the *Deseret News* had come to visit.

Craig Burton said, "Oh, you mean the *Desperate News*?"

Noorda looked to the amused reporter and said, "You've met all these other nice people and this one BIG mouth."

Surprisingly, Burton didn't say anything for the remainder of the meeting.

"Momentum Quarter"

Then Noorda settled into his discussion of the company as a whole. He said that this second quarter will be a real "momentum quarter" for Novell.

"In three years, we have met almost all of our projections and now we have set new, higher goals," Noorda said. He said that the targeted production of $10 million is being met each month.

In addition, he said that this quarter is an important part of the business cycle for Novell. He said that this next cycle requires a lot of communications support.

He then made reference to the "Shoot-Out" which is taking place in April. The Shoot-Out will be a grand debate between Novell and 3Com. Noorda described the event as "Taking on the competition with our own bare hands.

"When we participate in seminars, people try to see who the leaders are. They know that it is between Novell, IBM, and 3Com.

"Well, we're going to eliminate 3Com and we have a good relationship with IBM, so then there will only be NOVELL!"

1170 Members Meeting

After the preliminary phases of MEMBERS Meeting, the Novell president treated the group with some Noorda philosophy.

"Most of this quarter has been spent in preparation," he told the crowded group in the lunchroom. "We are getting prepared for a great future."

Noorda stressed the vast product development that has been taking place here at Novell. "Right now products are coming in fairly consistently with a consistent quality."

He told the employees about the sales campaign that will be going on in April. "We're calling it the 'April No Fool, Real Saver Month,'" he said. The purpose behind the campaign is to "help build momentum", he explained.

Noorda then touched on the issue of product inventory, saying that by next quarter most of the inventory for Novell will be out in the field—at the NetWare Centers.

"This movement will give better support and service to our customers."

"This month will be the forerunner of several great months to come," Noorda said, closing his speech.

Then he opened the meeting up for questions. One employee asked about the new building.

"We're still on schedule," Noorda said. "But no one knows what the schedule is!"

After teasing the bunch, Noorda acknowledged that the East Bay facility will be constructed by Nov. 1, 1986.

Referring to the occasional high waters in that area of town, Noorda suggested, "Everybody in this room should invest in a canoe." Another employee hinted that there may be a "Ray's Ark".

Engineering Humor

Another story of that time: The Engineering department at Novell was a stronghold for Gary Larson's *Far Side* cartoons.

One in particular that gained widespread circulation had the nerdy little kid going into the school for the gifted with a door labeled "Pull", and he was pushing as hard as he could. The label of the school name would get changed by almost each displayer of it. So one for instance had "Microsoft School for the Gifted".

CHAPTER SEVEN
Corporate Decisions

International

Throughout Novell's history, its international operations have played a smaller role in company politics and direction than their annual contributions to revenue might suggest. Since 1983, international operations have accounted for an average 30% of total company revenues. Indeed, in the early years, Novell might not have survived at all had it not been for international sales. Yet for most of Novell's history, the international staff has been relegated to the bench, compelled to look on from the sidelines as the real players clashed on the field.

Novell's assault on international markets was in many ways more challenging than the growth of its US business. Abroad, the company faced the same obstacles it did at home: Market confusion over disk server versus file server technology, customer fears about the reliability of LANs, aggressive competition from other LAN vendors, a shortage of software applications, and so on. But the global market presented new problems as well: Language differences, different engineering standards, the logistics of product shipping, and a smaller pool of qualified candidates for LAN support jobs.

And like Novell's US field offices, International faced a challenge that at times seemed insurmountable: Dealing with headquarters.

The Beginnings of International

In 1981 and '82, Reid and Craig had perambulated through Europe and the Middle East on behalf of Novell Data Systems. Indeed, one of the first sales of a Novell LAN was to a company in Cairo; when Reid revisited the company a year later, the LAN was still functioning, though it had been operating under rather primitive conditions.

198

Although NDSI was hemorrhaging badly in 1982, at least 40% of its income that year derived from international sales. Manufacturing and shipping problems plagued international orders as well as domestic orders. By the time Ray took over, Novell was known to a number of distributors internationally, but its reputation abroad was as bad as or worse than its reputation in the US.

In July 1983, Ray sent Jonathan Whiteley to Europe to turn this situation around. Jonathan arrived in Düsseldorf with his wife, Maureen. For the first six months, he worked out of his home, with his wife serving as receptionist.

Jonathan's job was first to interest distributors in carrying NetWare, then to make sure they were getting the support they needed to sell it.

Although the office locations changed several times over the years, Düsseldorf remained the major center of Novell's European operations. In December 1983 Jonathan obtained Ray's permission to rent office space. Two years later, in June 1985, he moved into larger 200-square-meter offices on Niederkasseler Lohweg, and in June 1986, Jonathan opened a new European NetWare Center which included 400 square meters of office space and 560 square meters of warehouse space.

The Düsseldorf office at first covered all of Europe, the Middle East, and Africa, providing sales, training, and technical support to distributors abroad. In 1985, an additional tech support office was opened in Frankfurt and a sales and tech support office was opened in Maidenhead, about 30 miles west of London. Andrew Zoltowski joined Novell in 1985 as general manager of Novell UK. In 1986, Andrew moved his offices from Maidenhead to nearby Slough and began to stock inventory, thus creating the UK NetWare Center.

In some respects, Germany was an odd choice for Novell's first European office, probably involving personal connections. At the time, the United Kingdom had the most developed market after the United States. The UK had about 50% of all PCs in Europe, while Germany and France were still heavily dominated by minicomputers.

Some important successes were scored by the UK team in 1985. Among Novell's top customers for September 1985 were the British Railway Board and a distributor, Novell Data Systems, Ltd. By the end of 1986, British Railway had the largest NetWare network in the world: Over 2,000 workstations networked on 170 S-Net LANs. A year later, the number of S-Net systems had grown to more than 300.

199

From the beginning, European sales contributed significantly to Novell's revenues. International sales—most of which were from European distributors—contributed 30% ($1.2 million) in 1983 and 21% ($2.45 million) in 1984 to total revenues. In 1985, Europe alone contributed almost 18% ($6 million).

By the end of 1984, Novell had about 15 active foreign distributors, mostly European. A year later 41 international distributors, about 20 of which were based in Europe, were buying from the company. By March 1986, the number of European distributors had grown to more than 30.

Novell Gets Serious about Europe

Publicity

1986 was an important year for Novell's European operations. Until that time, Novell had relied heavily on its European distributors for marketing, sales, and technical support. After three years of this approach, Ray felt ready to increase Novell's investment and presence in this key market. In 1986, he allowed Judith to spend one-fourth (roughly $1 million) of her corporate communications budget on European promotions. Most of this money went on trade shows and conferences.

On March 6, Judith and Promotions Manager Anita Reece helped Andrew launch the first annual United Kingdom NetWare Affiliates Conference. Representatives from over 30 European software developers attended—16 of them newcomers to Novell and NetWare. "The whole day was a tremendous success," said Andrew. "The entire concept of a manufacturer addressing software developers in this way is totally unique in this country. We were talking at their level and about things of relevance and interest to them. The overall reaction was one of great enthusiasm for this approach."

Judith and Anita then proceeded to Germany to set up Novell's booth at the CeBIT Hanover Fair, the world's largest trade show for office, electronic, data, and communication technology. This was the first time Novell exhibited at the show, and its booth featured two LANs connected by an SNA Gateway: A 286A file server running NetWare ARCnet on three workstations linked with a NetWare 68B file server running S-Net on five workstations. The company also presented five seminars and played host at a dinner for distributors and another dinner for software developers.

One of the guests at the distributor dinner said, "The time is ripe for Novell to take the load in Europe. Novell's presence at the show, combined with the support offered to distributors and resellers here, indicates the company's total commitment to the European LAN market."

At both the UK conference and the Hanover Fair, representatives of the International NetWare Users Group (INUG) made presentations. This group, like the user groups in the US, was organized with Reid's help in 1985. It was important not only as a source of ideas and feedback to the NetWare designers but also as a demonstration of NetWare's acceptance by major customers, so speeches by INUG members were important at gatherings of the independent software developers ("NetWare Affiliates") whom Novell was trying to impress.

One result of the Hanover Fair was an OEM agreement between Novell and Bertelsmann AG of Hanover, where Bertelsmann translated both the manuals and screen text of Advanced NetWare 2.0 and marketed a German language version of Advanced NetWare for IBM PC networks. This was the first official foreign language version of NetWare.

Novell's booth at Hanover Fair was followed by participation in two more European shows in 1986, both in London: The PC User Show in July and Compec in November. The booths featured two LANs linked by an SNA Gateway, similar to the demonstration at Hanover Fair. NetWare Affiliates also exhibited their LAN applications in the booths. "NetWare Everywhere" stickers and banners announced Novell's presence throughout the booths.

Novell also took its first steps into international advertising in 1986. The first of a series of "Milestones Ahead" ads, released in May, appeared in translation in the various European markets. Although advertising was quite limited in 1986—it gradually expanded through 1987 and 1988—this was the first time the company had directly advertised its products to international end users. In 1986, the NetWare Centers in Germany and the UK also hired their own public relations companies (Henschel and Stinnes in Germany and Tom Burgess and Company in the UK) to issue press releases, handle media relations, and help with other PR activities.

The Market

In a *LAN Times* article (June/July 1986, p. 24), Joseph Wolf, an employee at the Düsseldorf NetWare Center who gave technical training sessions for distributors and dealers, described the market in Europe:

In Germany and France the computer industry has given local area networks (LANs) a lukewarm reception. The main interest there has been in minicomputers. Novell is meeting this challenge by showing that NetWare, with its ability to communicate with a variety of hardware systems, can be a valuable asset to such companies.

Spain, Italy and Great Britain, on the other hand, are eager for LANs, and NetWare has incredible potential in those countries, according to Wolf.

One of the areas of investigation is in utilizing NetWare to run large automated machining and milling operations. Though still no more than an idea, the concept of adapting a PC to run a lathe or other device, for instance, appeals to German heavy industry.

"When you have to coordinate the activities of an entire factory, the use of a stripped-down PC attached to a NetWare LAN to run one of the multimillion-dollar machines offers a very inexpensive and universal communication tool. Even when we have different types of machines from different countries, NetWare can talk to all of them," said Wolf.

...

Wolf summarized by saying, "How many major computer firms do you have in the United States? Three? Four? In Europe, we have those same firms as well as three or four of our own, none of whose systems can talk with the others. Europe *needs* NetWare."

From the same issue of the *LAN Times* (June/July 1986, p. 23).

While the London NetWare Center is finding success with its new distributors, the European NetWare Center is seeking distributors for Israel and Kuwait. Last year, the number one distributors in Europe were Holland, Germany, and France, respectively. The Scandinavian countries were also large sellers, [Jonathan] Whiteley said. He also pointed out that Spain and Italy are becoming more active.

In 1986, Novell's international operations, like the rest of the company, were reorganized to incorporate the NetWare Center concept. As already mentioned (p. 199), two NetWare Centers were established in Europe: Slough and Düsseldorf. Suddenly these offices no longer confined their activities to sales and technical support; they became stocking distributors of NetWare and other products as well. The *LAN Times* article just quoted reported that the UK center was even "looking at the possibility of buying disk drives inside the United Kingdom; the center would then supply UK and perhaps other European customers with the disk drives."

By mid-1986, Novell had lined up an impressive array of European and other international distributors, and the focus of activity had shifted to the ongoing business of training and supporting resellers and end users. Although 120 German dealers were selling NetWare by the summer of 1986, only 4 of these were authorized dealers who met the company's training requirements and demonstration capabilities.

The other major focus of activity for Novell Europe in 1986 was the development of the International NetWare Affiliates group. By the summer, over 900 independent software vendors (ISVs) belonged to the group worldwide. The Düsseldorf NetWare Center sponsored a series of five seminars in various European capitals during the fall of 1986.

By the end of 1986, Novell was estimated to control at least 30% of the European LAN market—at least twice as much as its closest competitors. UK rivals—Torus, Apricot, Research, and others—trailed far behind the company from Utah. By mid-1988, according to that September's *LAN Times* (p. 20), Novell's share of the European market was estimated at 50%.

By 1988, Novell's European operations (including the Middle East and Africa) accounted for about 75% of all international revenues, which, in turn, accounted for about 30% of all company revenues.

Novell's ROW "Rest of World" Operations

Other world markets did not receive the same attention as Europe. Yet progress was made in these areas.

John Harris was a key player in all international operations. He joined Novell in 1984 and by 1986 was working as International Distributor Manager, a job which took him around the world. By 1987 he was serving as Director of International Sales, and by 1988 he was responsible for all Novell sales in Canada, Asia, and South America.

In June 1987, Clifton Ashley was named Director of Regional Sales for Latin America.

Another key player in the growth of Novell's Asian and Pacific Rim market was Andrew Lai, who joined Novell in May 1984. He undertook the unenviable task of developing Novell business in Asia—from company headquarters in Orem! Ray would not authorize an Asian office for Novell until 1987, when Andrew opened the regional headquarters in Hong Kong in July. His region included 15 different countries about 10,000 miles from Utah, with a time difference of 14 to 15 hours.

Yet Andrew accomplished a great deal during the three years he was based in Utah. Like his counterparts in Europe, he relied heavily on distributors for customer training, sales and tech support, and sponsorship of seminars. For example, a seminar held in May 1985, dubbed "Brainstorm '85", was hosted by Advanced Computing Resources, Novell's Hong Kong distributor. Andrew assembled a program of three other American speakers besides himself and attracted about 100 end users to the event. In October 1986, he put together a two-day Pacific Region Distributor conference in Hong Kong, again with sponsorship by a Novell distributor, and he delivered none other than Ray as the keynote speaker.

By the end of 1985, Andrew had signed up 11 distributors in the Pacific region. With the opening of the Hong Kong office in July 1987, Andrew was able to increase his sales and technical support, educational offerings, trade show presence, advertising, and other local promotions. By the end of 1988, four years after Andrew started, Novell commanded an estimated 90% of the LAN operating systems market in Taiwan and at least 70% of the market in the rest of the Pacific region.

In an interview at the end of 1988, Andrew recalled, "We spent most of that first year just finding resellers and doing very little business. I am still looking for good resellers, but we have certainly developed the business."

In many areas of the world where Novell decided it could not afford to maintain a large corporate presence, the distributors became the principal company representatives. As late as 1989, this was still the case in the Pacific region.

"Most of our distributors look at themselves almost as being Novell, and they are the source of everything from top to bottom," Andrew said then. "Novell doesn't sell anything direct in this region so our bare-bones headquarters operation has the role of support."

For all of Novell's success in the Pacific region, Japan remained virtually closed to NetWare through the 1980s. In 1990, Novell established Novell Japan, Ltd., a joint venture with Canon, Fujitsu, NEC, Sony, and Toshiba, that sold NetWare products in Japan.[13]

NetWare Centers and NetWare Everywhere

The Life and Death of a Big Mistake

In the 1985–87 period Novell went through huge cultural changes associated with its growth and success. It grew from a small hopeful company with a big dream into a large successful company that made that dream come true. It grew from Utah-centric to polycentric, from a company in a converted truck dealership to a company that built its own buildings in a new industrial park, from a company that few people had heard of into a company that was making a brand new multibillion-dollar high tech industry. These were stupendous changes, and there were many growing pains associated with the transition.

Businesses are not run in a state of perfection. The real world is a messy place. What happens in the real world is that multiple attempts are made to solve real world problems. Many of those attempts are quietly successful and are used for years and years without notice. Many more are quietly unsuccessful and are quickly replaced with new efforts to solve the problem.

Once in a while there is a spectacular success or a spectacular failure. Novell as a whole was a spectacular success, but within that success were many quiet, and a few spectacular, failures.

The story of one spectacular failure, the NetWare Centers of the mid-'80s, shows how an idea can evolve from good in concept and precedent to sour in execution, and how the sour result was ultimately dealt with.

---

[13] http://ecommerce.hostip.info/pages/804/Novell-Inc.html.

Before NetWare Centers

Growing the Industry

Ray was always a man in a hurry. Each of his companies has been a company in a hurry. This is especially true of Novell. At first the scramble was for survival. Two years later, the company was rushing to accomplish a larger goal: Growth of the LAN industry.

In 1985, Novell began to spend time and money defining and supporting that fledgling industry. It formed an international users group. It held its first conference for independent software developers. It rolled out its first reseller authorization program. It expanded the distribution of *LAN Times*. And the idea for the Networld trade show was born.

Of course Novell saw itself as the leader of the new industry. The management team had always prided itself on having technology that was least two years ahead of the competition. In 1985, Judith started publicizing this two-year lead in *LAN Times* and company advertising. The idea of LAN milestones was articulated. Indeed, in this year, Novell invented an historical perspective for an industry that was barely two years old. Players in this business weren't just selling product, they were making history.

The self-consciousness, self-definition, and sense of purpose that Novell promoted in defining the LAN industry was, in a way, as important a contribution as its technology.

Novell was not merely catering to an established market; it was creating a new market by exciting public demand for an altogether different kind of product. This new market for LAN products had to be carved out of the existing market for office automation machines, minicomputers, and mainframes. To get the end users excited about LANs, Ray and his team had to motivate business partners in the new industry such as resellers, distributors, systems integrators, software developers, and other manufacturers.

Growing NetWare

The key to it all was the proliferation of NetWare. Ray saw a window of opportunity that would remain open for just two or three years. If Novell could attain a critical mass of installations in that time, its technological claim would prove lucrative indeed and Novell could find itself the dominant player in an important industry. If Novell failed to create momentum and rally both its allies and its competitors to the cause, its moment in history would pass. Either other LAN companies would overtake Novell or the entire LAN industry would die aborning as alternative technologies were developed and presented to the market.

In the speeches he gave from 1984 to 1989, Ray often compared Novell to a mouse among elephants. His point was that Novell and the entire LAN industry existed at the pleasure of the titans of the computer industry. For the moment, the LAN industry was allowed to grow. Why? The LAN companies had caught the giants napping, in some cases, and in other cases the giants were content to let the small fry pay the costs of developing the new technology. When the fruit was ripe the giants would come in and buy the orchard.

Ray was very solicitous of the giants and tried to make Novell helpful wherever possible. If he played his cards skillfully, he could sell Novell when the time was right and then do again what he loved best: Building up small companies.

Marketing

So there was to be NetWare Everywhere—the slogan reflected the company's marketing strategy. Ray pronounced that all channels would be flooded with NetWare products—it would be unfair to keep the end users waiting for this revolutionary technology! No business was bad business.

In this spirit, Novell not only sought marketing agreements with OEM customers, distributors, and resellers; it also lined up a number of retail accounts. This manifestation of the "NetWare Everywhere" strategy was spurred by IBM using retail dealers to market its slow and cumbersome PC Network Program network operating system, along with other Big Blue PC products.

In 1985, Byron Kirkwood was appointed Retail Sales Manager and worked with Ray, Harry, and Craig in making deals. His staff also began to grow, to include Rob Walton, David Chung, Lee Love, Sue Barrett, and Judith's second son, Jay Zwicky. By the end of the year, NetWare was being sold by Businessland (62 stores), ValCom (240 stores), MicroAge (170 stores), and ComputerLand and Entre (more dozens of stores).

Training and Support

Having secured a retail channel, there still remained the question of how hard these retailers would push NetWare. If the retail outlets were going to be effective at NetWare sales, they would have to have considerable training and technical support from Novell. For that matter, training and tech support were sorely needed by most of Novell's distributors and resellers. The typical reseller salesperson had less than a year of computer experience and jumped ship frequently. High turnover among reseller salespeople was a big problem for Novell as well as for the VAR (Value Added Reseller) as versus those who just "moved boxes".

Training and tech support had been a problem for Novell from the early days, but rapid growth in the number of customers was making this problem ever more insistent. "Customers" included salespeople from all sales channels as well as end users. Novell employees and other interested people were also among the trainees.

From 1983 until the Education Department was created the following year, Jared Blaser and Jim Bills did all the training. (Jared subsequently became Director of Marketing Technical Services and Jim became Director of Sales.) In May 1984, John Harris and Sandy Searles were hired to head Education. By early 1986, the Education Department was staffed by 18 employees based in Orem and the regional offices. Most trainees were unable to come to Utah for their lessons, so the Education staff members spent almost half of their time on the road.

As for tech support, Jim Stallsmith had joined the company in December 1983 as Manager of Customer Service. When he was promoted to Director of Field Service two years later, one of his first assignments was to increase the number of field technicians from 9 to 25. Most of these were stationed in Novell's four regional offices: Mountain View, California; Dallas, Texas; Vienna, Virginia; and Düsseldorf, West Germany.

The Birth of NetWare Centers

Ray became convinced, as he analyzed the capabilities of his resellers, that Novell would have to offer systems integration services to resellers and major end users if LANs were ever going to take off. High end tech support and sales support would have to come from Novell, at least until NetWare matured as a product and the level of LAN expertise increased in the world.

At the end of 1985 this need to address the training and support issue, coupled with Ray's interest in developing a strong retail channel, led him to make one of his more conspicuous mistakes, which would ultimately imperil the company. That decision was to create a chain of regional "NetWare Centers" to handle training, tech support, sales, and even some manufacturing operations. As the concept evolved over the next six months, it changed in some dangerous ways.

The NetWare Centers idea also became a bone of contention for the different factions within Ray's management team. Until the NetWare Centers became an issue, Ray's Novell had been a relatively homogenous, cohesive organization. Its challenges and frustrations had mostly come from outside the company. There had been differences of opinion—strong advocacy of different courses of action—but these differences had not been truly rancorous. All that began to change in 1986, imperceptibly at first. In a sense, the NetWare Centers represent Novell's first real growing pains as it expanded from a small to a medium-sized company. Although no one was aware of it at the time, the advent of the NetWare Centers marked the passing of Novell's "Golden Age" or "Age of Heroes". As this program soured, things would never be the same.

This also involved Novell's first experiment with acquisitions—an experiment that was not altogether successful and which presaged difficulties that attended later acquisitions.

Two outside events caused the NetWare Centers idea to gel in Ray's mind: In November 1985, two Novell distributors went belly up, owing Novell several hundred thousand dollars in unpaid bills. One was Jersey Micro in Saddlebrook, New Jersey, and the other was a distributorship in Memphis, Tennessee, called Micro Source Technologies, owned by Carl Orellano.

In spite of the failure of Micro Source, Ray had been impressed with Carl and wanted to find a place for him in Novell. After thinking the matter over, Ray thought he saw an opportunity to take these lemons and make some lemonade. He announced the NetWare Center concept, put Harry in charge of them, and let Carl head the new NetWare Center in Memphis. Ray also took over the Saddlebrook location, although he dumped the management.

These were Novell's first acquisitions.

Ron speculated on Ray's reasons for setting up the NetWare Centers:

Ray actually wanted to have inventory in every NetWare Center. He didn't ever really explain this, but it might have been based upon what Businessland was doing. I think everybody realized that in the PC world, everything is sort of an off-the-shelf sale. You know, something in a shrink-wrap or box, and people just walk into a Businessland store and buy it off the shelf. So Ray was thinking in terms of having "NetWare Everywhere" and having inventory everywhere.

It was a short jump in reasoning: If retail outlets are important, why not set up our own chain in addition to using independent chains? We have to find a way to improve our field support anyway, so why not create some regional offices that will be retail outlets as well as training, tech support, and sales support centers? Then there's the advertising and PR value. We'll call them "NetWare Centers", and before long "NetWare" will become a household word!

Of course, the distributors and resellers will grumble about Novell increasing its regional presence and making additional direct sales. But they need to understand that as NetWare proliferates, more opportunities will eventually come their way. The direct retail customer we sell to today will need the reseller's value-added services when he upgrades or expands his NetWare installation. Furthermore, the NetWare Centers will be regional inventory warehouses serving both distributors and resellers. Regional inventories will shorten delivery times to our distribution customers and allow them to reduce their inventory carrying costs. We can also offer them sophisticated systems integration services as sales support.

In talking the concept over, Ray and Harry saw yet another opportunity in the centers. Novell shipped many of its hardware components in from other areas of the country, like Silicon Valley. These components were then assembled in Orem and shipped right back to the regions whence they came. Why not use the NetWare Centers as assembly points and eliminate all this back-and-forth shipping?

In retrospect Ray was widely criticized for his NetWare Centers, yet at the time the concept had ample precedent. For one thing, the idea of regional inventories is a time-honored one which many manufacturing companies—especially smaller ones—still use today. For example, in the electrical industry in the early 1980s manufacturers felt pressured to maintain far-flung networks of regional inventories, because if contractors were unable to find the brand they were looking for they simply switched to a competitor's line.

"It was like an auction out there," said John Monter, Vice President of Sales for Panduit Corp, a hardware manufacturer. "We reasoned if our products weren't immediately available in the marketplace, we would lose the sale."

As Novell's hardware became more and more a commodity item, it too could become subject to such brand-switching.

And as noted above (p. 207), IBM was also marketing its LAN product through retail dealers at this time. Ray felt he had to fight fire with fire.

Even the idea of getting deeper into the distribution business had been pioneered by other manufacturing companies. Ray's old employer, GE, had years ago created a nationwide chain of electrical wholesaler-distributors known as the General Electric Supply Company (GESCO). GE had been competing with its own independent distributors for years. There was also precedent in the computer industry. For example, in 1984, Apple acquired its four largest distributors.

So early in 1986, Ray announced that Novell would be establishing nine NetWare Centers: Seven in the US, one in Great Britain, and one in West Germany. An article on the subject appeared in the January/ February issue of *LAN Times*:

> "The goal of the NetWare Centers is to provide an effective supply of hardware and software LAN products to Novell's customer base. The idea is to bring all the services now available only at our corporate headquarters out into the field to provide faster, more effective solutions," explained Noorda.
>
> The centers will stock inventory for Novell's distributors and dealers, cutting down on the inventory they'll have to carry, speed up delivery to the entire customer base, and provide better service, field support and technical training.
>
> ... According to [Harry] Armstrong, "The centers will be regionally accessible and will create a bridge of better communication and support for our customers."
>
> ...

Having NetWare Centers in the field will cut product lead times and this should eventually lower costs. "Many times we receive hardware from our suppliers and then turn around and send it right back to the same area. NetWare Centers will allow us to cut down shipping expenses," stated Noorda.

The present regional offices of Novell in Mountain View, CA, Dallas, and Vienna, VA, will expand to become NetWare Centers. Other company expansion in this area recently included the acquisition of MicroSource Technologies in Atlanta and Memphis, and Jersey Micro in Saddlebrook. ... Novell plans to have all the NetWare Centers operating by the end of the company's current fiscal year in October 1986.

Ray added a resolute yet upbeat message for his resellers and distributors:

All channels will benefit from a more localized service organization. ... Ultimately the customer is the end user. All the channels serve as a means to reach the end user and we must always keep in mind that we will be selective in using those routes that serve him effectively—now and in the future.

Seeing the Dark Side

Is Novell Cooperating or Defecting?

Manufacturers, distributors, and retailers in all lines of business must cooperate to get product to the customer. But cooperation adds substantial cost, so it is worthwhile only if it makes the total of everyone's profit much bigger than it would otherwise be. Some organizations instead reach out to capture a larger piece of what the end user pays for product. Some manufacturers "go direct" to retailers or customers, some distributors start manufacturing, some retailers buy up or create a "captive distributor". Their risk in grasping these opportunities is that other players will see them as a defector—someone who is no longer cooperating—and in return they will no longer be cooperated with.

From the beginning Novell distributors and resellers didn't buy the NetWare Center concept, and they had good reason to be fearful of it. In the distributors' and resellers' eyes, every direct sale Novell made was a lost opportunity for them. There was grousing. Novell could not afford to be seen as a defector, and Harry hit the road to do some hand-holding. He had to show that the NetWare Center concept was in fact not defecting against the other sales channels. His remarks at one of these explanatory seminars were reported in the next issue of *LAN Times* (Apr/May 86, pp. 48-49):

"We want to make it much easier to deal with Novell. ... So the idea of the NetWare Center is to put our product, our people, our technical knowledge in the field, and get closer to our dealers and distributors.

"Originally we thought we'd have seven locations worldwide. I believe now there will be at least 10 and possibly more."

Harry dangled the systems integration services before resellers:

"The NetWare Centers are going to be squarely in the middle of the systems business, and as such will require more specialists. ... The systems engineer can be almost anything. He is generally a person that works with major end users, sits down, talks with them, finds out what their needs and requirements are, and configures the system for them. He is a consultant, he can be industry specific, he can be product specific."

Regional inventories and assembly will shorten order delivery times for resellers:

"The NetWare Center operations people will be doing systems integration and testing—almost what we call assembly. ... Each NetWare Center's goal is to be able to ship products within 48 hours of receiving an order."

Resellers can bring customers to the centers for product demonstrations:

"Each NetWare Center will have a product demonstration center where customers may observe our products, and receive operations demonstrations and educational classroom experience. Education is becoming a much larger portion of Novell sales as we grow."

Armstrong concluded by reassuring his audience that these centers were really in everyone's best interest:

"The number one purpose of the NetWare Centers and ourselves is to provide excellent customer service."

In 1985 Novell's channel partners grudgingly accepted the Centers. They had no choice, and perfect happiness always eludes distributors and resellers in any industry.

According to the article, Harry also gave some idea of the major role the centers were expected to play in the future of Novell:

Armstrong expects the centers to be accounting for 50% of Novell sales by the year's end [1986]. [This would hardly have been reassuring to resellers!]

On the personnel side, Armstrong estimates that the number of NetWare Center employees located outside of the home base in Orem will equal the number at the corporate office.

By the end of the year, he projects that 80–90% of all products in the centers will be Novell products, with non-Novell products being such items as uninterrupted power supplies (UPS), terminals, software application programs and communication boards.

There will also be an authorized Novell product catalog, which will include all Novell products and the approved non-Novell products sold at the NetWare Centers. Non-Novell products listed in the catalog will be peripherals selected and provided to enhance Novell systems. It will be the first time non-Novell products are included in a Novell products listing.

Red Flags Are Waved within Novell as Well

Not every member of Ray's management team was as enthusiastic about the NetWare Centers as Harry. Craig and Ron both had misgivings, primarily because it seemed to get Novell deeper into low-margin hardware. The NetWare Centers concept became part of the old hardware vs. software argument. As Craig recalled:

I didn't care if they sold hardware; I just wanted to get out of the mentality that was where our revenue was going to come from. I didn't care if they used hardware as a means to move software as long as it was understood that software was what we were after.

That is why I never tried to stop it. Not because it took a long time for it [the phase-out of hardware] to happen but that the mentality needed to change, which it did. We were motivating people to sell software, and that was really clear that was where our bread and butter was.

It was tiring having to fight the same battles over and over again—having to remind the same people of what had been discussed and keeping them on track. For Craig, personally, it was also a bit disheartening to see Harry taking the lead in the centers.

214

Ron was frustrated at the importance of the role the centers were cut out to play. He had been pleading with Ray to add more staff to key administrative areas such as accounting, information systems, and human resources. Ray was a brick wall. Now plans were being made to double the staff—and all those new bodies would be in the field!

The Concept Balloons and Novell Defects

In May 1986, Ray took another step deeper into the NetWare Center quagmire. Novell acquired yet another distributor, Cache Data Products, based in St. Louis, Missouri. Cache Data had 41 employees, three locations, and 1985 sales of about $6 million. The newly acquired company would change its name to the St. Louis NetWare Center.

But there was more to the story. Cache Data had been Novell's first distributor, and in the three years they did business together, Ray had been impressed with the company's President, Ken Kousky. Ken had been a teaching fellow at the Wharton School and was a Ph.D. candidate. When Ray talked about him in staff meetings, he called Ken a genius. Integrating Ken and his team into Novell was an early example of Ray growing his management by acquisition.

With Ken on board, Ray restructured Novell quite dramatically. Corporate functions were divided between two separate operating divisions: Novell Utah, with Harry as executive Vice President and general manager, and a new, wholly-owned subsidiary company called NetWare Centers International, Inc. (NCI), with Ken as President. By this time, the number of NetWare Centers had expanded to 11 US locations and three international locations.

Ray explained the changes:

The Novell Utah operating division assumes the responsibility for providing proprietary hardware and software products to all channels of distribution. Its sales focus will be on new products and new channels of distribution.

NetWare Centers will have the capability of supporting their customers with uniformity of training, field service, sales programs and inventory.

Then came the shocker. The thing that Novell resellers had feared from the first announcement happened.

The NetWare Centers will not be limited to the provision of proprietary products from Novell Utah. This gives the overall company continued emphasis on making price/performance selections of products and services to the LAN market that are not necessarily bound by Novell proprietary products.

Ray had moved beyond the original plan for the NetWare Centers. The centers would no longer be mere regional warehouses for Novell products; they would be full-fledged distributor operations. Just a few months earlier, Harry had said that 80% to 90% of the centers' inventories would be Novell products. Now Ray had taken the concept a step further, and Novell would be competing directly against its distributor customers.

This new move was Ken's idea. When Ray bought Jersey Micro and Micro Source in November 1985, he acquired those first two distributors' inventories of non-Novell products in New Jersey and the southeastern US. The Cache Data acquisition brought in additional non-Novell inventory stored in that company's three warehouses in Chicago, Minnesota, and St. Louis. As a result of the three acquisitions, Novell had become a de facto distributor, and now Ray decided to make it official.

This is a good example of what can happen when a new manager is brought into an organization, particularly through an acquisition. Being brought in to make change, their first change will usually be to try implementing their past success in the new organization. Ken had made a name for himself as a distributor, and Novell now had the tools and business connections in place to become a distributor. With Ray's blessing, Ken took those tools and ran with them at NCI.

Implementing old ideas in a new organization is always a challenge to the new manager. Sometimes the implementation is completely successful and sometimes not.

Another example of this is when one of Ray's successors, Eric Schmidt, came to Novell in 1997 and brought ideas from his previous work at Sun Microsystems, which developed Java, an operating system–independent programming language. The first Java implementation at Novell was a bloated file server–management application that earned Java a lot of derision in Engineering and Technical Support.

Storm Clouds Brew

Novell's selling partners grew increasingly uneasy at the evolution of NetWare Centers. One example of this dissension was revealed at a

216

meeting on August 2, 1986 at the Radisson Hotel in St. Louis. At the dinner on a riverboat ride, Ken said:

Much of the concern and speculation regarding the NetWare Centers as relevant to our resellers has centered around the role the centers play in sales of Novell products. We believe we are proposing a program of appropriate levels of channel management and intend to maintain your business loyalty through providing sound economic value in the marketplace.

In that speech, Ken also gave a brief history of Novell's NetWare Centers. In 1985, he said, the first real roots of the NetWare Centers were put in place when Novell's field service offices began expanding their functional responsibilities.

From the fall of 1985 through the spring of 1986, numerous variants of NetWare Centers were established in the marketplace. Some of these experiments were dictated by economic necessity. In New York, the loss of a distributor in a crucial market area forced Novell to respond instantly with sales and marketing resources capable of fulfilling the lost channel. In Memphis and Atlanta, a distributor was acquired, giving Novell broader product offerings and presence in the market.

There were many other efforts to soothe the unease of NetWare Centers.

"Authorized distributors will deal directly with the regional NetWare Centers, thus receiving more personal attention. Authorized resellers may purchase products and receive support from authorized distributors or, by making a volume commitment, from the regional NetWare Center. NCI's support of resellers will be based wholly on the reseller's volume and, therefore, specific need for strong support," explained NCI President Ken Kousky.

In addition, for any authorized reseller that begins to buy directly from a NetWare Center, Novell will pay his distributor a commission for having found and trained that reseller, [Director of Technical Services Jim] Bills said.

As the computer industry grows, Noorda said, so will Novell. Challenges Novell will meet in the industry are lower hardware prices, copycat products from competitors, and new technology. In order to combat these challenges, Novell will concentrate on marketing its software systems and customer services.

At Networld 86, announcing that NCI would distribute Data Flex, a 4GL (4th-generation language) application development tool, Ken declared:

> The marketing of non-Novell software emphasizes the value added to a LAN installation. A LAN is only as useful as the increased productivity it can provide. The catalysts for LAN productivity are the software applications that directly support day-to-day activities.

Moving MIS and Other Issues

Another important anomaly of the integration of Cache Data and the creation of NetWare Centers was that the St. Louis facility became a center for Novell's MIS (management information system) operations.

Ron explained how that evolved:

> Two of our distributors went bankrupt the same month. One was Jersey Micro in New Jersey, and the other was Carl Orellano's distributorship out of Memphis, Tennessee, called Micro Source Technologies. So we lost a few hundred thousand on the Jersey Micro one, and we merged Carl's business into Novell, because Ray wanted Carl.
>
> In May of '86 we acquired Cache Data Products in St. Louis. That was the Ken Kousky company. It was in August of that year that Ray transferred all of the shipping and marketing and accounting functions for sales out to St. Louis—the MIS function, everything. Cache Data Products had been a business that was doing about $5 million a year. And in August of '86 when all this got dumped on them, we would have been doing about a $90-million annual rate. So naturally they came out with a list of about a hundred people they wanted to hire to deal with this. And over a period of months, Ray gave them everything they asked for, which was very disturbing to me.

Craig also had problems with this evolution.

> First of all I didn't think it made a lot of sense to put all that out in St. Louis; secondly, I was just desperately needing people all along to handle the growing network in Provo. It was like pulling teeth to get anybody. I think we got John Strang hired in the fall of '86, but he didn't—none of us—we didn't have the

accounting support or the MIS support that they ended up having in St. Louis.

This was crazy. We're the headquarters, and he's sending all the resources out to St. Louis, to a company that was doing $5 million a year. It made no sense to me at all.

The End of NetWare Centers

In 1987 Ray finally gave up on the idea of NetWare Centers. But dismantling them was not quick or easy. In his interview, Craig discussed how that was handled.

Craig: I guess it was about a year later that Lon Davis was hired, and Lon was Senior VP of Human Resources. He was a kind of a bright guy, and he said to Ray, "What in the world are you doing out in St. Louis? You've got a whole other company with a whole headquarters staff. You're producing stuff in Provo, you're shipping it to your central warehouse in California, then you're shipping it to St. Louis and some of it to Virginia. You're handling this stuff three times, and this is hardware, big boxes, heavy stuff."

So thanks to Lon Davis, we finally got St. Louis dismantled. And I'm trying to remember if that was '88 or '89 that we did that. It was in March of '87 that we had the acquisition of CXI [a Silicon Valley company that was itself the fruit of many acquisitions] and SoftCraft [the Austin, Texas, company mentioned above, pp. 123 and 161]. And with CXI, we got their management, Jerry Thompson, who had been their CFO, and Lou Cole, who'd been the President, so those two were given the job of dismantling St. Louis ... very, very sad.

This dismantling was a very critical problem to handle because they had the MIS system upon which all the shipping and billing was conducted. If we did it wrong and caused a mutiny, that could have shut down the entire company, just like that. We were very, very nervous about that.

What we worked out was a program of paying the people either several weeks' or several months' pay, depending on how long we wanted to keep them, and kind of phasing it down. So I think once the employees got resigned to the fact that they were going away, that they were being treated decently—you know, being given enough money that they'd be able to survive in the transition—fortunately it kept the place operating until we got it all transferred back to Provo. That was probably the highest risk position the company was ever in.

Interviewer: And Ken Kousky, what happened to him?

Craig: Lou Cole was given the job of asking him to leave.

Interviewer: Ray must have thought very highly of Ken to trust him with such a critical function.

Craig: Well, Ken is a very, very intelligent man. He's ... Ray used to say in meetings, "Ken is a genius"; he's really extremely intelligent. But the problem, as always, was politics, and Ken Kousky and Vern Mann, his CFO, had visions of taking their company public, spinning it off from Novell, and doing grand and glorious things, and they just had a different agenda than Ray had.

And Ray wanted to get out of the hardware business, as you know, and Kousky got us not only into our own hardware, but into everybody else's. We were remarketing third-party hardware, which has a margin of about zilch. And so the inventory started ballooning, and the margins started going down, and Ray was just fighting it on all fronts, so he finally decided, with Lon Davis's little boot, "Yeah, let's shut this one down. It's more trouble than it's worth."

In the end the activities of the NetWare Centers were quietly folded back into Novell, or cut loose, and Ken left and went on to Wave Technologies.

But all during the NetWare Centers interval, Novell had been growing, and acquiring, and there were now many other bright aggressive managers available to take his place at Novell.

In Conclusion

The purpose of this story is to show that even in white hot success stories such as Novell's, many mistakes are made.

But unlike other aspiring high tech companies that continued to wander in the small-company wilderness, Novell made and successfully exploited more right choices and cut off the wrong ones with minimal damage to the company.

220

PART THREE
Novell Matures, 1988–94

CHAPTER EIGHT
The End of the Visionaries, 1988–89

The Countdown on Craig and Judith

The Triumvirate

All through 1988 the political situation at Novell grew more important to those at Novell. The success was bringing new money to the table, the acquisitions were bringing new players into the organization. The company goals were transforming from just interconnecting PCs to connecting PCs to many kinds of networks. These, and the growth of Novell's importance to its customers, all conspired to make what happened at Novell "important". These changes attracted ambitious people, made the corporate vision more complex, and made defector behavior more rewarding. "Politics", in the pejorative sense, is defector behavior that isn't seen as contributing to the company good, and Novell was becoming political in that sense.

Ray did little or nothing to stop this politicizing trend in Novell management—his management style was such that he did not see it as a problem except where it led to his fourth "E" in the five stages of morale: Euphoria, which blinds management and leads to Extinction.[14]

From 1983 on there had been continuing changes in personnel at Novell, but the three constants at the top had been Ray, Craig, and Judith. Ray had provided the unifying vision, business acumen, cost control, and credibility. Craig proved an exceptionally good planner and articulate spokesman for the open systems marketing and technology approach. He spread the gospel within and without Novell. Judith implemented a style and an education communications campaign that not only made Novell a place to turn for information on the emerging

---

[14] For those who don't want to hunt back to p. 88: Ray's first three Es were Enthusiasm, Excitement, and Exuberance.

LAN industry, but also helped analysts and other opinion makers believe there was an industry.

The other major role Craig and Judith jointly assumed was apologists or "spin controllers" for Ray. At some points, such as the NetWare Centers execution souring, what happened just didn't fit into the company vision. Craig and Judith took on the task of making it fit. They issued press releases referring to statements made in older press releases and talked to analysts explaining how what had happened was actually consistent with Novell's long-term vision. It required a lot of creativity and fast footwork, and Craig and Judith did it well. Analysts left feeling warm and fuzzy about what Novell was up to, even when as soon as their backs were turned Craig and Judith were scratching their heads and shrugging, still trying to figure out what had really happened.

But in 1988 the triumvirate cracked, and in 1989 it shattered, leaving Novell with a palace revolt, layoffs, and the end of Novell's Legendary Period.

High Tech Trap: The Car Phone Conversation

Craig and Judith both liked being on the forefront of communications technology. They were among the first to get car phones in Utah Valley. (This is the pre–cell phone era when portable phones were still expensive and exotic.) But they were not the only enjoyers of high tech communications. A Utah Valley ham hobbyist had a radio scanner and a tape recorder, and this person tape recorded a conversation between Craig and Judith in which disparaging remarks were made about Ray. Utah Valley being the tight-knit community that it is, this tape found its way to Ray's ear in December 1987. There was no immediate effect but the stage was being set.

Later, through this same tight-knit community, Craig and Judith found out that Ray had overheard something. They didn't know what, but they assumed that Ray had got whatever it was by bugging their phones, so yet another veil of suspicion was drawn between the triumvirate.

Choosing Sides

By April 1988 people in the community were starting to take sides. Two new management hires into Communications were told that part of their work was to suppress any nasty rumors they heard about senior managers.

On one side were Craig and Judith—young, aggressive, hard-working superstars of the LAN industry. They were also evolving into a nouveau-rich lifestyle that was raising eyebrows. On the other was Ray Noorda—old, hardworking, pinch-penny "Uncle Ray", the savior of Novell and the person who finally made the computer industry happen for Utah Valley.

So it was a painful but not a hard choice to make for people in the Utah Valley community as to whose side to believe. When the time came, all but a handful sided with Ray.

Within the company and within the industry the split was just as painful but more evenly divided.

Networld 88

By October 1988 the stress of the politics and the pace of the ever larger Novell were wearing Craig and Judith thin. At Networld Dallas their fast-and-loose style stumbled and led to some severe unraveling of the image that Craig and Judith had been working so hard to build. This is what Tom Vitelli of Communications saw:

The height of the crisis came at the Reseller Dinner.

First problem: Craig and Judith were there, but Ray hadn't been invited.

Second, there had been bad news for the resellers announced earlier in the show and they were out for blood.

Third, there was a noisy party with a band playing below on the atrium floor [of the Infomart] and the noise level at the dinner was high.

Fourth, Craig was tired. As was often the case he had been up until 2 AM the night before and had already put in a full day. But this time he couldn't pull it off. By the time he was making his presentation at the dinner he was distracted, belligerent, and his speech was slurred. If I hadn't known he wasn't a drinker I'd have pronounced him drunk. The audience didn't appreciate him either. They wanted Ray and when they found out he wasn't going to show, many walked out.

Ray heard about this the next morning.

Judith Plans for the Future

Novell's ambitious people weren't all imported by acquisition. Judith had plans of her own. She talked with Tom one evening about how it was time to position Craig as Ray's successor.

As Tom was putting together the annual report for 1988 she directed him to put Craig's picture next to Ray's on the "Report to the Stock-holders" page, and he did as he was told.

But it turned out that Judith's timing for these positioning ploys was poor—and she had a hard choice to make. When Ray saw the draft and questioned the positioning, she ducked responsibility. This cost her credibility with her staff as well as with Ray.

The Action Technologies Contract

The decisive crisis for Craig and Judith came in December 1989. Craig tried to solve the nagging Action Technologies/Message Handling Service (MHS) problem by terminating their contract with Novell. He signed an agreement without consulting either Ray or the legal depart-ment, which it turned out was going to cost the company millions of dollars in termination fees.

Craig wasn't Ray, and this wasn't an acquisition. Losing that kind of money that way was considered a big mistake.

Troubleshooters or Loose Cannon?

Craig was the technology enthusiast made good at Novell. Unlike Ray, whose office rarely contained even a single personal computer, Craig's was rarely equipped with less than a Mac and a PC and a laser printer. As the latest in personal computer accessories became available, there would be one in his office. Scanners and big-screen color displays for the Macintosh were some of the items that could first be seen at Novell by looking in Craig's office.

His staff also reflected Craig's passion for the products of the indus-try. It was just three people and they were techno-junkies as well.

Craig used them as troubleshooters to help him introduce new tech-nological ideas. Steve Pelfrey, for instance, was "Mr. MHS" within Novell; his mission was to proselyte for the its use within Novell and to make it an industry standard. Craig saw his staff's role as one of initiating vital projects and then handing them off to the proper rank and file department to carry through with. ELS (Entry Level System) NetWare got its start this way.

When the ambitious newcomers to the company turned on Craig, one of their strategies was to use these people against him. In the eyes of the newcomers these people weren't initiators, they were loose cannon—bumbling loose cannon at that—and they took pains to discreetly portray them as such to outsiders, to Ray, and even to Craig.

Trying an End Run

In 1988 Ray announced that it was time for a management review. This one had a different twist. One item was that each manager was to name his or her successor in the event of sudden departure. In a stable environment this would have been just another bit of paperwork, but in the superheated political situation of Novell in 1988 it became a major signal of who was "in" and "out". Ray set the example: He named Jim Bills, then Director of Sales, as his successor.

When Craig and Judith found this out they realized that their positioning efforts of the last few months were about to be nullified. In response they took a risky step: They tried to end-run Ray by appealing directly to the board that Jim Bills wasn't his proper replacement.

It was a step of hubris. They felt they had done just as much as Ray to grow Novell and grow the industry. They felt they knew the industry as well as he. If Ray was leaving, why should "newcomer" Bills be favored over "founder" Craig?

The board listened but took no action. This was still Ray's company and in spite of the political hysterics that had brought about this strange appeal, Novell was still growing profitably and Ray was showing no signs of leaving.

In making this effort Craig and Judith may have also forgotten Ray's roots. At Novell Ray was finally part of a company where he was the founder—the guy that had the weight of organization tradition behind him. After having worked at four other companies where as the "newcomer" he was forced to leave as part of a management struggle, he was not about to lose Novell in this management struggle—ill-timed and launched by a couple of people who were still amateurs to this phase of company evolution.

The First, and Last, Vacation

Finally in October 1988 Craig took a six-week vacation and Judith followed suit two days later. As they were leaving someone asked Ray if they would be coming back. "I just don't know" was his surprising reply.

Michelle Swaner, Tom Vitelli's wife, remembers that time. (More language color, this time not Utah-based: She pronounces her first name McHaley.)

> It was so sad. Craig and Judith's leaving happened just before the Novell New Year's celebration in October. The party was at the Red Lion Inn and the theme that year was a Mardi Gras costume ball. The uncertainty about what their leaving meant and the sadness made the party seem more like something out of Poe's "Masque of the Red Death".

The Final Days

The Rumor Floodgates Open Wide

When Craig and Judith left, the gossip mills cranked into high gear. The simultaneous departure of Craig and Judith for their first vacations in three years signaled major changes were afoot, even to those unaware of the heat of the politics coursing through Novell's top management.

The first effect was shock. Craig and Judith had always had critics, but it was unclear that Novell's stupendous growth could continue without them. Certainly there were day-to-day questions that needed to be answered and the organization had to adjust to those.

Then the gossip began to fly. What had been talked about discreetly before came out into the open: Craig (married) and Judith (divorced) had been having an affair.

And the worse nastiness began: Craig and Judith had conspired against Ray. Ray had conspired against Craig and Judith.

And the speculations: Ray had driven Craig and Judith out because he'd found out about their infidelity. Craig and Judith felt Ray was holding Novell back.

But the facts remained remarkably hidden. Jim Bills spoke darkly about "trusts having been broken".

The Return

In February of 1989 Craig and Judith returned. Their return made as much news within the company as their departure had.

It was quickly announced that Novell was being reorganized yet again. Judith's domain—the *LAN Times* and the trade shows—were being spun off into a separate profit center called NetWare Enterprises. For Judith this was purgatory—her strength was communicating an image, not controlling costs. But she agreed to the arrangement.

Craig's return didn't result in such a dramatic change. He resisted taking the electronics industry's traditional exit door position: VP of Special Projects. Craig said later:

> I'd seen Ray dispose of managers from Santa Clara, CXI, and Novell. Heck, I'd helped. He would start by putting him [or her] in charge of a special project—something that was outside the normal lines of responsibility and accountability. The manager would be given lots of encouragement and favorable feedback, and at the same time the project would be adjusted until it was paralleling something already going on within the company mainstream. The manager would finally see himself or herself as redundant, get the message and leave.

The return was temporary. The trust that had held the triumvirate together was shattered. Craig's blunt ways of dealing with media people and analysts were no longer ameliorated by his being a mover and shaker at Novell—just because he said something no longer meant it was so. Drew remembers an episode.

> We were at an analysts meeting in New York. When Craig got up to make his presentation he rambled on about how the new NetWare we were designing for 386-based servers shouldn't be called NetWare 386. It should just be called another version of NetWare.
>
> This was the wrong audience for this kind of thing. What difference did naming NetWare make to these analysts?

In 1988 what Craig said was likely to happen, and outsiders appreciated listening to him. In early 1989 what Craig said was "an image problem". Ray put pressure on Craig and Craig responded by not appearing. As far as Novell was concerned he went into limbo in March of '89 never to return. His employment officially ended in May.

It was about the same for Judith.

No announcement was ever made at a MEMBERS Meeting.

Dismantling Craig- and Judith-ism

Dismantling Craig's Planning Arm

When Craig left, Novell as a whole was shaken, but organization-ally there was little impact. Craig had only a handful of people working directly for him, and they scattered to other departments before the final blow fell. Mark Calkins assumed his product-specifying functions, Daryl Miller assumed his communications functions, and in the new Novell, no one needed to assume his visionary functions.

Dismantling Judith's Education Arm

Judith, unlike Craig, had built a substantial organization under her. She had assembled the MarComm (marketing communications), Trade Show, and Publications departments. Publications had staffs for the *LAN Times, NetWare Technical Journal,* and *Selling Red*—over fifty people in all.

In Ray's eyes these functions were all too large for a Novell which no longer needed to educate the world on what a LAN was, so the challenge was how to best get rid of them. The same close-knit com-munity that supported Ray in his crisis with Craig and Judith would turn on him if he just hacked the department off cold, and he knew it. He once commented, "Laying off people in Utah is tough. When I had to let 20 people go from Manufacturing I got a call from the governor."

Opportunity knocked when McGraw Hill contacted Ray about buying the *LAN Times*—they wanted a publication to compete in this newly emerging industry. Ray sat down with their representative and came away smiling. They would take not only the *LAN Times* but the rest of Novell's Publication Group and pay him good money to boot! Once more Ray had proved his business acumen.

The Scars

For Ray, Craig, and Judith, Novell was their baby. They'd made it happen, and they'd made it happen together. For six years they'd trusted each other, worked together, spilled blood and tears together, and their baby had become something very special: A company that had made an industry.

This baby had generated a lot of money, a lot of pride, and a lot of good times, and breaking up that special relationship was no easier than breaking up any other special relationship.

Those close to Ray have said that the breakup aged him. Those close to Craig and Judith have commented on their bitter feelings towards how things turned out.

But given what was at stake, it went very smoothly indeed. Lawsuits were threatened but never materialized. Novell continued to grow under Ray's tutelage. Craig and Judith got married in the summer of 1989 in a picturesque wedding at their new home in the foothills near Little Cottonwood Canyon—home to some of Salt Lake's best ski resorts. They went on to found Clarke Burton Corporation as a way of offering their expertise to the industry at large.

Perhaps in this case money solved some problems: Novell was still profitable. Novell continued to grow. Boat rocking by either side would have threatened that. Perhaps, in this case, money and success bought peace.

CHAPTER NINE
The End of the Revolution, 1989–90

The Organizational Phase Change and After

The departure of Craig and Judith marked the beginning of the end of Novell's revolutionary period. After they left Novell would make money, but not history. But that was not clear at the time, and Ray was not about to give up "shaking the world" just because Craig and Judith were gone.

The Layoffs of Summer '89

One of the amazing things about this free market system we live with in America is that people do make a difference. Novell without Craig and Judith continued to grow, but in a different way than it would have with them. The Novell of Ray, Craig, and Judith had concentrated on defining what a LAN was and educating customers as to its benefits. The Novell that followed concentrated on embellishing what a NetWare LAN was and on making money by concentrating on Ray's three S's: service, software, support.

But before that transition could happen, the remaining influences of "Craig-and-Judithism" had to be exorcised. This was the company goal for 1989.

The crisis surrounding their exit had been distracting and had depressed earnings growth. This gave Ray the excuse he needed to assume the role of "company doctor" and announce layoffs in June and July of 89. Those layoffs, plus the departure of the Publications Group, left Ray firmly in control and with a new generation of senior managers who were ready to pursue Novell's new goals.

Roger Bourke White Jr.

Taking on Microsoft

As the late '80s turned into the early '90s, Ray acted as if he'd decided that the minicomputer companies were beat—Novell had done its job against them and a new battlefield was needed.

Novell was not the only PC-oriented company that was rising over the collapse of the minis. Microsoft was another. Not only was Microsoft prospering mightily, Bill Gates had personally vexed Ray on at least half a dozen occasions while Novell and Microsoft were both carving out identities and market share in the '80s.

Microsoft became Ray's next target, and he chose to take it head on. He was going to out-Microsoft Microsoft.

This was an ambition truly worthy of the billion-dollar company Novell had become, and Ray's acquisitions and attempted acquisitions of the early '90s reflected it: Lotus, for a spreadsheet to compete with Excel (though this acquisition was not completed); WordPerfect, for a word processor to compete with MS-Word, plus a groupware package, Groupwise, to replace what Notes would have brought from the Lotus merger; Digital Research, for a workstation operating system to compete with Windows; and UNIX from Bell Labs, for a server OS system and development tools. Venerable NetWare would remain the LAN system.

The spirit was willing, but Ray without visionary Craig and presenter Judith was weak. All the companies Ray acquired had been leaders in their market at one time, but that was a couple years to a decade ago—none had adapted well to the Windows environment that was fast becoming standard. They were now in second or third place, putting out "me too" products that followed Microsoft's lead. To out-Microsoft Microsoft, all these new acquisitions were going to have to perform heroically, stretching to reclaim past glory. Getting them to march to that drummer was the job for visionaries.

But while the senior managers Ray had brought into Novell in the late '80s were highly qualified and steeped in industry experience, it was minicomputer industry management experience, not personal computer industry history-making experience. They had seen the PC industry swallow their previous companies, but hadn't understood why. Ray tried, but he found that they were not personal computer visionaries, and he could not call on them to do what Craig and Judith had done.

233

What this new generation of senior managers did understand well was company politics. People are the same no matter what industry they are in, and these people had risen in the minicomputer industry because they were good with people.

Ray's management style was not particularly visionary. He was the deal maker, and a deal maker functions best when he keeps his hand close to his chest. It was Craig and Judith who had compensated for that and kept the Novell rank-and-file looking outward—out at the market they served, out at the technology that was growing around their industry, and out at how they were building an industry.

Novell Turns In on Itself

When Craig and Judith fell out of favor, it was a sign that looking outward was not the road to success at Novell any longer. Those who stayed with Novell after Craig and Judith left found their fortunes depended much more on what was happening within Novell than in the outside marketplace.

This was a condition the new senior managers had all seen before— some many times—so they adapted very quickly. Within weeks the "glib defectors" were making new policies in order to protect their incipient fiefdoms. There was a flurry of memos describing how Novell employees should communicate with others, and those memos all ended with an ominous paragraph announcing that anyone ignoring these new policies was "subject to immediate termination". This was the first time this kind of wording had shown up in Novell memos. It marked a distinctive change in the company ground rules.

With startling speed, Novell became a rather average billion-dollars-in-sales high tech company. Most of the senior management worked out of the Silicon Valley area, to keep up appearances and to stay in touch with the flow of ideas in that valley. Production parts of the company were farmed out to lower cost hinterlands, such as Utah and Texas. At the new Novell it was not important that the production people have access to the idea flow that senior management did, and ideas generated within the production areas of the company received no more consideration than ideas that flowed around Silicon Valley.

The result was a steady loss of anything distinctive about Novell ideas and implementation.

234

Ray "Lets the Company Breathe"

Another Ray practice exaggerated the problem of Novell turning in on itself.

When Ray was in "company doctor" mode, he thought he was making surgical layoffs. In his words, and a different metaphor, he wanted a company to breathe.

But layoffs are a tool that cuts many ways. When a company is in a life-threatening crisis—and if most members of the company feel that the crisis is real—layoffs can do what they're supposed to: "Get rid of deadwood" so the company can cut costs and survive. Layoffs in such a time of crisis work because the company as a community sees the necessity of getting more efficient, and the company acts as a community to make layoff decisions within that survival context. This was the mood of most of the companies when Ray came into them to turn them around, so his first rounds of layoffs at these companies worked.

But when most of the community company members see layoffs as a periodic ritual, serious crisis or no, different thinking emerges. Layoffs become a tool for solving factional disputes. "Deadwood" is redefined: The first definition becomes "people who are threatening to those with layoff power" and the second, "those people whom those with layoff power just plain don't like".

In the early '90s Ray would announce layoffs and justify them as happening because a quarter was soft and earnings weren't rising fast enough. This was hardly a life-threatening crisis to the Novell community, so factionalism was given a great boost. Workplace priorities changed: In the early '90s at Novell, time and attention devoted to protecting yourself from layoffs was time and attention well spent.

In sum, watching what happened within Novell was important to survival at Novell, so the company watched itself a lot.

While the Novell layoffs were traumatic for anyone who got caught up in them, they had one silver lining: A lot of good people with a lot of good ideas found themselves hitting the pavement in Provo. The Novell alums started a whole bunch of new companies that became the core of Utah's Silicon Valley.

Acquisitions and Strategic Partnerships

While all this internal politics went on, Novell also pulled some of the outside world in.

As reported in the online *Free Encyclopedia of Ecommerce*:[15]

Novell benefited from strained relations between IBM and Microsoft in 1991, when IBM agreed to market NetWare in an effort to limit Microsoft's increasing control over PC standards. In other deals, both Hewlett-Packard Corp. and Compaq Computer Corp. agreed to work with Novell to develop and market computer-networking technologies for their machines. Acquisitions that year included Digital Research Inc. for $136 million and a five-percent stake in AT&T Corp.'s UNIX System Laboratories. Novell and UNIX also founded Univel, a joint venture that developed UNIX-based products. Noorda restructured Novell into three units: NetWare; general operations; and a division working on the development of extensive corporate networks that would later become known as intranets.

Lotus and Novell agreed to increase the compatibility of NetWare and the Lotus Notes networking software in 1992. By then, Novell had become the world leader in computer networking. Its products included operating software, network management software, hardware, and services. Novell acquired UNIX System Laboratories from AT&T in 1993. Eventually, the UNIX operations were folded into Novell's NetWare division. NetWare 4.0 was shipped that year. In 1994, Novell paid $1.4 billion in stock for WordPerfect, a leading word processing software maker. The firm spent another $145 million on the spreadsheet operations of Borland International, which formed the basis for the Quattro Pro spreadsheet.

The Sharks Eat Ray

As company doctor, Ray was—to take a term from my essays on politics—being a "ruthless leader". Ruthless leaders thrive on crisis and perceived threats.

---

[15] At http://ecommerce.hostip.info/pages/804/Novell-Inc.html. A few misspellings—"Netware" (which is also sometimes correct as NetWare) and "Word-Perfect"—have been corrected.

But by laying people off in times of plenty with no apparent crisis, Ray stepped over the line of appropriate behavior for a ruthless leader and he lost support. Each time he made enemies in the company, and those enemies would do their best to stop the terror of more layoffs in the future.

This behavior strengthened the powerful, experienced faction leaders who did not owe Ray much loyalty, and he lost the naive young people whom he had "made" and who had been loyal to him. Finally in 1994, an all-too-familiar theme in Ray's business career happened again: He lost control of the company. Robert Frankenburg became CEO, Chairman, and President.

In the end, it seemed that Ray needed Craig and Judith as much as they needed him. Novell of the '80s truly was a "magic moment" in the history of business, and when it shattered, everyone had to move on.

Exorcising Ray-ism

When Ray left, as when Craig and Judith left, his legacy had to be dismantled. The vision of out-Microsofting Microsoft was abandoned and the acquisitions of his final three years were dismembered.[16] This burden fell to the new President, who spent two years at it and then moved on. As with the necessary layoffs in Dave Guerrero's presidency, it was a thankless task, and no one thanked him for it.

With Ray's departure, Novell became totally immersed in the flow of professional ideas, and has made no history since.

Novell as a Standards-Sustaining Company

The Transition

In the 1990s Novell transitioned from being a standards-introducing company to being a standards-sustaining company. In 1990 the LAN vision was complete: A network operating system standard had been

---

[16] For example, from the previously cited article in the *Free Encyclopedia of Ecommerce,* http://ecommerce.hostip.info/pages/804/Novell-Inc.html: "Taking a huge loss, Novell sold WordPerfect and Quattro Pro—both of which were struggling to compete with Microsoft's word processing and spreadsheet programs—to Corel Corp. for $186 million in 1996. The firm then refocused on its core network platform operations."

devised, it had been promoted successfully, and it had created a billion-dollar industry.

The organization that sustains a standard isn't the same kind as the one that first parades it in front of the world. Audaciousness and single-minded vision are necessary qualities for bringing a new idea to life. Consensus and orderliness are necessary for keeping it useful.

In the 1990s Novell transitioned to becoming a "Statue of Liberty" company—a company that holds a standard high for all to see, a company that is marveled at and envied by its contemporaries, a company of importance, but a company that doesn't move much.

In the 1990s Novell's vision base widened. Instead of being centered around the Ray-Craig-Judith-SuperSet axis, it widened to include top management from many of the companies Novell and Ray had acquired. It transitioned from a monocentric vision to a polycentric vision, and from a vision originating within management to a vision supplied to management by professional visionaries. The new senior managers didn't so much create visions as they picked and chose which visions to support from the many presented to them by consultants and middle managers.

In the 1990s, many of the top management moved to or were appointed out of the California area. At one point in 1991 the only company officers living in Utah were Ray and Jim Bills.

The result was a company that was highly profitable but very hard to figure out. There was a lot of talent at Novell, but the company produced no leader who could explain what that talent was supposed to be doing.

In yet another way, Novell turned inward.

Introducing a New Product

A standards-sustaining company is dominated by the slogan "No surprises". It doesn't need surprises any more—they just cause lots of dislocations between the various constituencies that the standards are serving. Consider how Novell treated NetWare 386.

This was Novell's last breakthrough product in the visionary era. It was the last to originate the way the original NetWare had: As a feeling on the part of the SuperSet people that new technology—in this case the 386 chip—could support the LAN vision in a better way.

238

NetWare 386 was a complete rewrite. In many ways it didn't act the same as NetWare 286—which was both a blessing and a curse. The blessing was that it could work better. The curse was that supporting it would be different than supporting NetWare 286.

In 1988 and '89, as the product developed, Novell had some hard choices to make in marketing it. The challenge was to reach Novell's many different kinds of customers in ways that allowed Novell's many marketing channels to do so profitably.

One possible solution followed the very traditional path of bringing in a high-performance solution at a high margin and appealing to a limited segment of the market. In this scenario NetWare 386 would be brought out as a high-end-only operating system. It would be positioned to compete with minicomputer operating systems and priced accordingly—higher than NetWare 286—so that it would appeal only to those customers developing very large networks using high-performance equipment.

This solution had the support of people in Novell's West Coast divisions, for many of whom networking was something that minicomputer operating systems had claimed to do for years.

The alternative was to supplant NetWare 286 with NetWare 386 by introducing a range of NetWare 386 products designed to service low-performance as well as high-performance markets. The advantage of this solution was market penetration. A lot of NetWare 386 going out quickly would send a strong signal to the third-party applications software developers that 386 was going to become the mainstream LAN operating system and they should commit their design work to it. This would insure that NetWare 386's most visible competitor, Microsoft's LAN Manager, would have a hard time getting established.

One of NetWare 386's distinctive features was that it was much easier to install than NetWare 286. Marketing it across the board, high and low, would give all NetWare users a product that was much easier to install and the convenience of a very smooth migration path. This PC-centric–oriented marketing was championed by Craig and those within Novell who had a lot of direct experience with the personal computer marketplace. But pursuing this strategy meant making a lot of change. It meant transitioning Novell's service, training, and support arms from 286-based expertise to 386-based expertise. It meant

Novell's third-party applications developers would have to transition quickly too.

Craig's demise in 1989 put an end to talk about a multi-tiered 386 introduction. The survivors felt there was no reason not to "skim the margin cream off the top" that this new technology offered, as they had always done in the minicomputer industry.

Novell introduced NetWare 386 in 1990 as a high-end operating system, and NetWare 286 has remained a viable product for many years. Rather than supplanting NetWare 286 with a low-price version of 386, Novell chose to modify 286 so that it acted more like 386.

And LAN Manager became a formidable competitor.

Transforming the Open Systems Approach

With Craig's leaving, the meaning of "open systems approach" changed considerably at Novell. Early Novell viewed open systems as a form of "corporate jujitsu". It was a way of thinking that let Novell develop policies and products so that the successes of other players became successes for Novell as well. Craig was particularly good at devising those kinds of tactics, and none of his successors had the frame of mind to match his skills in following that theme.

Novell in the '90s remained firmly committed to "open systems", but the meaning of the phrase changed. In the new Novell, the open systems approach referred to the details of making connectivity happen between various minicomputer communications systems—say, a connection between the TCP/IP communications protocol and a Net-Ware file server. It was transformed from a strategic business style to a strategic suite of products.

The Installed Base Anchor

Many times in the middle '80s Novell "bet the company" on an idea. The most spectacular of those ideas became the company "milestones".

By the late '80s Novell had a large installed base and was reaching the Fortune 1000 marketplace it had targeted. It listened to its customers and it found that they were happy with the current product. It was no longer necessary to bet the company on a new idea to make these people happy. They wanted NetWare to do what it was doing now only better. By the late '80s Novell had reached and was beginning to

240

find acceptance with the customers it wanted to cater to; it had an installed base; it was time for the revolution to stop.

The End of Novell's Visionary Era

Making History

What a ride Novell was!

From nothing in 1983 to a half-billion-dollar company in 1989.

From the wrong dream in 1980 to 65% market share in a billion-dollar industry in 1989.

This by every definition was history making, and for those on board, it felt like history making. It was a wonderful experience.

Sadly, it was hard to repeat. Many Novell alums, and Novell itself, have tried to make the magic again. Almost all have made some magic, but the Novell experience was unique in its magnitude.

The Epilog

The Novell that Craig and Judith departed from in 1989 did $422 million in sales. The Novell that Ray departed from in 1994 did $2 billion in sales after his final acquisition binge, but it was unstable. When Ray's successor moved on, what he left behind was a company that spent years hovering near a billion in sales.

By the time of Frankenburg's departure, the Internet Boom was in full swing, and it was a technology revolution that was pushing LAN technology into IT (Information Technology) backwaters. NetWare's moment in the sun was finished and Novell had to reinvent itself. It did so successfully enough to remain a large and profitable company, but not enough to keep making history.

The Novell of the late '90s and the 2000s could attract the finest talent—one of its Presidents, Eric Schmidt, went on to preside over Google's explosive growth—but that talent couldn't find a replacement for NetWare as a history-making product. Instead, the company moved up into the "niche hills" and thrived there. It could ably support those markets it had already carved out, but it was lackluster about carving out new marketplaces.

The people of '80s Novell steadily moved on. Thanks to Novell's success, and its habit of shedding both good people and bad, Utah Valley thrives as a high technology incubator.

Craig and Judith's Clarke Burton Corporation became the Burton Group. It has prospered as a technology consulting company and grown to hundreds of people by 2010, but this happened under Jamie Lewis, another Novell alum. Craig and Judith moved on.

After Ray left Novell he continued to work with computer-related high technology startups until his death in 2006. Caldera Systems in Utah was his most prominent vehicle, but he had many other interests as well.

The Lessons

Here are the lessons I have drawn from this experience.

First, a business organization is a delicate beast. It must constantly watch the marketplace and constantly respond to changes. As a result, much of running a business is exploring: It's researching what are right ideas and right implementations of ideas.

Second, when the business process is working well, it is quickly and efficiently filtering out poor implementations and poor ideas, and a few people suffer. When it stops doing this well, a lot of people suffer.

Third, there is a big difference between running visionary companies and well managed companies—so big that few people can do both. This means that you, as a potential employee, manager, or owner, need to decide which of these environments is going to suit you better. And you need to be watching management to see if they are well-suited for the company environment.

Fourth, there are exciting things happening around us all the time, and dull things, too. So be aware of the world around you. If you want to play with exciting things, look for the people conduit—where are people moving to? While Novell was exciting, it grew mightily. If you wanted to be part of Novell in its visionary period, it wasn't hard. But if you choose a visionary company, fasten your seatbelt, I guarantee you the ride will be wild!

242

www.ingramcontent.com/pod-product-compliance
Lightning Source LLC
Chambersburg PA
CBHW051228050326
40689CB00007B/840